Vegetables from the Sea

Low Calorie, High Nutrition

VEGETABLES FROM THE SEA

To help you look and feel better

by Seibin Arasaki, D. Agr.
and
Teruko Arasaki, D. Sc.

Japan Publications, Inc.

Published by JAPAN PUBLICATIONS, INC., Tokyo

Distributors:
UNITED STATES: *Kodansha International/USA, Ltd., through Harper & Row, Publishers, Inc., 10 East 53rd Street, New York, New York 10022.* SOUTH AMERICA: *Harper & Row, Publishers, Inc., International Department.* CANADA: *Fitzhenry & Whiteside Ltd., 150 Lesmill Road, Don Mills, Ontario M3B 2T6.* MEXICO AND CENTRAL AMERICA: *HARLA S. A. de C. V., Apartado 30–546, Mexico 4, D. F.* BRITISH ISLES: *International Book Distributors Ltd., 66 Wood Lane End, Hemel Hempstead, Herts HPZ 4RG.* EUROPEAN CONTINENT: *Boxerbooks, Inc., Limmatstrasse 111, 8031 Zurich.* AUSTRALIA AND NEW ZEALAND: *Book Wise (Australia) Pty. Ltd., 104–8 Sussex Street, Sydney 2000.* THE FAR EAST AND JAPAN: *Japan Publications Trading Co., Ltd., 1–2–1, Sarugaku-cho, Chiyoda-ku, Tokyo 101.*

First edition: January 1983

LCCC No. 79–91516
ISBN 0–87040–475–X

Printed in Japan

Preface

Seaweeds, or benthic marine algae, include many useful species that may be eaten directly or from which certain elements may be removed for nutritional purposes. The appropriate term *sea vegetable* was first used by Miss Judith Cooper Madlener in her work *The Sea Vegetable Book*, in 1977. Considering it suitable, I have employed it in this book. In the Japanese language, all plants growing in the sea are designated by the Chinese character 藻 (pronounced *mo* in Japanese and *zao* in Chinese), which can be broken down into three parts: 艹, which refers to plants; 氵, which is the radical for water; and 喿, which, representing three mouths above a tree, suggests the noise of many small birds chirping in tree tops. These three components together can be interpreted as plants buffeted by the waters under the roaring waves. The combined two components 澡 mean cleansing. This refers to plants that cleanse themselves in water. The general impression of the total character is one of gentle motion, like that of water.

Japan uses many more sea vegetables prepared in a wider range of cooking methods than other countries. The history of their use in this country is very long. Reference to sea vegetables appears in the *Ritsuryō* or code of laws enacted at the beginning of the eighth century; in the *Manyōshū*, an eighth-century poetic anthology; and in topographies from various regions edited in the middle of the eighth century. All of the species mentioned in these works are still eaten today and include such fronds as *amanori* (purple laver); *wakame* (*Undaria*); and *miru* (*Codium*), which are eaten directly, and *korumoha* or *tengusa* (*Gelidium*), from which an agar thickening substance is prepared. It can be assumed that the method for manufacturing such agar has been known since ancient times. The genus name *Gelidium* was first employed by the French scholar J.V.F. Lamouroux (1779–1825). Its Latin root *gelidus* (to congeal after boiling or maceration) is similar in meaning to the Japanese name *korumoha*.

Like land plants, sea vegetables contain photosynthetic pigments and develop by means of photosynthesis performed using the sun's rays. But, since they are undifferentiated into root, stem, leaves, and so on, as the land plants are, sea vegetables utilize the sun's rays more efficiently and are usable by man in all their parts. Such total, uniform usability is rare in land plants.

Interestingly enough, low-level plants like the algae are a greater source of natural fuel energy than more elaborate, sophisticated plants. Coal, which is produced largely from ferns, is a better fuel than firewood. And petroleum, which is formed from living organisms, including unicellular, low-level algae from the sea vegetables, is superior to coal as fuel.

Scientific research on sea vegetables lags far behind that on agricultural land products. Current knowledge concerning them is mainly based on practical experience gained over a long period. As mentioned previously, the potential power of the lower-level plants is greater than that of higher-level plants; but, only after many scientific investigations, was it discovered that this potential in the form of petroleum can be turned into kinetic energy. Once this was known, the kinetic power of petroleum came to play a major role in the advancing of human culture. Probably utilization of sea vegetables can have the same revolutionizing effect on human diet that the use of petroleum has had on human industry and civilization.

The ancient Mesopotamian Gilgamesh epic states that a plant with thorns growing on the sea bottom was a commonly known rejuvenator. This is, of course, no more than an interesting part of a myth; but it is a fact that, according to recent surveys, people living in areas where large quantities of sea vegetables are consumed live longer (high percentages of the populations of such zones live over seventy years). Further, according to results of nutritional studies, the components of sea vegetables effectively prevent hypertension and arteriosclerosis and promote the cerebral activity that keeps people healthy. Future research will probably show that sea vegetables are even more valuable as foods than has been thought till now.

This first overall evaluation of sea vegetables from the biological, biochemical, and nutritional-chemical standpoints deals with their practical applications, cultivation, and preparation as foods. Since seaweeds have nondiet applications too, the following publications investigating their many other aspects are interesting reference.

Chapman, V.J. *Seaweeds and Their Uses*. London; Methuen & Co., Ltd., 1950 (first edition) and 1970 (second edition).

Newton, L. *Seaweed Utilization*. London; Sampson Low, 1951.

Tressler, D. K. *Marine Products of Commerce*. New York; Reinhold Co., 1923, 1954.

The following books deal with sea vegetables as foods.

Abbott, I. A. and Williamson, E. H. "Limu, an ethnobotanical study of some edible Hawaiian seaweeds," *Pacific Tropical Botanical Garden*, 1974.

Madlener, J.C. *The Sea Vegetable Book*. New York; Clarkson N. Potter, Inc., 1977.

The following books discuss botanical forms of sea vegetables.

Dawson, E. Y. *Seashore Plants of Southern California*. University of California Press, 1966.

Guberlet, M. L. *Seaweeds at Ebbtide*. University of Washington Press, 1956.

Dewes, C. J. *Marine Algae of the West Coast of Florida*. University of Miami, 1974.

Dickinson, C. I. *British Seaweeds*. The Kew Series. London; Eyre and Spottiswoode, 1963.

I obtained various interesting suggestions from the above publications for this book, in the preparation of which thanks are due to Mr. Iwao Yoshizaki, president of Japan Publications, Inc., and to Mrs. Asako Kishi of the Editors Publishing Co. for her assistance with the color photographs.

Seibin Arasaki

Contents

Part 2: Cooking with Sea Vegetables

1. Sea grapes (*fusaiwazuta*, or *Caulerpa okamurai*).
2. *Ulva* zoospores.
3. *Laminaria religiosa*.
4. *Codium divericata*.
5. *Gelidum amansii*.
6. Farm for raising the *nori* (*Porphyra*) in Japan.

7. Harvesting giant kelp (*Macrocystis*) in Southern California.

Fancy Kombu

Techniques for the manufacture of these products, which have long been popular in Kyoto, were known as early as about 1620.

8. *Jabara* (snake-belly) *kombu* used as a wrapping decoration or on occasions when congratulations are in order.
9. *Kombu* baskets, made of slender strips of *kombu* and deep-fat fried, are used as garnishes or containers for other foods.
10. *Kombu* bows, tied from strips of vinegar-softened *kombu* and slow dried in a special charcoal kiln (*hoiro*).
11. (left) *Kombu* rolls.
    (middle) Shredded *kombu*, made from lower-grade, thin-leaf *kombu*, has been produced since about 1620.
    (right) *Nattō kombu* is shredded *kombu* of the *tororo* variety, which is viscuous.

7

When soaked in water it becomes sticky like fermented soybeans, or *nattō*.

12. A famous old Kyoto dealer in sea vegetables. Most of the wide variety of *kombu* and other sea-vegetable products—including the ones shown above—sold in this shop are prepared in time-honored fashions.

8   9   10

11   12

13

14

13. Marinated *wakame* and cucumbers (p. 153).
14. (top) *Wakame* and bamboo shoots (p. 155); (bottom) *Wakame* and bamboo-shoot soup (p. 151).
15. *Kombu* rolls with sweetfish (p. 144).
16. Sea-vegetable salad, a variation of the

recipe for *wakame* and cucumbers in sesame-mayonnaise (p. 153).
17. *Hijiki* and soybeans (p. 159).
18. Assorted sushi. (top and bottom) Sea bream and *sanshō* sushi (p. 148) and mackerel sushi (p. 147); (middle) *nori*-wrapped sushi (p. 173).

15

16

17

18

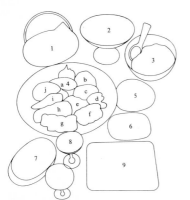

19. Party foods using sea vegetables.
   (1) Tempura and fried *kombu* (p. 143).
   (2) Almond jelly (p. 187).
   (3) Rice for sushi (p. 171).
   (4) Assorted sushi: a. young yellowtail, b. *ogonori*, c. julienne-cut *daikon* radish, d. shrimp, e. *wakame*, f. squid Hakata roll (p. 167), g. tuna roll, h. green *tosakanori*, i. yellowtail, j. red *tosakanori*.
   (5) Toasted *Asakusa-nori* to wrap around sushi.
   (6) *Nori*-wrapped sushi (pp. 173–75).
   (7) *Wakame* salad (p. 154).
   (8) Crab cocktail with *tosakanori* (p. 178).
   (9) Fillings for *nori*-wrapped sushi.

19

Part 1 | General Information

Introduction

Though their history as part of the human diet is long, seaweeds have in fact been eaten only in limited areas by relatively few peoples. Some once had the mistaken idea that only backward races with low cultural levels eat seaweeds. At present, however, when much research has been done on them, sea vegetables are better understood; and their great values are beginning to be appreciated.

Generally, sea vegetables are taxonomically low-level plants with low-level organic differentiation. As a whole, their fronds are undifferentiated living bodies and include all of the substances required for life, especially large amounts of the minerals and vitamins useful to human beings: iodine (I), iron (Fe), and calcium (Ca), which are found in smaller amounts in land plants. Because their carbohydrates are indigestible, they are not a source of calories. They are very low in fats. In other words, sea vegetables are low-caloric, highly nutritious foods that help promote health and longevity. This is of immense importance in the industrialized countries, where today overnutrition is a threat.

The food values of sea vegetables are currently being reconsidered in the hope of coping with future food shortages caused by population explosion and damage done to plants by intensive use of artificial fertilizers and other agricultural chemicals. This situation is the background against which this book explains sea vegetables and their importance.

Chapter 1 describes uses of sea vegetables as food in various countries, with special emphasis on current conditions and the history of utilization in Japan, where seaweeds have been eaten from primitive times. Of particular interest are regions where and periods when sea vegetables have played important roles as sources of salt, a vital element in human physiology.

Chapter 2 discusses chemical characteristics of sea vegetables (especially polysaccharides), chemical composition, nutritional problems, minerals, and vitamins as well as colors and flavors. The use of sea-vegetable components in drugs—origins in folklore and recently obtained scientific evidence of usefulness as antihypertensive agents and anthelmintics and in the new field of antibiotics—is examined. In addition Chapter 2 relates folklore concerning the utilization of seaweeds and longevity.

Chapter 3 concerns sea-vegetable biology and outlines differences between their living conditions and those of land plants, especially differences in photosynthesis caused by marine environmental conditions and the problem of sunlight. In photosynthesis performed on land, the only changes involve amounts of light and dark. In the sea, on the other hand, light quality—wavelength and color—as well as light quantity is important. Differences between land-plant and sea-plant photosynthetic products (polysaccharides); differences among green, brown, and red seaweeds; and environmental differences are discussed.

Chapter 4 outlines the ecology of typical important sea vegetables, the relation between growth history and harvesting season, and seasonal changes in environmental conditions. The theory and practical techniques of sea-vegetable cultivation are described in detail. Seaweed cultivation in Japan started with *Porphyra* (purple laver) and expanded to include *Monostroma* (green laver) and such larger kelps as *wakame* and *kombu*. Amounts of cultivated sea vegetables far outstrip those naturally raised in the wild. Cultivation techniques may be applied to large-scale production of seaweeds for nondiet applications. This book describes the theory on which these cultivation techniques are based for the first time.

Chapter 5 stresses the need for care in the storage of seaweeds, since they tend to change color and quality more rapidly after harvesting than land plants do. The reasons for this are described in connection with the special characteristics of pigment and polysaccharide components of seaweeds. Changes in physical properties of the polysaccharides in red algae, which form the basis of agar manufacture, too are discussed.

Chapter 6 presents line drawings of major sea vegetables (eleven species of green algae, thirty of brown algae, and forty-five of red algae) together with simple descriptions and chemical compositions.

1. In the Human Diet

In General

In ancient times, primitive men who lived by the sea probably ate seaweeds as well as the fish and shellfish they found in the waters. Remains of *arame* (*Eisenia bicyclis*), *hondawara* (*Sargassum*), *hijiki* (*Hizikia fusiforme*), and *wakame* (*Undaria pinnatifida*) in excavated archaeological sites dating from about ten thousand years ago indicate that such was the case in ancient Japan. In 1951, Professor Lily Newton reported that, in England wild deer, foxes, and bears habitually eat seaweeds. On the coast of Iceland, she photogaphed domestic cattle pushing kelp aside with their muzzles as they searched for dulse (*Palmaria palmata*), *Alaria esculenta*, and Irish moss (*Chondrus crispus*). Others of her photographs show sheep eating seaweed that had been cast up on shore. In 1962, Professor R. F. Scagel noted seeing cattle and deer eating seaweeds at low tide on the coast of British Columbia. Probably, valuable salts were derived from seaweed by primitive men and wild animals. But it is unlikely that the search for salt was what drove them to eat these seaweeds. Simple hunger, no doubt, was the sole stimulation. In general, domestic animals must be trained by starvation habits to eat seaweeds. But once accustomed to them, they eat them willingly.

Since animals—as well as human beings—require such nutrients as proteins, vitamins, iodine, calcium, and iron in which seaweeds are rich, once tried, sea vegetables probably became favorite foods. In Europe for a number of years people have been feeding domesticated animals on seaweeds when regular fodder is insufficient. They probably got the hint for this policy from watching wild animals feed on sea vegetables. Incidentally, sea vegetables stimulate animal appetites.

The history of seaweeds, especially kelp, as fertilizer is very old. In Europe, kelp meal was effectively put to this use in the twelfth century. In the seventeenth century, on the west coast of France, certain species of kelp meal (that from the brown algae, *Laminaria* and *Fucus*) were burned to form ash, a source of soda used in making glass. This industrial need stimulated remarkable growth in European kelp ash industry. At about the same time, a number of other uses for kelp ash were discovered. Potassium from kelp ash was used in chemical fertilizers and in the production of gunpowder. Iodine from kelp ash, discovered by B. Courtios, in France, in 1811, became indispensable for use in photography. Beginning as part of the glass industry, the production of kelp ash was a source and stimulus for the later growth of the Western chemical industry in general. Although it fell off for a while in the late nineteenth century, when soda, potassium, and iodine were derived from mineral sources, the kelp-ash industry was restored in the twentieth century because of the great demand for gunpowder stimulated by World Wars I and II. It is ironic that an industry started for the beneficial purposes of producing iodine and potassium should have been resuscitated for the aims of war.

As these paragraphs indicate, in spite of the brilliant development of a kelp-ash industry for chemical and other uses, in Europe, except in some coastal regions, sea vegetables as food were largely ignored. In terms of who does and who does not eat sea vegetables, the world may be divided into two large segments. People who as a rule consume no seaweeds inhabit Europe and North America. Those who do eat seaweeds live in Japan, China, Korea, Southeast Australia, New Zealand, Polynesia, and South America. In Japan, China, Korea, Southeast Asia, and Polynesia, many kinds of seaweeds cooked very simply are important to the diet. This is especially true in Japan, where more seaweeds are consumed now than in ancient times. The traditional fondness for sea vegetables in many kind of foods has stimulated the cultivation of *nori, kombu, wakame,* and *hitoegusa* along almost all Japanese coasts. Indeed in spite of the diversification of products derived from sea vegetables, in Japan today, 90 percent of the total output of such plants is used for food.

In some parts of the world, modern civilization has so improved and varied the human diet that people eat too much. This tendency results in such illnesses as diabetes and cardiac ailments as well as obesity, which could all be called indicative of our times. Since I believe that modern industrialized man, with his oversophisticated diet, should reconsider these virtually noncaloric sources of proteins, vitamins, and minerals, in the following pages, I explain the transitions that have taken place in seaweeds consumption in various parts of the world in the hope that this information will be interesting and informative reference.

Europe

The ancient Greeks and Romans took no notice of seaweeds as sources of food or medicine. Indeed, in ancient times, only in limited coastal areas were they used in primitive ways for foods, drugs, and fertilizers and even then only in small quantities. Though, according to Professor Valentine J. Chapman, seaweeds have long been eaten in limited quantities in Scotland, Wales, Ireland, Norway, Iceland, and the Mediterranean coastal areas and though some ancient recipes persist in use, these plants have never and are not now widely popular in this part of the world. The situation seems to be changing a little today, since an increasing amount of seaweeds forms and indirect element in many diets. For instance, algin obtained from brown algae and a polysaccharide named carrageenan obtained from red algae are employed in many processed foods.

Among the seaweeds eaten in limited amounts in this part of the world are dulse (*Palmaria palmata*), laver (*Porphyra laciniata*), sea lettuce (*Ulva lactuca, Enteromorpha* sp., *Monostroma* sp.), *Laurencia pinnatifida, Iridae edulis, Laminaria saccharina,* and *Alaria.* Sea lettuce is used in salads. Dulse, which becomes sticky when boiled, is used in soups. Laver is eaten in soups and stews or deep-fat fried. The other seaweeds listed are used in soups or salads. There are reports that *Enteromorpha* and *Monostroma* were eaten in salads during World War I: and Lily Newton says that Welsh housewives in Pembrokeshire collect laver at low tide and send it to town to be boiled and processed into a substance called black butter. Professor Chapman comments on the consumption of seaweed in Scotland about a hundred years ago, when "dulse tangle" and other sea plants were sold in the Edinburgh streets. At about the same time, in Scotland and Norway, a jellylike substance called seaweed bread was made from *Laminaria saccharina* or *Chondrus crispus*. In South Wales, today, the most commonly eaten seaweed is laver (*Porphyra*), which is used in salads or as a garnish with roast meat. In the eighteenth century, whaler crews relished seaweeds fried in deep oil.

In Ireland, dulse (dillisk, dillesk, or crannogh, as the much prized young dulse is called) is the most popular seaweed. Even in ancient times it was eaten either separately or with dried fish, butter, and potatoes. During famines, dried Irish moss (*Chondrus crispus*) was boiled and mixed with milk. Today an important food **additive (carrageenan)** is derived from this same Irish moss. In addition, in the past in Ireland, as today in some parts of Alaska, seaweeds, washed, dried, and rolled, were used as a substitute for chewing tobacco.

The Americas

The most prominent use of seaweeds in the diet of the United States is in the form of carrageenin and algin, which play an important part in food processing. Irish moss was imported for the production of these substances until it was learned that the same seaweeds grow along the Atlantic Coast of the United States and Canada. Along the Pacific Coast of North America, some people eat *Ulva*, *Porphyra* (laver), and *Palmaria*. In Polynesia, including the Hawaiian Islands, seaweeds are eaten in the oriental manner. The Chinese and Japanese Americans living in California collect and consume great amounts of laver, which is dried for use in Chinese restaurants and for export to China.

Polynesia, including the Hawaiian Islands

Of the seventy varieties of aquatic algae, marine and freshwater, produced in this region, about forty are normally used for food. The Hawaiian word *limu* (it is used in Samoa too), the Tahitian name *rimu*, and the Guam term *lumut*, all of which mean seaweed, are apparently derived from the same linguistic root. The following varieties are eaten raw, baked with salt or other spices, or mixed with other foods, sometimes after having been pickled in salt or soaked in water to remove bitterness or astringency: *Enteromorpha prolifera*, *Ulva fasciata*, *Codium edule*, *Dictyopteris plagigramma*, *Sargassum echinocarpum*, *Porphyra* sp., *Asparagopsis sanfordiana*, *Grateloupia filicina*, *Gracilaria coronopifolia*, *Ahnfeltia concinna*, and *Laurencia nidifica*.

South America

South American aborigines eat *Ulva* and *Durvillea antarctica*, or giant kelp, a brown algae of the Fucaceae genus reaching more than ten meters in length. Special stress is put on certain kinds of seaweeds—called goiter sticks—in areas where goiter is a common local disease. In the 1930s, Caucasians on the southern Pacific Coast of Chile ate *Ulva* and giant kelp in soups or as vegetables.

Australia

The consumption of seaweeds as food in this part of the world is very uncommon, though aborigines eat *Sarcophycus potatorum*, *Durvillea potatorum*, and *Durvillea antarctica* after soaking them for twelve hours in freshwater, drying them, and roasting them.

New Zealand

Among the green seaweeds that the Moaris traditionally favored in soups and salads is a kind of *Porphyra* called *karengo*.

Asia

Seaweeds have long been and continue today an important part of the diets of many Asian peoples, especially the Japanese, Chinese, and Koreans. Even among these three, however, Japan, where these sea vegetables have considerable market value, is the most important seaweed consumer. Fortunately, the extensive Japanese coastlines produce enough to supply at least a major part of the nation's great demand for these foods.

Indonesia
The following are some of the many seaweeds eaten raw or cooked in Indonesia: *Turbinaria* sp., *Sargassum* sp., *Gelidiopsis rigida*, *Sarcodia montagneana*, *Gymnogongrus javanicus*, *Gracilaria lichenoides*, *Gracilaria taenoides*, *Corallopsis minor*, *Hypnea cervicornis*, *Laurencia obtusa*, *Acanthophora specifera*, *Caulerpa lataevirens*, *Caulerpa peltata*, *Caulerpa racemosa*, *Caulerpa racemosa* var. *clavifera*, and *Codium tomentosum*.

The Philippine Islands
In the Philippines, green algae (*Caulerpa racemosa*, *Chaetomorpha crassa*, and *Enteromorpha intestinalis*), brown algae (*Hydroclathrus cancellatus*), and red algae (*Gracilaria verrucosa*) are eaten raw in salads or boiled with other vegetables.

Burma
The Burmese eat a boiled red alga (*Catenell nipae*), which is collected along the Tenasserim Coast and sold daily in the markets of Rangoon.

China
In spite of its long coastlines, China is deficient in kinds of seaweeds. Nonetheless from ancient times, *Sargassum* tea has been drunk; and powdered *Monostroma* and *Enteromorpha* have been sprinkled on foods as a seasoning. From the earlier parts of this century, the Chinese imported large quantities of laver (*Porphyra* sp.) and *kombu* (*Laminaria* sp.) from Japan; but *kombu* has a much longer history in China. Iodine deficiency in the diet caused goiter to be prevalent in ancient China, and the people combatted it by taking a medicine made of *kombu* imported first probably

from the northern districts of Siberia on the coast of the Japan Sea. Ancient records state that in about the first century, during the Latter Han dynasty, fish, shellfish, and seaweed were imported from Japan. Later, when the Japanese sent envoys to the Chinese court, they continued to include *kombu* in the tributes they offered. A report made in 1980 indicated that China has made remarkable recent progress in the artificial cultivation of kelp and laver along its coastlines. In addition, *Undaria pinnatifida*, *Eucheuma gelatinae*, and *Gracilaria* sp. have been successfully cultivated. The following are the main kinds of seaweeds eaten in China: green algae—*Enteromorpha* sp. and *Monostroma* sp.; brown algae—*Sargassum* sp., *S. fusiformis*; and red algae—*Eucheuma gelatinae*, *E. edule*, *Gracilaria verrucosa*, *G. ligulata*, *Hypnea cervicornis*, *Porphyra* sp., *Gelidium* sp., and *Gloiopeltis furcata*.

Korea

Most of the roughly forty kinds of seaweeds eaten in Korea are among the ones the Japanese eat. Furthermore, the manner of eating them is the same. Laver is cultivated in considerable amounts and exported in dried sheets to Japan, though it is considered inferior to true Japanese laver. The following kinds of seaweeds are eaten by the Koreans but not by the Japanese: green algae—*Ulva japonica*, *Codium cylindricum*, *Codium divaricatum*, brown algae—*Ecklonia stolonifera* and *Alaria esculenta*.

Japan

From the distant past, long coastlines and a rich and abundant variety of sea vegetables have made it possible for the Japanese to take full advantage of this source of food. Today too they are known as perhaps the sole people on earth that put seaweeds to very good use, especially in the diet. So popular are these foods that in recent years natural crops of laver, *kombu*, *wakame*, and *hitoegusa* have been insufficient to the demand; and artificial cultivation has been essential.

As the following tables of annual production of primary edible seaweeds and the per-capita consumption of these seaweeds indicate, marine algae play a vital role in Japan's coastal fishery industries.

Probably the Japanese are the only highly civilized people who consume as much seaweed as this. In 1973, 9.6 billion sheets of dried laver (25,920 tons when each sheet weighs 2.7g) was produced; and per-capita consumption was about 96 sheets or nearly 259g annually.

In prehistoric times, before the introduction of agricultural cultivation, the hunting-

Table 1   Production of Edible Seaweeds in Japan (unit tons)

Aonori, hitoegusa	3,130	
Hijiki	2,000	
Kombu	32,042	
Wakame	97,211	
Mozuku	3,000	
Tengusa	15,150	
Asakusa-nori	20,790	(7.7 billion sheets)

Sources: Fishery products statistics, 1969–1974.

Table 2   Per-capita Annual Consumption of Seaweeds by the Japanese
(1969–71) (unit grams)

Aonori, hitoegusa (Enteromorpha sp., Monostroma nitidum)	31
Hijiki (Hizikia fusiforme)	20
Kombu (Laminaria sp.)	320
Wakame (Undaria pinnatifida)	972
Asakusa-nori (Porphyra sp.)	208
Mozuku (Nemacystus decipiens)	30
Total	1,581

and-gathering forefathers of the modern Japanese ate large amounts of seaweeds; and the practice has survived to the present day. Throughout the stages of Japanese history, seaweeds have continued to be popular with most of the people. When the court aristocrats of Kyoto held major political power, seaweeds were always found on their tables. At one time there was even a tax on them. The warriors who ruled the nation for centuries found seaweeds excellent foodstuffs, as did the vegetarian Buddhist warrior-monks who contributed to the strife that ripped Japan asunder until final unification and the establishment of the Tokugawa shogunate, which ruled in peace from 1600 until 1867. During this time, seaweeds enjoyed increasing popularity with all classes of society.

The complexities and cosmopolitan nature of the modern Japanese diet might seem to suggest that such old-fashioned foods as seaweeds are on the way out. But the production and consumption figures in the preceding tables give the lie to this assumption. For a better understanding of the ways the Japanese have taken advantage of a great source of potential nutrition for other parts of the world, I offer the following historically organized sketch of Japanese seaweed-eating practices.

In Japan

Ancient Japan

The population of ancient Japan is believed to have consisted of two main strains: fishing people who came from islands in the south and hunting people who crossed to Japan from the Asian mainland. Although the ways in which the Japanese ate seaweeds in prehistoric times (Jōmon, Yayoi, and Tumulus periods, or up to the fourth and fifth centuries of the Christian Era) are uncertain, since the fishing people settled near the sea and made a living by catching fish and shellfish, it is likely that they gathered and ate seaweeds as well. Such seaweeds as arame, hondawara, hijiki, and wakame have been found in remains of burial mounds and in peat dating from ten thousand years ago; but there is no way to determine the ways in which these vegetables were consumed. Obtaining salt from them was probably one of the main reasons why primitive Japanese people ate seaweed. It is known that dried hondawara and hijiki were articles of barter with hunting people who lived further inland.

In a later stage of development, the Japanese learned the art of cultivating rice;

and seaweed became an important source of fertilizers. In addition, ways of obtaining salt by burning seaweed were devised. These two uses greatly stimulated trade in seaweeds between coastal and inland peoples. Before the Japanese began cultivating food crops, seaweeds were probably an important source of vegetable foods, especially because they are abundant along the coasts.

In the sixth century, Buddhism was introduced into Japan from Korea; and a sophisticated culture based on Chinese models grew up around the court. The aristocrats of this age ate great amounts of seaweeds, which were subject to taxation. *Kombu* was part of the tribute offered by Japanese envoys visiting the Chinese court. For the next six centuries seaweeds continued to be important in the diets of court aristocrats, and evidence of their use are found in main aspects of the culture of the time.

Seaweeds in the poetic *Manyōshū*

This famous anthology, compiled in the eighth century, is filled with interesting information about the daily lives of the Japanese of the sixth and seventh centuries. Of the roughly four thousand poems in the collection, about one hundred mention seaweeds. The wide geographic range associated with these references—the Kinki area, Hokuriku, Sanin, Tōkai, Kantō, and Kyūshū—proves that seaweed consumption was widespread. *Ama*, or fisherwomen, figure prominently in the poems. Burdened with heavy taxes requiring that they present large amounts of seaweed as tribute and required to make a living by toiling in the search for abalone, shellfish, and seaweeds, these women had little time to beautify themselves. Even courtiers gathered edible seaweeds, as is related in a poem by Kakinomoto-no-Hitomaro, one of the most famous representative poets in the *Manyōshū*. But they were not the only ones to do so, for all people living by the sea considered this one of their every-day chores. Although specific names of seaweeds are rare in the *Manyōshū*—only *wakame*, *miru*, and *hondawara* are called by name—because of the thirty kinds mentioned as tributes in the Taihō Laws (A.D. 701), it is certain that varieties used for food, salt, or fertilizer were numerous.

Seaweeds burned for salt

The eating of animal organs probably provided sufficient salt in the diet of the Japanese of the time when hunting and gathering were the main methods of obtaining food. Later, however, when the people began cultivating crops and relying on the grain they raised, they probably experienced salt deficiency; and some way to produce this vital seasoning artificially became necessary. The *Manyōshū* mentions fishermen of Suma district in modern Hyōgo Prefecture who burned seaweed to obtain salt. This method, which was used in other places as well, consisted in spreading seaweeds (*Sargassum*) and eel grasses (*Zostera*, sea grass) on the beach, sprinkling them with seawater several times, drying them to condense the brine on them, and then burning them to ashes. The ashes were collected in pots and mixed with freshwater. This dissolved the salt from the ashes into the water, which was boiled until crystallized salt was produced. But this method, which was time-consuming and laborious and which produced salt of poor quality, was abandoned later for the saltern system. Nonetheless, seaweed burning for salt production persists in the religious rituals of the Shiogama Shrine in Miyagi and gives an idea of the ancient process.

Religious rituals

In addition to the seaweed-burning rites of the Shiogama Shrine, a number of other Shinto shrines perform rituals associated with seaweeds. Most of these shrines are connected with the imperial family or *ama* fisherwomen; and the rites are designed to ensure a bountiful harvest, to protect the sources of seaweed, and to guard against overharvesting. The following shrines conduct such rituals: Ise Shrine, Mie Prefecture; Sumiyoshi Shrine, Yamaguchi Prefecture; Hayatomo Shrine, Fukuoka Prefecture; Hinomisaki Shrine, Shimane Prefecture; Norishima Shrine, Shimane Prefecture; and Shiogama Shrine, Miyagi Prefecture. Interestingly, all of these Shinto shrines were founded before the eighth century.

Offerings to the gods

During the Nara period (710–784), Chinese influence was felt in many aspects of Japanese life especially in the stipulations of elaborate rituals for such things as banquets and offerings to deities. Everything was rigidly detailed, including the kinds of food and wine to be served during festival. The offerings themselves, which reflected the diet of the people of the time, always included several kinds of seaweed. A work entitled the *Engishiki* (edited in 905–967) stipulates the details of religious ceremonies that continued to be carried out and therefore exerted an influence on the people's lives for a long time. Seaweeds are included in these rituals too, as the following table shows:

Ise Shrine (*Shinjo* festival)	*Amanori* (*Porphyra* sp.), *miru* (*Codium, fragile*)
Court festivals (*Kashiko-dokoro* festival)	*Wakame* (*Undaria pinnatifida*), *murasaki-nori* (*Porphyra* sp.), *miru* (*Codium fragile*)
Thanksgiving at the Imperial Ascension	*Kombu* (*Laminaria* sp.), *wakame* (*Undaria pinnatifida*), *murasaki-nori* (*Porphyra* sp.), *miru* (*Codium fragile*)
Kasuga Shrine	*Wakame* (*Undaria pinnatifida*)
Iwashimizu Hachiman Shrine	*Kombu* (*Laminaria* sp.), *wakame* (*Undaria Pinnatifida*), *tosakanori* (*Meristotheca papulosa*), *aonori* (*Enteromorpha* sp.), *Mishima-nori* (*Porphyra* sp.), *amanori* (*Porphyra* sp.), *miru* (*Codium fragile*)

Kamo Shrine

Wakame (*Undaria pinnatifida*), *Mishima-nori* (*Porphyra* sp.), *tengusa* (*Gelidium amansii*), *hondawara* (*Sargassum confusum*), *amanori* (*Porphyra* sp.), *kombu* (*Laminaria* sp.)

Taxation

The Taihō Laws (701) set forth an elaborate system of taxation on land and foods, including several varieties of seaweeds: *amanori, tengusa, wakame, miru, arame, manakashi,* and *kajime*. Great amounts of these seaweeds demanded as tax from each fisherman were an onerous burden involving cruel labor. In the tenth century, the varieties of taxable seaweeds and the regions subject to such tax were increased to cover much of the nation, though per-capita amounts of each variety were reduced to about one-third of what they had been in the Taihō Laws. *Nori* was the most important seaweed for taxation purposes; and the second was *manakashi*, an old name for a kelp meal made from the sprouts of *arame*.

Seaweeds collected as tax went to the imperial court and civil and military officials as well as to temples and shrines. Fortunately seaweed may be stored without perishing for a long time, and the government was able to dispose of surpluses in Kyoto markets. Priests, aristocrats, and officials did the same thing, though secretly. In the eighth century special shops were authorized to deal in seaweeds and agar jelly, a great favorite in those days, which was produced in temples and elsewhere from *tengusa*. But the wares of these shops—such high-class seaweeds as *wakame, amanori, miru,* and *kombu*—were enjoyed only by the upper classes and remained too costly and rare for the ordinary people.

Heian seaweed cookery

During the Heian period (784–1185), rice was eaten by the aristocracy; but there were few regularly raised vegetable crops. Consequently, as poetry anthologies of the time reveal, people gathered fresh wild greens to amplify their diets.

Seaweeds too—twenty-one varieties, according to a work entitled *Wamyōshō*, written in 934—were used for variety. Very much the same as the culinary methods used with them today, preparations for seaweeds involved expensive luxuries like vinegar, soy sauce, bean paste, starch jelly, liquor, and salt and were therefore possible only in the homes of the rich. Though this was the period in Japanese history when seaweed consumption reached a peak, most of the dishes prepared from them for the imperial court, the aristocracy, and religious ceremonies were unvaried. Aside from raw seaweed seasoned with vinegar and grilled seaweed, most of these so-called delicacies were no more than dried seaweed plain or sweetened. Interestingly enough, seaweeds prepared in these fashions were hard to digest. When the warrior class seized power from the court aristocracy—a process that was completed with the establishment of the Kamakura shogunate (1185–1333)—consumption of seaweeds dropped sharply. Apparently, the warriors could produce enough land foods to meet their nutritional needs.

Middle ages and premodern times

When the court aristocrats lost power, the seaweed taxes they had imposed ceased to be collected. But the new warrior government set up regional lords who were quick to reinstate this taxation in kind and to market the seaweeds they received, thus expanding the range of trade in such commodities. The warrior government made the city of Kamakura, on the eastern coast of Honshū, its capital. This shift in the location of the national administrative center stimulated the flow of people and goods—including seaweeds—between east and west regions.

Buddhism developed considerably along strictly Japanese lines in this period. Since Buddhist priests were then largely vegetarians, they came to incorporate seaweeds in their foods. This demand in part made up for the loss of popularity for sea vegetables among the ruling class.

The Kamakura shogunate collapsed in the fourteenth century to be replaced by the Muromachi shogunate (1392–1573), which returned the capital to Kyoto. Trade between the east and west, however, not only continued vigorous, but also expanded as sea routes were opened up with Hokkaidō in the north and with the Japan Sea coast. As maritime commerce developed, certain ports became famous for their seaweeds (especially *kombu*). Though increased availability of land and sea products caused seaweed consumption to decrease, their popularity with Buddhist monks, in the meals served with the tea ceremony, and as garnishes for fish and shellfish steadily grew. Furthermore, by this time, seaweeds were enjoyed by the ordinary classes as well as by their overlords. In addition to agar jelly, long a popular favorite, other seaweeds, prepared in the following ways, found their ways to many tables:

> Blue powder—*aonori* roasted, powdered, and sprinkled on glutinous rice cakes.
> Hawk's wings—*arame* baked in patties of fish paste shaped to resemble hawk wings.
> Seaweed rolls—quenelles of ground fish parboiled, rolled in black *nori* and served in soup.
> *Miru* and *nori*—used as garnishes for soups and other foods.

Preserved seaweeds were popular as confections or light foods in the tea ceremony —especially, because of their durability—from as early as the Kamakura period. *Kombu*, kept for from two to five years, or until brown and soft, was treated with vinegar, cut in strips, tied into bows, and roasted. Parched beans were covered with *aonori*. Sometimes *nori* was cut into strips and salted for a light food.

The Edo period (1600–1867)

Great sophistication and elaboration in seaweed cookery took place at this time. The *Kan'ei Cookbook*, written in the time of the third Tokugawa shogun, Iemitsu (1623–1651), contains recipes for baking, pan frying, vinegaring, using in soup, and preparing raw for salads of twenty-one kinds of seaweeds. From about this time, *kombu* came to be used in preparing basic broths for other soups and foods—it continued to be a popular source of broth to the present. The following seaweeds were used in the ways given.

> *Kombu* (*Laminaria* sp.)—in soups, boiled, in sauce, as a confection, steamed, boiled to produce stock, deep-fried, and so on.

Wakame (*Undaria pinnatifida*)—in soups, raw, lightly toasted, shredded, marinated in sakè, and so on.

Arame (*Eisenia bicyclis*)—in soups, boiled with fish.

Kajime (*Ecklonia cava*)—in cold soups, lightly toasted.

Hondawara (*Sargassum fulvellum*)—boiled, vinegared in salads, in sauce, pickled.

Hijiki (*Hizikia fusiforme*)—boiled and in sauce.

Mozuku (*Nemacystus decipiens* or *Tinocladia crassa*)—in cold soups, raw.

Amanori (*Porphyra* sp.) and *Asakusa-nori* (*P. tenera*)—in cold soups or lightly toasted.

Aonori (*Enteromorpha* sp.)—in soups, lightly toasted in confections, marinated in sakè, steamed.

Tosakanori (*Meristotheca papulosa*)—raw or marinated in vinegar.

Miru (*Codium fragile*)—fried.

Agar jelly—raw, pickled, as a summer confection.

During wartime and famine

Exigencies of warfare demand supplies of portable, durable foods nutritious enough to keep soldiers in good health. Traditionally, for centuries, Japanese soldiers have been fed on parched rice; dried boiled rice; rice cakes; salt; bean paste; pickled plums; dried and salted fish; dried abalone; and such seaweeds as *kombu* (*Laminaria* sp.), *arame* (*Eisenia bicyclis*), *amanori* (*Porphyra* sp.), *hijiki* (*Hizikia fusiforme*), *wakame* (*Undaria pinnatifida*), and *mozuku* (*Nemacystus decipiens*). Military lords included seaweed storage spaces in their castles because this fine food became highly important in time of battle or siege. Established connections between *kombu* and religious ceremonials naturally led to the inclusion of this kind of seaweed in triumphal military celebrations. It is still an essential part of Japanese weddings and New Year festivities.

Famine relief

With the coming of peace at the establishment of the Tokugawa shogunate in the early seventeenth century, military demands for food were drastically reduced. But food storage policies were nonetheless necessary to provide for famines that struck frequently, the three most tragic being those of the Kyōhō period (1732–33), the Tenmei period (1783–87), and the Tempō period (1833–36). During the especially severe Tenmei famine, farmers of the Northeast (Tōhoku) region were reduced to filling their stomachs with mud and dirt. Documents of the time explain how to prepare more or less edible substances from earth. The shogunal government and the various clan lords encouraged the cultivation of such supplementary foodstuffs as foxtail, millet, and buckwheat grains and such nuts as acorns and horse chestnuts to provide supplies to fall back on in time of distress. Efforts were made to cultivate sweet potatoes for the same purpose. Such seaweeds as *kombu, wakame, arame, kajime,* and *hijiki* were sources of nourishment; and a book written in 1839 describes eighteen specimens of seaweeds consumed by the people during food shortages.

In spite of such steps, however, major famines reduced local populations by half, especially in the Tōhoku region, where relief policies had little effect.

The seaweed industry

The immense seaweed industry of modern Japan dates back as far as the fourteenth and fifteenth centuries, when, as has been explained, seaweeds were an important foodstuff for the soldiers involved in the almost continual civil strife raging at the time. After the establishment of nationwide peace in the seventeenth century, the shogunal government and local clan lords encouraged agriculture, fishery, and seaweed collection and processing. Not only did these products assist in relieving popular distress in famine periods, they also became highly desirable additions to the ordinary diet and gifts worthy of presentation to Buddhist temples, Shinto shrines, and the imperial aristocracy. The founder of the Kamakura shogunate, Minamoto no Yoritomo (1147–99) presented *Izu-nori* (*Porphyra*) to the retired emperor Goshirakawa on three occasions; and the tradition of such gifts persisted long thereafter.

Various regions of the country developed their own distinctive seaweed products, which became favorite souvenirs for travelers to take home. This stimulated distribution of these foods, as did the Tokugawa shogunate's policy of requiring feudal lords to spend alternate periods in Edo and in their own fiefs. The lords, their families, and retainers often took back home or brought to Edo various local seaweed products. As time passed, commercial routes for trade in these items were established and expanded. Ōsaka, which was directly under the control of the Tokugawa government, became a great commercial center. *Kombu* from Hokkaidō was shipped first to Ōsaka and then distributed throughout the nation. The Asakusa district in Edo became famous for the collection of seaweeds that were then processed into thin sheet known as *Asakusa-nori*. In the early period, these seaweeds were actually gathered at the mouth of the Sumida River in the Asakusa region. But, as increasing land reclamation made this impossible, the raw material came to be brought in

Fig. 1 An eighteenth-century dealer in sea-vegetable products.

Fig. 2 *Nori* farm in the nineteenth century; wood-block print by Katsutora.

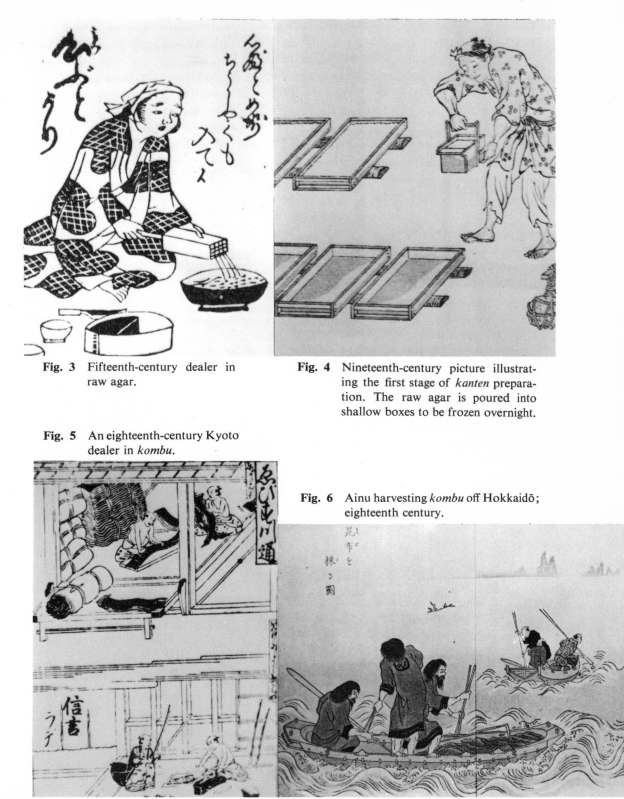

Fig. 3 Fifteenth-century dealer in raw agar.

Fig. 4 Nineteenth-century picture illustrating the first stage of *kanten* preparation. The raw agar is poured into shallow boxes to be frozen overnight.

Fig. 5 An eighteenth-century Kyoto dealer in *kombu*.

Fig. 6 Ainu harvesting *kombu* off Hokkaidō; eighteenth century.

from such other places as Fukagawa, Kasai, Shinagawa, and Ōmori, though the sheets of seaweed were still called *Asakusa-nori*. The shogunate, which had earlier established Asakusa as a food-distributing center to ensure good steady supplies in the city, strictly controlled the numbers of shops that could deal in this merchandise and stipulated that cultivation of the seaweeds needed for it be restricted to Edo (Tokyo) Bay. Such measures kept prices of *Asakusa-nori* high.

Kombu too remained expensive and did not become widely available to the general populace until the twentieth century. Formerly used to make confections of a kind distinctive to Kyoto, *kombu* was regarded as something suited only to religious ceremonies or to the imperial court.

Some of the other local seaweed products that gradually became items of commercial trade in many parts of the nation include agar, first produced in Ōsaka and later in Kyoto and Nagano Prefecture, and locally produced *wakame, arame, hijiki, tengusa,* and *funori,* which came to be sold on a nationwide basis.

Though the use of seaweeds for industrial purposes was slow starting in Japan and never developed to the level of its Western counterpart, consumption of seaweeds as food in Japan has remained at a high level. Production figures show that today four times as much *Asakusa-nori,* eleven times as much *wakame,* and twice as much *aosa* and *aonori* are produced and consumed in this country as were produced and eaten twenty years ago. Although the ways in which seaweeds are eaten today (Table 3) have altered, some of the old-fashioned preparation methods persist. Obviously production of edible seaweeds has reached the status of a major industry; but, in spite of increases in output, commensurate increases in demand keep prices high. Nonetheless, seaweeds, with their high vitamin and mineral content and low calorie count, are vital to the Japanese and can make an important contribution to the better nourishment of peoples everywhere.

Fig. 7 An inscription written in 1890 by Prince Akihito Komatsu stating, "Sea vegetables are beneficial in the lives of the people."

Table 3   Applications of Major Edible Seaweeds in Japan

	Seaweeds	Application
Green algae	*Enteromorpha linza* *Enteromorpha intestinalis* *Enteromorpha clathrata* *Enteromorpha compressa*	Food (*Asakusa-nori* or powdered)
	Ulva (U. pertusa, U. fasciata)	Domestic animal fodder
	Monostroma nitidum	Food (*nori* simmered in soy sauce)
	Codium fragile *Caulerpa fastigiata (C. racemosa)*	Food
Brown algae	*Nemacystus decipiens* *Hizikia fusiforme* *Heterochordaria abietina* (*Analipus japonicus*) *Endarachne binghamiae* *Undaria pinnatifida*	Food
	Laminaria sp. *Ecklonia cava* *Sargassum confusum* *Eisenia bicyclis*	Food; domestic animal fodder; raw material for alginic acid, iodine, and potassium; fertilizer
Red algae	*Porphyra* sp. (laver) *Porphyra suborbiculate* *Porphyra crispata* *Porphyra dentata* *Porphyra umbilicalis* *Porphyra pseudolinearis*	Food (natural *Asakusa-nori*)
	Porphyra tenera (P. yezoensis)	Food (cultivated)
	Gracilaria verrucosa *Meristotheca papulosa* *Gymnogongrus flabelliformis* *Eucheuma muricatum*	Food
	Bangia fuscopurpurea	Food (powdered)
	Gelidium sp.	Agar raw material
	Chondrus ocellatus *Gloiopeltis furcata*	Paste
	Digenea simplex *Chondria armata*	Insecticide
	Ceramium kondoi *Grateloupia filicina*	Paste

2. Dietary and Medical Applications

Chemical Compositions

Though, when living in their natural habitat, sea vegetables are composed of from 80 to 90 percent water, dried, they contain only from 10 to 20 percent water and consist of from 80 to 90 percent carbohydrates, proteins, and minerals. In this state, they contain only from 1 to 2 percent fats. Vitamins, nucleic acids, and pigments similar to those found in land plants occur in sea vegetables too. As Table 4 shows, sea vegetables are especially rich in carbohydrates (from 50 to 60 percent in their dried states) and include high percentages of minerals (sometimes as much as 30 percent) and vitamins. In addition, they contain characteristic mucilages.

Table 4   Chemical Composition of Sea Vegetables (unit grams)

Seaweeds (per 100 g)		Water	Raw proteins	Fat	Carbo-hydrates	Fiber	Ash
Blue green	*Nostoc commune*	10.6	20.9	1.2	55.7	4.1	7.5
Green	*Ulva* sp.	15.2	23.8	0.6	42.1	4.6	13.7
	Enteromorpha sp.	3.7	20.7	0.3	61.5	7.2	6.6
	Eisenia bicyclis	19.3	7.5	0.1	50.8	9.8	12.5
Brown	*Hizikia fusiforme*	16.8	5.6	0.8	29.8	13.0	34.0
	Heterochordraria abietina (*Analipus japonicus*)	13.1	19.4	0.4	40.3	5.5	17.2
	Undaria pinnatifida	16.0	12.7	1.5	47.8	3.6	18.4
	Laminaria sp.	18.0	6.7	1.6	49.1	5.4	19.2
	Gracilaria sp.	12.9	7.9	0.05	58.4	3.0	17.8
Red	*Chondrus crispus*	16.1	11.2	2.6	54.8	2.4	14.2
	Porphyra tenera (lower)	13.4	29.0	0.6	39.1	7.0	10.9
	(middle)	11.1	34.2	0.7	40.5	4.8	8.7
	(upper)	11.4	35.6	0.7	39.6	4.7	8.0

From food analysis tables.

Polysaccharides

The polysaccharides of the thick, soft cell walls of seaweeds are specialized in structure to control entry and exit of inorganic ions. This is very important because of the high concentrations of salt in the seawater environment. A characteristic mucilaginous cell-wall framework surrounding both sides of the cellulose protect the fronds, which, because of their soft walls, would naturally suffer damage as a result of the

Table 5 Polysaccharides in Marine Algae

Polysaccharides		Green algae	Brown algae	Red algae
Cell wall				
	Structural	Cellulose Xylan Mannan	Cellulose Chitin	Cellulose Xylan Mannan
	Intercellular	Heteropoly- saccharides	Alginic acid	Galactan sulfate
	Matrix (mucilage)	Sulfate 1) Polyuronides 2) Neutral Polysaccharides	Fucoidan	1) Agar 2) Carageenan 3) Funoran 4) Porphyran type galactan
Storage		Starch (α-1, 4 glucan) Fructan (2, 6-β fructo- furanose)	Laminaran (β-1, 3 glucan)	Floridean starch (α-1, 4 glucan)

Note: Words in parentheses indicate kinds of polysaccharides in marine algae.

constant swaying motion of the sea. In addition, these mucilages admit ions needed for the plant's survival and reject unnecessary ones.

Seaweed polysaccharides are of three functionally differentiated kinds: structural polysaccharides in cell walls, intercellular mucilages, and storage polysaccharides. Constituent components of these polysaccharides (Table 5) not only differ from those found in land plants, but also vary among blue-green, green, brown, and red algae. Mucilages account for as much as from 40 to 50 percent in some cases. Table 5 shows the kinds and locations of polysaccharides in seaweeds.

At present, alginic acids made from brown algae and agar carrageenan from red algae are widely used in food additives, glues, and drugs.

STRUCTURAL CELL-WALL POLYSACCHARIDES

As is true in land plants too, the seaweed cell-wall skeleton is mostly cellulose (β-1, 4-glucan). But in blue-green algae, which have structures closer to those of bacteria than those of other sea vegetables, the cell wall, while including cellulose, consists mainly of the peptide glucan (polysaccharides bound with peptides). Red and green algae contain xylan (*Caulerpa* sp.) and mannan (*Codium* sp.) in addition to cellulose. The physical properties of cellulose in green algae are closer to those of land plants than those of cellulose in green and brown algae. In seaweeds, cellulose content ranges from a minimum of about 1 percent to a maximum of 14 percent.

INTERCELLULAR OR SECRETED MUCILAGES

Brown algae—Phaeophyta

Alginic acid

Alginic acid, a polymer of two different units of uronic acids (D-mannuronic acid and L-glucuronic acid), is found in the mucilages of brown-algae cell walls. A high degree of polymerization indicates a high percentage of β-1, 4-bound polyuronides. Uronic acid differs from the C-6 alcohol group of sugars in that its $-CH_2OH$ is oxidized carbonic acid $-COOH$. Structurally, alginic-acid resembles a pectin found in the hemicellulose of land plants, which is a polymer of D-galacturonic acid.

A very viscous solution is obtained by treating such brown algae as *Laminaria* sp. and *Macrosystis* sp. with dilute sulfuric acid and then extracting it with warm dilute alkaline solution. Addition of acid precipitates alginic acid, which, when dried, produces the alkaline salt of alginic acid. White and odorless, alginic acid shows acidity because of its free carboxyl group. Since it is a polysaccharide, it is called alginic acid. It is insoluble in water, though its sodium salt is swollen by absorption to from ten to twenty times the amount of water in which it is placed. Its calcium salt too is insoluble.

Though it differs with the species and is subject to seasonal survival, alginic-acid content in dried brown algae is high (from 10 to 47 percent). This content is at a peak from September to November and falls to a minimum in March and April.

The binding property of alginic acid to divalent metallic ions is correlated to the degree of the gelation or precipitation in the range of Ba$<$Pb$<$Cu$<$Sr$<$Cd$<$Ca$<$Zn$<$Ni$<$Co$<$Mn$<$Fe$<$Mg. For this reason, heavy metals taken into the human body are gelated or rendered insoluble by alginic acid in the intestines and cannot, therefore, be absorbed into body tissues.

Applications: Since no known intestinal enzyme digests it, alginic acid cannot be used as a nutrient for mammals. It does, however, have the following other applications.

1. Its soluble alkali salts (especially sodium salts) are used in the textiles industry for printing, finishing, and waterproofing of fabrics.
2. It is a water softener.
3. It is a bonding agent for briquettes and a mixing agent for mortar and cement.
4. It is used in the manufacture of activated charcoal.
5. It is used in processing such foods as jellies, jams, and ice cream.
6. It is used as a clarifying agent in the production of sugar, sakè, beer, and so on.
7. It is used to glaze and size paper.
8. It is a mixing agent for rubber production.
9. It is used in the production of water-based paints.
10. It is an electrical insulator.
11. It is used in gelation in film production.
12. It has an extensive range of applications in other fields, especially manufacture of pharmaceuticals (see p. 58). Its versatility derives largely from the possibility of preparing various metallic salts from it and from its high viscosity in aqueous solution.

From the nutritional and food-processing standpoints, in addition to its use as an emulsion stabilizer for ice creams, jams, mayonnaise, condensed milk, soup, and so on, alginic acid, in combination with soybean protein, is being employed in the production of plant proteins to replace meat proteins in the diet.

Industrial development: Discovered by an Englishman named Stanford, in 1886, alginic acid was first commercially manufactured, under the name of Norgine, in Norway, in 1919. Somewhat later, production started in England and the United States, where it began being widely used after World War II. Today, the United States and England lead in production of alginic acid; they are followed by Japan, West Germany, Spain, Australia, South Africa, and Canada.

Sources: In England, France, and Norway, alginic acid is produced mainly from *Laminaria* sp.; in the United States and Australia, from a giant kelp called *Macrocystis*; in Canada, from a similar kelp called *Nereocystis*; and in Japan from Laminariales (brown algae) called *arame, kajime,* and *kombu.* Although *wakame* has the highest alginic-acid content of all of the Japanese seaweeds, it is popularly eaten and therefore not used as a source of this substance.

Since the same seaweeds that produce alginate provide kelp ash (for iodine and potassium), fertilizer, and feed, there has been some competition among the related industries for supplies. Recently, alginate, which is used mainly in the adhesives and food industries, is replacing carrageenan (see p. 38).

Fucoidan

First isolated from *Fucus vesiculosus*, fucoidan, which is a polymer of fucan sulfate with units of L-fucose-4-sulfate bound to the 1, 2 positions containing the 1, 3 or 1, 4 positions, contains, in addition, small amounts of galactose, xylose, and uronic acid in some instances. Fucoidan content, which changes with the season, is closely connected with habitat. For instance, *Pelvetia canaliculata*, which grows in comparatively deep waters, has a content of 23 percent, whereas *Laminaria*, which grows in littoral regions, contains less than 7 percent on a dry basis.

Fucoidan contains a fairly high percentage of sulfate ester (about 30 percent in some cases). This substance is known to have the same anticoagulant action as heparin. A 1-percent aqueous solution of fucoidan obtained from *Sargassum linifolium*, for example, has been shown to have greater antithrombic action than the same concentration of heparin.

Red algae—Rhodophyta

Galactose as an intercellular substance in red algae forms various viscous polysaccharides, or galactans, which are all acidic and which include sulfate esters. Hot water will extract them all from algae fronds. The resulting liquid is viscous and, if allowed to stand, gelates. The gelation power of agar is strong, whereas that of funoran and carrageenan, which are used as glues, is weak. The amount of sulfate ester in the polysaccharide determines its gelation capacity: no coagulation occurs when the sulfate-ester content exceeds 10 percent. This content varies from species to species. For instance, the sulfate ester content is about 20 percent in *Gigartina*, from 4 to 6 percent in *Ceramium*, and less than 3 percent in *Gelidium*. The red algae in which a 1-percent solution gelates at a temperature of from 15°C to 20°C are used as agar materials. The ones that do not gelate at these temperature are used for glues.

Agar

The Gelidiales, Cryptonemiales, Ceramiales, and Gigartinales—known as agarophytes among red algae—contain some cellulose in their inner cell-wall layers. The outer layers and intercellular spaces consist of mucilage.

Agar, which is the main component of the mucilage in the agarophyte and a cell-wall structural component, has semipermeable properties with ion exchange. It accounts for about 35 percent of air-dried *Gelidium*. Agar consists of two different components: agarose and agaropectin in a ratio of 7:3. Agarose is a neutral polysaccharide with a linear structure of repeated units of the dissacharide agarobiose, which consists of D-galactose (D-Gal) and 3, 6 anhydro-L-galactose (3, 6 ALG) with such linkages as [–D-Gal-(β-1, 4)-3, 6 ALG (α-1, 3)]. Agaropectin is an acid polysaccharide containing sulfate ester, pyruvic acid, and D-glucuronic acid in addition to agarobiose. The sulfate content of agar is comparatively low: from 3.5 to 9.7 percent.

Properties: Though it does not dissolve in cold water, agar absorbs water and becomes soft and swells. Heated to 80°C or more it melts to become a viscous liquid. It coagulates at from 25°C to 35°C and at low concentrations of from 0.5 to 1 percent.

Generally a mixture of various kinds of agarophytes is used in making agar: 48 percent *Gelidium amansii*, 25 percent *Gracilaria verrucosa*, and 26 percent of another agarophyte (see Table 6).

Origins: For the past 1,200 years the Japanese have eaten a dish called *tokoroten*, which is made by boiling *Gelidium* species and allowing them to coagulate. In the late seventeenth century, the lord of the Satsuma clan, on a periodic journey between his fief and the shogunal capital in Edo (Tokyo), stopped at the home of a certain Tarōemon Minoya, in Fushimi near Kyoto, and was served *tokoroten*. The leftovers, when thrown out, froze in the cold winter night. A few days later, the frozen *tokoroten* became a spongy, white, dry material. Some brave soul added water to it and boiled it. It became whiter than the original *tokoroten* when it congealed, but tasted good and had few impurities. The local inn started serving it to travellers under the name dried *tokoroten*. Upon eating it, a famous priest from the temple Mampuku-ji gave it the name of *kanten*, by which it is known today. *Kanten* is agar. This accidental occurrence was the origin of the freeze drying method which is used today and which made Japan the leader of the world's agar-producing industry.

Applications: In Japan today 30 percent of the crops of *tengusa* species (Gelidiales) is used to produce *tokoroten*, and the other 70 percent to produce agar. One-third of the locally produced agar is exported.

Agar is used as a stabilizer for jams and marmalades, in the manufacture of confections (jellies and Japanese bean jelly or *yōkan*), and as filler for canned meats.

Table 6 List of Agarophytes

Order	Species
Gelidiales	*Gelidium amansii* *Gelidium decumbensum* *Gelidium japonicum* *Pterocladia tenuis* *Acanthopeltis japonica*
Cryptonemiales	*Grateloupia filicina* *Grateloupia divaricata* *Grateloupia turuturu*
Gigartinales	*Gracilaria verrucosa* *Gracilaria edulis* *Hypnea charoides* *Gigartina tenella* *Gigartina mamillosa*
Ceramiales	*Ceramium kondoi* *Campylaephora hypnaeoides*

In addition it is used as a substrate for bacterial culture since only a few bacteria are capable of decomposing it. In addition, it is used in cosmetics.

Carrageenan

Carrageenan is a sulfated polysaccharide included in the Gigartinaceae order of red algae, including *Chondrus crispus* (Irish moss) and *Gigartina stellata*. A viscous polysaccharide, it contains 3, 6-anhydro-D-galactose instead of the 3, 6-anhydro-L-galactose in agarose. There are at least two types: κ- and λ-carrageenan. When the algae is extracted in hot water and fractionated with 0.25M KCl, κ-carrageenan precipitates out in a gel form; and λ-carrageenan remains in the mother liquor. The κ-carrageenan consists of D-galactose, 3,6-anhydro-D-galactose and sulfate ester in a ratio of 6:7:5. The λ-carrageenan is a polysaccharide with mainly α-1, 3 binding of D-galactose and sulfate ester units. It has a high sulfuric acid content (35 percent).

Dried *Chondrus crispus* (Gigartinaceae) is boiled by the coastal people of Ireland and mixed with milk. An unpurified, commecrcial product called carrageen has long be sold in Ireland. The name is said to originate from the village Carragheen on the coast of Waterford in the south where this Irish moss is gathered and distributed. It is widely used in folk medicine as treatment for respiratory disease. Furthermore, it is a clarifying agent in the production of wines and beers.

Algae species used in producing carrageen are harvested from May to August, washed in seawater, spread on the shore to dry for twenty-four hours, and then collected. This entire process is repeated several times until the sunlight bleaches the algae to white or light yellow. At this stage, the dried algae have hard edges. If rain falls during the drying process, the product is of poor quality without jelling properties. In the early period, the United States imported algae for carrageenan production from England and France. In the mid-nineteenth century, however, it was found that algae growing along the Atlantic coast of the United States and Canada produce the material; and the local carrageenan industry got under way.

Properties: Carrageenan, which has high viscosity in dilute solutions, mixes well with various liquids and is a better stabilizer, emulsifier, and filler than such substances as alginic acid, agar, and pectin. Its already extensive use in the food industry has recently been increasing. It reacts with proteins with especially strong viscosity. Its excellent stabilizing properties make it widely popular for use in ice cream, confections, cocoa, sherbets, fruit syrups, pies, puddings, cheeses, and instant soups. Use in the glue and textiles industries and in the manufacture of cosmetics too is on the increase.

Green Algae—Chlorophyta

Green-algae intercellular polysaccharides include two water-soluble polysaccharides: one consisting of sulfated uronic acid, and the other of sulfated neutral sugars. The former is obtained from such species as *Ulva lactuca*, *Enteromorpha compressa*, and *Acrosipinia arcta*.

STORAGE POLYSACCHARIDES

Green-algae starches

Though starch is a common photosynthetic polysaccharide in the green algae, Dasycladales contain fructan—a polymer of fructose—too. This substance has a dry-weight content of from 6.5 to 12.5 percent.

As in land plants—with which the green algae have more in common than do any of the other seaweeds—green-algae starches consist of polysaccharides of amylose and amylopectin, both of which have properties like those of potato starch, though their polymerization degree is much lower (about one-tenth). Furthermore, the starch of green algae shows no significant double refraction. Algae-starch dissolves readily in hot water without becoming gluey.

Laminaran

One of the storage polysaccharides in brown algae, laminaran (β-1, 3 glucan) is a polymer of D-glucose, Its main chains consists of β-1, 3 bonds and its subchains of β-1, 6 bonds. This is different from the main chain (α-1, 4 bonds) of starch. Laminaran was first isolated from Laminariales by Schmiedelberg (1885), who named it for the species of origin. At its highest, in mature fronds, laminaran content reaches from 20 to 30 percent dry weight. Among species growing in sublittoral regions, laminaran content ranges between 2 and 10 percent; but, in species from upper littoral regions, it is generally less than 7 percent. The laminaran molecule contains mannitol, though insoluble laminaran contains less mannitol than soluble laminaran.

Floridean starch

Floridean starch, a red-algae polysaccharide, has a structure similar to that of starch amylopectin, though it produces a redder iodine reaction. It is decomposed by β-amylase. Though its properties are somewhere between those of animal glycogen and plant starch, in terms of physiochemical properties, floridean starch shows stronger gelation when heated in aqueous solution than amylopectin does.

Proteins

Nitrogen content of sea vegetables ranges from 1.5 to 7.6 percent dry weight. When raw protein is calculated by multiplying nitrogen content by 6.25, the protein range becomes from 10 to 48 percent (Table 7). Since they grow uncultivated, if this protein

Table 7 Nitrogen Contents of Some Sea Vegetables

	Algae	Nitrogen %
Blue-green	*Nostoc commune*	3.34
Green	*Codium fragile*	2.50
	Codium latum	2.94
	Chaetomorpha spiralis	2.63
	Enteromorpha compressa	1.98
	Enteromorpha linza	3.09
	Ulva pertusa	3.26
	Ulva lactuca	2.38
Brown	*Eisenia bicyclis*	1.82
	Endarachne binghamiae	2.34
	Hizikia fusiforme	1.69
	Analipus japonicus	3.80
	Laminaria japonica	2.47
Red	*Chondria crassicaulis*	3.28
	Chondrus ocellatus	4.37
	Chondrus crispus	1.80
	Gelidium amansii	3.25
	Gymnogongrus flabelliformis	4.31
	Porphyra tenera	7.63

can be used as food, seaweeds can be an important substance in solving man's food crisis, particularly in improving the diets of the one-third of the population of the world today suffering from protein deficiency. Sadly, however, almost no nutritional research is currently being conducted on their utilization.

According to some of my own recent research, protein purified by alkaline extraction from some of the seaweeds harvested along the Japanese coast has an almost constant nitrogen content of from 11 to 14 percent. Amino acids in these proteins are about the same as those in ordinary proteins, and the amino-acid composition is actually better than that of land plants. Interestingly, this amino-acid composition closely resembles ovalbumin—egg-white protein (Table 8). Though some questions about digestibility remain, in general, previous animal experiments and experiments on artificial digestion indicate that alkaline-extracted seaweed proteins—especially

Table 8   Amino-acid Composition of Proteins in Sea Vegetables and Ovalbumin
(g of amino acid-N/100 g of protein-N.)

Amino acid	Green		Brown		Red		*Ovalbumin
	Ulva pertusa	Codium fragile	Eisenia bicyclis	Undaria pinnatifida	Porphyra tenera	Grateloupia turuturu	
Tryptophan	0.3	1.2	1.3	0.8	1.3	0.8	1.0
Lysine	4.5	4.1	7.8	4.3	4.5	4.3	7.7
Histidine	4.0	1.5	4.0	2.7	1.4	1.8	4.1
NH₃	1.9	3.4	3.2	2.5	5.1	1.9	5.3
Arginine	14.9	12.3	18.6	7.5	16.4	15.8	11.7
Aspartic acid	6.5	6.4	5.0	5.6	7.0	5.7	6.2
Threonine	3.1	2.9	2.3	2.4	4.0	3.0	3.0
Serine	3.0	2.8	2.3	2.8	2.9	2.8	6.8
Glutamic acid	6.9	6.1	7.6	5.1	7.2	6.3	9.9
Proline	4.0	3.6	4.5	2.8	6.4	5.1	2.8
Glycine	5.2	5.1	6.5	4.4	7.2	5.0	3.4
Alanine	6.1	6.6	7.0	4.8	7.4	5.5	6.7
Cystine	1.2	0.6	0.7	0.5	0.3	0.7	1.4
Valine	4.9	5.8	5.9	4.1	6.4	4.9	5.4
Methionine	1.6	2.0	2.4	2.2	1.7	1.7	3.1
Isoleucine	3.5	3.4	4.4	2.9	4.0	4.4	4.8
Leucine	6.9	6.6	7.3	5.1	8.7	6.3	6.2
Tyrosine	1.4	1.2	2.1	1.6	2.4	0.9	1.8
Phenylalanine	3.9	3.3	4.0	3.7	3.9	3.7	4.1
Total	83.8	78.9	96.9	65.8	98.2	81.2	95.4
N %	13.2	13.7	10.6	11.6	13.6	14.4	15.8

Source: Arasaki, T., *Larsen B. A.

Table 9   In-vitro Digestibility of Alkali-soluble Proteins from
Analipus japonicus and *Laminaria japonica*

Enzyme	Time (hours)	Analipus japonicus (%)*	Laminaria japonica (%)*
Pepsin		42.7	8.8
Pancreatin	5	68.3	54.0
Pronase		97.8	69.2
Pepsin		85.0	25.1
Pancreatin	24	100.0	71.2
Pronase		100.0	83.8

*Percentage on the basis of casein digestibility.   Source: Arasaki, T., 1979.

from such old Japanese favorites as *Asakusa-nori* (*Porphyra tenera*), and *matsumo* (*Heterochordaria abietina*, recently renamed *Analipus japonicus*)—are both good and highly nutritional.

Extracts obtained from seaweeds by means of a 70-percent aqueous-alcohol solution contain amino acids; peptides; nucleic acids; and such sugar alcohols as mannitol, sorbitol, and dulcitol.

Amino Acids and Peptides

Free amino acids

Some twenty or thirty types of free amino acids in fairly large amounts are found in seaweed ethanolic extracts. In addition, there are some special amino acids peculiar to seaweeds. The nonprotein nitrogen originating from amino acids, peptides, amines, and nucleotides accounting for from 10 to 20 percent of the nitrogen in seaweeds is thought to be an intermediate or final product of nitrogen metabolism in plant tissues. Habitat, and especially seasonal variation, have an effect on amino acids and peptides in seaweeds.

Nonprotein, free amino acids in the cells include β-alanine, α-and γ-aminobutyric acid, taurine, 2-aminocapylic acid, ornithine, citrulline, lanthionine, phenylserine, and hydroxyproline. Their contents differ with the species. Table 10 shows some

Table 10   Composition of Amino Acids in Ethanolic Extracts from Various Algae (mg% on dry basis)

Amino acid	Ulva pertusa	Entero- morpha linza	Undaria pinna- tifida	Sargassum confusum	Chondria crassi- caulis	Neodilsea yendoana	Laurencia nipponica
Alanine	17.7	23.8	617	278	71.4	25.8	61.4
Alloisoleucine	0	0	2.7	0	0	0	0
Arginine	2.5	1.9	36.5	1.6	trace	1.3	1.4
Aspartic acid	4.4	13.7	5.4	27.5	87.1	6.1	42.2
Chondrine	28.7	43.0	41.0	22.8	193	29.0	24.7
Citrulline	0	0	0	0	0	40.7	0
Cysteic acid	35.5	13.1	4.8	3.7	13.3	9.8	8.7
D-Cysteinolic acid	152	73.4	1.9	2.2	57.4	0	0
Glutamic acid	31.8	55.0	89.8	28.5	49.5	0.7	219
Glycine	9.1	5.2	455	3.7	29.1	5.6	45.9
Histidine	0	0	2.1	0	3.3	0.6	0
Isoleucine	3.7	5.8	11.2	9.7	6.4	0.4	37.9
Leucine	6.6	6.8	19.6	14.3	5.3	1.7	11.6
Lysine	0.9	0.8	34.6	0	3.6	0.5	0.3
Methionine	0	0	1.7	0	trace	0	1.7
Ornithine	0	0	0	4.0	0	1.6	1.5
Phenylalanine	4.1	3.8	9.2	11.3	0	0	1.9
Proline	40.0	51.1	156	24.2	50.8	8.8	32.7
Serine	11.9	33.7	64.4	51.6	12.9	2.6	33.3
S-Hydroxymethyl-L-homocysteine	0	0	0	0	0	4.6	2.7
Taurine	1.8	2.0	11.8	9.7	14.5	218	24.9
Threonine	5.7	3.8	90.3	12.1	12.0	2.5	48.6
Tryptophan	2.4	1.4	5.8	8.0	12.6	0	3.3
Tyrosine	2.1	2.1	10.1	7.5	0	0	1.1
Valine	3.5	3.9	11.1	14.0	7.6	1.7	87.6
NH$_3$	3.7	3.4	16.6	4.0	10.5	4.2	5.3
Total	368.1	347.7	1698.6	538.4	640.3	366.2	697.7

Source: Takagi, T., Oishi, K., Okumura, A., 1967.

Table 11   Comparative Amounts of Free Proline and Citruline in Some Marine Algae
(Calcd. as % of total amount of amino acids)

Algae	Proline	Citrulline
GREEN ALGAE		
Cladophora rupestris	19.2	—
Enteromorpha compressa	41.1	—
RED ALGAE		
Delesseria sanguinea	51.9	—
Polysiphonia nigrescens	52.1	—
Palmaria palmata (dulse)	53.5	—
Dilsea carnosa	—	15.2
Furcellaria fastigiata	—	34.0
Gracilaria verrucosa	—	29.8
Chondrus crispus (Irish moss)	—	35.0
Gigartina stellata	—	53.9
Polysiphonia lanosa	—	58.3

Source: Citharel, J., 1966.

seaweed amino acids and their seasonal and species-related differences. In the red algae *Sarconema scinaidioides*, serine, which has a high content of as much as 0.6 percent, accounts for more than half of the total free amino acids. In *Porphyra tenera*, alanine amounting to about 25 percent of the total free amino acids, probably accounts for the faintly sweet taste. *Ulva pertusa* contains large amounts of cysteinolic acid, cysteic acid, proline, glutamic acid, and chondrine. *Undaria pinnatifida* contains abundant alanine, glycine, and proline. *Chondria crassicaulis* has high chondrine content; *Neodilsea yendoana*, has high levels of taurine and alanine; and *Gracilaria verrucosa* has a high arginine content. In addition, such amino acids as citrulline, proline, taurine, arginine, and ornithine accumulate in the cells.

Because of their saline seawater environment, taxonomically, seaweeds fall between bacteria and higher plants and, it is assumed, have a special metabolic system, which probably requires the presence of at least the ten known kinds of amino acids peculiar to them.

Peptides

Since Hass et al. (1931) initiated research on peptides in seaweeds by discovering octaglutamic acid in *Pelvetia canaliculata*, many other studies have been carried out, though few instances of successful peptide isolation have occurred. Toshihiko Ōhira isolated eisenine from *arame* (*Eisenia bicyclis*) in 1940, and Dekker et al. isolated L-pyrrolidonoyl-L-glutamyl-L-glutamine in 1949. Lews et al. (1962) found carnosine —which is present in animal muscles—in four species, including *Acanthophora delilei*. And I have found many peptides—including glutamic acid and aspartic acid—in aqueous extracts from *Laminaria japonica*.

Fats and Lipids

Though the fat content of seaweeds is low, approximately 1 percent dry weight, the fatty-acid composition differs from that of ordinary plant oils only in that there are more unsaturated than saturated fatty acids in it. The main fatty acid is oleic acid; some behenic acid is included too. Palmitic acid is the main saturated fatty acid, but myristic and stearic acids too are found. Nonsaponificating substances—sterols

Table 12   Algae Sterols

Order	Species	Sterols*	Reference**
	Green algae		
Ulvales	*Enteromorpha compressa*	Sito	(1)
	Ulva lactuca	Sito	(1)
	Brown algae		
Chordariales	*Analipus japonicus*	Fuco	(2)
Laminariales	*Alaria crassifolia*	Fuco	(3)
	Costaria costata	Fuco	(2, 3)
	Eisenia bicyclis	Fuco, Sarg	(3)
	Laminaria japonica	Fuco	(2)
	L. digitata	Fuco	(1)
	L. hyperborea (cloustonii)	Fuco	(4)
	L. saccharina	Fuco	(4)
Fucales	*Ascophyllum nodosum*	Fuco	(1, 4)
	Cystophyllum hakodatense	Fuco	(3)
	Pelvetia canaliculata	Fuco	(4)
	Sargassum ringgoldianum	Fuco, Sarg	(3)
	Red algae		
Bangiales	*Porphyra umbilicalis*	Fuco	(1)
Gelidiales	*Acanthopeltis japonica*	Chol, Chal	(6)
	Gelidium amansii	Chol, Chal	(6)
	G. corneum	Sito	(1)
	G. subcostatum	Chol	(5)
	Pterocladia tenuis	Chol, Chal	(6)
Cryptonemiales	*Gloiopeltis furcata*	Chol	(3)
	Grateloupia elliptica	Chol	(3)
Gigartinales	*Chondrus crispus*	Sito	(1)
	Gigartina stellata	Sito	(1)
	Iridophycus cornucopiae	Chol	(3)
Rhodymeniales	*Palmaria palmata*	Fuco	(1)
Ceramiales	*Ceramium rubrum*	Sito	(1)
	Rhodomela larix	Chol	(3)

* Key to abbreviations of sterols.
   Sito: sitosterol, Fuco: fucosterol, Sarg: sargasterol, Chal: chalinasterol, Chol: cholesterol

** Key to references.
   (1) Heibron (1942)   (4) Black and Cornhill (1951)
   (2) Ito et al. (1956)   (5) Tsuda et al. (1957)
   (3) Tsuda et al. (1958)   (6) Tsuda et al. (1958)

and lipid-soluble vitamins—play a greater role in relation to neutral fatty acids in algae than they do in land plants. Few sterols are specific to seaweeds. Fucosterol, one of these rare kinds, has a structure closely resembling those of vitamin D_2 and ergosterol. Carotene and lipid-soluble vitamins too are present (see Table 12).

Vitamins

High vitamin and mineral contents are the most outstanding nutritional features of sea vegetables. Table 13 compares their vitamin contents with those of some other foods. Aside from the ones shown in this table, such substances as lipoic acid, choline, and inositol are present in sea vegetables, though in small amounts.

Table 13   Vitamin Contents in Sea Vegetables and Other Foods

per 100 g	A* (IU)	B_1 (mg)	B_2 (mg)	Niacin (mg)	C (mg)	B_6 (mg)	B_{12} (μg)	Folic acid (μg)
Sea Vegetables (dry)								
Porphyra tenera (upper)	44,500	0.25	1.24	10.0	20			
(middle)	38,400	0.21	1.00	3.0	20	1.04	13–29	8.8
(lower)	20,400	0.12	0.89	2.6	20			
Ulva sp.	960	0.06	0.03	8.0	10		6.3	11.8
Enteromorpha sp.	500	0.04	0.52	1.0	10		1.3	42.9
Eisenia bicyclis	50	0.02	0.02	2.6	0			
Laminaria sp.	430	0.08	0.32	1.8	11	0.27	0.3	
Hizikia fusiforme	150	0.01	0.20	4.0	0		0.57	21.8
Undaria pinnatifida	140	0.11	0.14	10.0	15			
Tomatoes	200	0.08	0.03	0.3	20	0.11	0	28
Spinach	2,600	0.12	0.30	1.0	100	0.18	0	140
Apples	5	0.02	0.03	0.2	5	0.03	0	5
Cabbage	10	0.05	0.05	0.2	44	0.16	0	90

* Retinol potency.   From food analysis tables.

Almost all edible Japanese sea vegetables contain fairly large amounts of vitamins B_1, B_2, C, niacin, and β-carotene. Though there is no vitamin A in them, β-carotene has the same effects as this vitamin found in land plants. In the table, the value for vitamin A is actually a conversion of carotene content on the basis of effects.

Asakusa-nori (*Porphyra tenera*) is a virtual storehouse of vitamins with a vitamin A content twenty times that of green peppers, ten times that of spinach. Its vitamin C content is about the same as that of tomatoes but four times that of apples. In addition, it provides ample vitamin B_1. The better the color and flavor of the *nori* the higher its vitamin contents. Since dried or toasted *nori* must be stored out of the sunlight and in a dry place, it loses none of its vitamin C through breakdown.

Minerals

Sea vegetables contain more minerals than any other kind of food. Mainly because of the action of their surface tissues, polysaccharides absorb freely and selectively inorganic substances from seawater. An extremely wide range of minerals accounts for from 7 to 38 percent of their dry weight. All of the minerals required by human beings, including calcium, sodium, magnesium, potassium, phosphorus, iodine, iron, and zinc are present in sufficient amounts. In addition, there are many trace elements in seaweeds.

Calcium

The high amount of calcium in sea vegetables, if all nutritionally effective, would make them the richest food after milk. Unfortunately, however, at present insufficient information is available on the form calcium assumes in sea vegetables. If it can be shown that its utilization is as good as that of calcium in milk, sea vegetables will become an unrivaled source of this mineral.

Table 14   Calcium Content in Sea Vegetables and Other Foods (Unit: mg%)

Sea Vegetables (dry)		Other foods	
Hizikia fusiforme	1,400	Sesame seeds	1,100
Undaria pinnatifida	1,300	Dried sardines	330
Eisenia bicyclis	1,170	Soybeans	190
Analipus japonicus	890	Milk	100
Laminaria sp.	800	Spinach	98
Ulva sp.	730	Eggs	65
Enteromorpha sp.	600	Cabbage	24
Porphyra tenera	470		

Iron

Deficiency of iron is one of the causes of malnutrition and anemia brought on by reduction of food intake for the sake of weight loss. The iron content of sea vegetables is from two to more than ten times that of egg yolks and spinach.

Table 15   Iron Content in Sea Vegetables and Other Foods (Unit: mg%)

Sea Vegetables (dry)		Other foods	
Enteromorpha	106	Sesame seeds	16
Ulva sp.	87	Egg yolk	6.3
Hizikia fusiforme	29	Soybeans	7
Laminaria sp.	15	Sardines	10
Undaria pinnatifida	13	String beans	6
Eisenia bicyclis	12	Spinach	3.3
Analipus japonicus	10	Beef	3.6
Porphyra tenera	23		

Iodine

The Chinese for centuries have treated goiter, caused by an iodine deficiency, by means of iodine obtained from *kombu* (*Laminaria*) harvested from the waters around Japan, especially the vicinity of the northern island Hokkaidō. Brown algae are very high in iodine content. One gram of *kombu* kelp daily would provide the 0.1 to 0.2 milligrams required by a normal adult or the 0.2 milligrams needed by children and pregnant women. In Japan, because of the regular consumption of seaweeds, there is no need to iodize table salt, as is done in the United States and Canada.

Table 16   Iodine Contents (Unit: mg%)

Seaweeds (dry)		Other foods	
Laminaria sp.	193–471	Shell fish	0.29
Eisenia bicyclis	98–564	Crustaceans	0.15
Sargassum confusum	300	Fish	0.07
Hizikia fusiforme	40	Seawater	0.005
Undaria pinnatifida	18–35	Eggs	0.006
Gelidium sp.	160	Meat	0.0005
Chondrus ocellatus	1.1	Onions, carrots	0.002
Porphyra tenera	0.5	Butter	0.01

Nutritional Value

Sea-vegetable polysaccharides, which are very different from land-plant polysaccharides, cannot be digested by the enzyme α-amylase. For this reason, they provide the human system with no calories, though fish and shellfish have an enzyme that decomposes them for the sake of energy. Because they are satisfying, seaweeds are a good diet food. Their soft cell walls regulate intestinal action without damaging intestine walls. In terms of amino-acid composition, seaweed protein is similar to that of egg whites and legumes; but many questions remain to be answered about the digestibility of this protein. Low in fats, sea vegetables have more of such vitamins as A, B_1, B_2, B_6, B_{12}, and C; pantothenic acid; folic acid; and niacin than fresh fruits and land vegetables.

Table 17   Digestibility of Sea Vegetables (Unit: %)

	Crude proteins	Lipids	Carbo-hydrates
Laminaria sp.	56	31	83
Undaria pinnatifida	64	60	92
Porphyra tenera	72	14	75

Source: Kimura, N., 1952.

Laminaria sp.	16.4	7.3	42.7
Undaria pinnatifida	41.1	4.5	25.4
Hizikia fusiforme	44.9	7.4	47.8
Porphyra tenera	70.8	2.0	51.2

Source: Matsumoto, K., 1960.

Results on experimentation on sea-vegetable digestibility in humans and other animals over a long period of time have provided no conclusive results, and data often differ according to species and individual. Only *Asakusa-nori* (*Porphyra tenera*) shows digestibility of 70 percent of carbohydrates and proteins. This ratio is probably the result of the action of intestinal bacteria.

Pigments

Colors

Though sea-vegetable fronds are not as diversely colored as land-plant foliage, color is generally referred to in their name: blue-green, green, brown, and red. Like land plants, sea vegetables contain chlorophylls and carotenoids. They perform photosynthesis, which is aided by some special accessory pigments or phycobilins.

Chlorophylls and carotenoids

Carotenoids in sea vegetable include red, orange, and yellow pigments, carotenes (three isomers: α, β, and γ-carotene), and xanthophylls including many isomers. (See pp. 61–65 for information on the roles of these elements in photosynthesis.) Two xanthophylls—β-carotene and lutein—are common to all blue-green, green, brown, and red algae. Though chlorophyll a is found in all algae, chlorophyll b is limited to green and chlorophyll c to brown algae, in which it produces a green color.

Phycobilins

Found in red and blue-green algae, phycobilins, unlike chlorophylls and carotenoids, assume the form of biliproteins firmly bound to proteins. According to Lemberg (1933), the prosthetic groups have tetrapyrrole structures. Pigments of the bilirubin type include mesobiliviolin and mesobilirhodin. In sea vegetables, mesobiliviolin is known as phycocyanin (blue), and mesobilirhodin as phycoerythrin (red). Both are water-soluble proteins. Less stable than phycoerythrin, phycocyanin fades on exposure to strong sunlight. Phycoerythrin is comparatively stable, retaining it red color temporarily even in acidic solution. Heat, drying and acidic and alkali conditions affect these major pigments and alter the colors of seaweed fronds.

Flavor and Taste

When growing in the sea, sea vegetables have only a faint flavor; when they have been damaged or have washed up on the beach, however, decomposition of organic iodine compounds brought on by enzymes in the algae by the action of bacteria produce an irritating odor which accounts for their flavor. This flavor is produced by free iodine and such sulfur compounds as dimethyl sulfide.

Volatile elements in damaged and decomposing sea vegetables give off odors and tastes (Table 18). The amounts of these volatile components differ with habitat, species, and harvest time.

Table 18 Volatile Components of Sea Vegetables

	Green			Brown		Red	
	Ulva pertusa	Entero-morpha	Codium fragile	Lami-naria sp.	Sarga-ssum sp.	Digenea simplex	Porphyra tenera
Dimethyl sulfide	+	+	+	±	−	−	−
Methylmercaptan	−	−	−	+	+	+	+
Trimethylamine	+*	+*	+*	+	+*		+
Formic acid	+	+	+	+	+	+	+
Acetic acid	+	+	+	+	+	+	+
Acrylic acid	+	+	+	−	−	−	−
Propionic acid	+	+	+	+	+	+	+
Butyric acid	+	+	+	+	+	+	+
Isovaleric acid	+	+	+	+	+	+	+
N-caproic acid	+	+	+	+	+	+	+
Caprylic acid	+	+	+	+	+	+	+
Myristic acid	+	+	+	+	+	+	+
Palmitic acid	+	+	+	+	+	+	+
Linolic acid	+	+	+	+	+	+	+
P-cresol	+	+	+	+	+	+	+
Furfural	+	+	+	+	+	+	+
α-methyl furfural	+	+	+	+	+	+	+
N-valeraldehyde	+	+	+	+	+	+	+
Benzaldehyde	+	+	+	+	+	+	+
Furfuryl alcohol	+	+	+	+	+	−	−
1,8-cineol	+	+	+	+	+	+	−
D-limonene	+	+	+	+	+	+	+
Linalool	+	+	+	+	+	+	−
Geraniol	+	+	+	+	+	+	+
α-pinene	+	+		+	+		+
Carbon	+	+			+		+
P-cymene				+	+		
Terpinolene	+	+			+		+

Source: Katayama, T., 1961, *Arasaki, T., 1971.

Table 19 Main Volatile Components of *Laminaria* sp.
(Shown as mg in 100 g of dried material)

Methylmercaptan	0.13
Acetone and propionaldehyde	0.75
Trimethylamine	0.06
Other amines	1.38
Lower fatty acids	7.38
Higher fatty acids	3.75
Terpene	9.13

Dimethyl sulfide and methylmercaptan

Dimethyl sulfide, a volatile substance with a bitter taste, has a strong flavor like that of dried *Enteromorpha* raised to its boiling temperature (37°C). While sea vegetables are growing, it is present as dimethyl propiotetine, which is changed to dimethyl sulfide by enzyme action when the algae are damaged. Its characteristic

Table 20   Green and Red Algae Containing Dimethyl Sulfide

Green Algae	*Ulva pertusa*
	Ulva lactuca
	Enteromorpha linza
	Enteromorpha clathrata
	Enteromorpha intestinalis
	Codium fragile
	Monostroma sp.
	Cladophora rupestris
Red Algae	*Polysiphonia fastigiata*
	Polysiphonia nigrescens
	Ceramium rubrum

Source: Obata, Y. et al., 1951.

taste occurs mainly in green algae and in some species of red algae. Methylmercaptan, not dimethyl sulfide, is formed in brown algae and some species of red algae. In green algae (*Ulva* sp., *Enteromorpha linza*, *Enteromorpha clathrata*, and *Monostroma nitidum*) there is a very high dimethyl-sulfide content. Methylmercaptan is present in *Porphyra tenera*, though dimethyl sulfide is not. In some cases, *Ulva* and *Enteromorpha* are added to dried *nori* sheets to increase flavor.

Trimethylamine

Well known as the source of bad odors in fish, trimethylamine is found in sea vegetables as well. But the smell of this substance is not necessarily bad in small amounts;

Table 21   Distribution of Trimethylamine Oxide in Sea Vegetables and Fishes (mg%)

Algae		Trimethylamine oxide
Green	*Codium fragile*	227
	Enteromorpha linza	551
	Ulva pertusa	602
Brown	*Eisenia bicyclis*	210
	Hizikia fusiformis	149
	Undaria pinnatifida	144
Red	*Grateloupia elliptica*	377
	Porphyra suborbiculata	679
	Porphyra tenera	486

Source: Arasaki, T., 1971.

Fish	Trimethylamine oxide
Blue shark	1,000
Herring	210
Sardine	38–50
Salmon	26
Tuna	21
Squid	589
Shrimp	331

Source: Yamada, K., 1967.

indeed, it is the source of the aromas of flowers. As an oxide, in fresh fish, trimethyl-amine has no odor. The stench develops as this oxide is reduced to trimethylamine by bacterial enzymes as the fish grows old and stale. As is true in fish, enzymes from bacteria attached to the surface reduce the oxide in algae and produce trimethylamine depending on the condition of the plant itself. Since the values for trimethylamine oxide shown in Table 21 are the result of reoxidization of trimethylamine produced by reduction, they may be assumed to represent the total amount of trimethylamine produceable in the organism. The data in the table show that, in general, there is more trimethylamine in algae than in most fish, with the exception of the shark, in which this substance is abundant. It is interesting to note that there should be more trimethylamine in thin-fleshed algae like *Ulva*, *Enteromorpha*, and *Porphyra* than in the thicker *Hizikia*, *Undaria*, *Eisenia*, and *Codium*.

The faint odor of trimethylamine in dried sheets of *nori* (*Porphyra tenera*) increases radically when the seaweed is immersed in water because, as in the case of spoiled fish, the trimethylamine oxide is rapidly reduced to trimethylamine itself.

Organic acids

Such organic acids as formic, propionic, acetic, isovalerianic, caproic, myristic, pyruvic, and malic acids play a part in sea-vegetable flavors; unsaturated fatty acids give them their characteristic tastes.

Aldehydes and alcohols

Aldehydes found in sea vegetables include furfural, valeraldehyde, and benzaldehyde. The rare aldehyde 5-bromo-3, 4-deoxybenzaldehyde is found in red algae. Alcohols found in them include furfural alcohol and heptanol. These volatile substances contribute to flavor.

Terpene

Present in land plants too, terpene plays a role in the characteristic flavors of sea vegetables. Some of the many types include cadinene, geraniol, cineol, α-pinene, d-limonen, carbon, terpinolene, and p-thymine. The following are some of the components thought to be responsible for the distinctive flavors of sea vegetables, which, as has been explained, the people of Japan have loved for centuries.

Sugar alcohols

The main sugar alcohols in sea vegetables are mannitol in brown algae and sorbitol and dulcitol in red algae. Though sweet, these substances are not caloric as are sucrose or glucose. Mannitol (see Table 22) has a sweetness of about 60 percent that of sucrose and is often found as a white powder on the surface of kelp (*Laminaria*).

Table 22 Mannitol Contents of Seaweeds (Unit: %)

Laminaria sp.	23–24
Undaria pinnatifida	5.6–12.3
Eisenia bicyclis	10.6–13.5
Hizikia fusiforme	9.1– 9.7

Sorbitol, the most powerfully sweet of these sea-vegetable sugar alcohols, is used widely for diet and diabetes patients as a food seasoning.

Glutamic acid, 5′-inosinic acid, and 5′-guanylic acid

Glutamic acid, in the form of monosodium salt, is widely used to prepare stocks for various Japanese foods. It is an amino acid, whereas 5′-inosinic acid and 5′-guanylic acid are nucleic acids. All three are found in some sea vegetables.

Asakusa-nori (Porphyra tenera) and wakame (Undaria pinnatifida) too contain large amounts of glutamic acid. In addition, Asakusa-nori has been found to contain abundant 5′-inosinic and 5′-guanylic acids (5mg%). Research on these three components in other seaweeds is still insufficient. Glutamic, 5′-inosinic, and 5′-guanylic acids account for the taste the Japanese find appealing in Asakusa-nori.

Other amino acids

The contents and types of amino acids—for instance glycine and alanine, which are sweet, and leucine, isoleucine, and valine, which are slightly bitter—in multiple effects with inosinic and guanylic acids do much to determine the flavor of sea vegetables. Extracts (70 percent alcohol) of Asakusa-nori are rich in glutamic acid, alanine, and taurine. Those of Undaria pinnatifida contain a great deal of alanine and glycine, whereas Laminaria japonica has glutamic acid as its main extract amino-acid component and aspartic acid as the second most important.

Taurine, a kind of amino acid, is different from the common amino acids. An amidosulfonic acid containing sulfur and producing an acidic taste like those of aspartic and glutamic acids, it contains the sulfonyl group ($-SO_3H$) instead of the carboxyl group ($-COOH$) present in ordinary amino acids. Not included in proteins but existing only in a free condition, taurine can be derived from cystine, an amino acid that forms a protein. Found in squid, octopus, and shellfish (about 0.5%) and in fish, taurine occurs in higher percentages in sea vegetables. The methyl derivative of taurine (N-methyltaurine) has a sweet taste as a sodium salt.

Table 23   Taurine Contents in Sea Vegetables and Other Foods (Unit: mg%)

Sea Vegetables		Other foods	
Ulva pertusa	2	Bonito	80
Undaria pinnatifida	12	Squid	350
Neodilsea yendoana	220	Octopus	520
Porphyra tenera	480	Lobster	170
Chondria crassicaulis	20	Pearl oysters	800

Many of the amino acids in sea vegetables contain sulfur, and most of the ones that do contain it are sulfonic acids. Amino acids containing sulfur (like cystine and taurine) have a meaty flavor that plays a part in the characteristic tastes of sea vegetables.

Most of the low-molecular peptides in sea vegetables have a bitter taste that is actually good in small degrees. (Incidentally, the peptides formed in sakè during the brewing process are important to the flavor of the drink.) Arsenine (a tripeptide consisting of two molecules of glutamic acid and one molecule of alanine) is found in *Eisenia bicyclis*, and carnosine (a dipeptide of β-alanine and histidine) is found in red algae. Carnosine contributes to the flavor of meat extracts. Betaine, an important element in the flavor of fresh land vegetables is widely distributed among sea vegetables too.

Specific Japanese Seaweeds as Foods

Kombu (Laminaria japonica)

One of the most important uses for *kombu* (*Laminaria japonica*), as has been stated, is the preparation of stock to serve as the basis for many other foods. Monosodium glutamate, aspartic acid, alanine, mannitol, and iodine account for the flavor produced when *Laminaria japonica* is immersed in water (Table 24). Because it lacks

Table 24   Composition of *Laminaria* sp. Extract Solution (Unit: %)*

Components	Laminaria	Cold extraction (2.5 hours)	Hot extraction (0.5 hour)
Solids	100	56.3	59.5
Organic components	74.40	50.1	54.1
Ash	25.60	74.0	75.1
Crude protein	11.25	60.0	66.1
Mannitol	23.60	97.7	93.4
Iodine	0.40	90.0	87.5
Calcium	1.30	16.1	29.2
Magnesium	1.09	45.9	53.2
Sulfuric acid	1.35	68.9	95.6

* Indicates percentage of *Laminaria* sp. component appearing in extract solution.

the peptides produced in stock made from actual *kombu*, commercially sold chemical seasoning does not actually duplicate the original. *Kombu* must not be boiled long, since this releases unpleasant-tasting inorganic magnesium, calcium, and sulfuric acid into the water.

Asakusa-nori (Porphyra tenera)

The complex taste of *Asakusa-nori* results from an astonishingly large number of elements: two nucleic acids (5′-inosinic and 5′-guanylic acids in quantities from 3 to 5 times greater than in bonito or *shiitake* mushrooms) and several amino acids (glutamic acid, alanine, glycine, and taurine). Taurine and alanine are present in remarkably large amounts. Indeed, alanine, sometimes accounting for as much as 25 percent of the nitrogen in the extract, produces the slightly sweet taste of the fresh fronds of *Asakusa-nori*. There are from four to five times as much amino acid in *Asakusa-nori* extract as in the extracts of other sea vegetables.

Medical Applications

Modern medicine tends to regard the ancient Japanese and Chinese traditions of medical uses of sea vegetables as mere folklore. In Japan, only two recognized medicaments have resulted from this venerable tradition: the anthelmintic *Makuri* (*Digenea simplex*) and the antihypertensive agent laminin.

Though research on their medical use is still in an early, undeveloped stage, sea vegetables have been shown to contain antibacterial, antifungal, antiviral, antiprotozoal, and antineoplastic elements. In addition they are toxic to certain insects and fish. The antibiotics they contain help preserve the ecological system of the sea and must be studied for use in preventing that system from falling into the polluted state that large-scale use of chemicals has created on the land masses of the world. In the following pages some of the medically promising components of sea vegetables are discussed.

Antilipemic and Blood-cholesterol Reducing Substances

Since about 1960, medical understanding of the long-standing Japanese belief that some sea vegetables are effective against organic diseases of the myocardium and the vascular system has been forthcoming, though the process is still complex and cannot be explained in terms of a single, simple concept. It is known, however, that administration of such thyroid hormones as thyroxin reduces cholesterol and lipids in the blood of elderly people when the thyroid functions decrease. The following points are interesting in this connection.

(1) **Carrageenan.** Subcutaneous injections of carrageenan inhibit arteriosclerosis in guinea pigs four or five weeks after treatment. Daily oral administrations (20mg/kg) of carrageenan inhibit increase of lipids and cholesterol in rabbits.

(2) *Laminaria japonica*. Oral administration of *kombu* (*Laminaria japonica*) inhibited the progress of hyperlipemia, hypertension, and arteriosclerosis even in rabbits to which cholesterol had been administered.

(3) **Sitosterol.** Like plant sitosterol applied to white Leghorn chickens, sitosterol from sea vegetables (fucosterol from *Laminaria* and sargasterol from *Sargassum*) effectively reduces blood cholesterol.

(4) **Mixture of *Entermorpha* and *Monostroma* and *Porphyra tenera* in feed** (5 percent of the total) caused cholesterol reduction in the blood of white mice. Increased cholesterol in the feces of mice fed *Porphyra tenera* suggests that cholesterol absorption in the digestive tract was inhibited.

(5) **Iodoamino acids.** Among the numerous iodoamino acids in sea vegetables, thyroxin and similar substances with thyroid hormonal actions are especially widely distributed. For instance, T. Tsuchiya (1971) reported great amounts of thyroxin in the brown algae *Analipus japonicus*. The effects of powders and extracts of *Fucus* and *Laminaria* on goiter patients and of sea-vegetable powders and pills in weight reduction apparently result from the antilipemic actions of such components as

iodoamino acids. In the past few years, a Spanish soap containing brown algae has been gaining considerable for cosmetic effects and contribution to weight reduction.

Blood Anticoagulants

Sea-vegetable polysaccharides have been shown to have blood anticoagulant actions similar to those of heparin. For instance, S. Kimura (1941) observed such actions in twenty-one of seventy-nine sea-vegetable varieties found in Japanese waters. Though laminaran sulfate (sulfated polysaccharide laminaran isolated from the brown algae *Laminaria digitata*) has only one-third the effect of heparin, this presents problems only in cases of long-term use. The red alga *Dilsea edulis*, which has strong anticoagulant action in vivo and in vitro, is especially promising since it is cheap and nontoxic.

Carrageenan, which is widely used as a food additive, has a fairly weak blood anticoagulant effect (λ-carrageenan 1/13 and κ-carrageenan 1/34, when the effect of heparin is taken to be 1). Fucoidan, the polysaccharide obtained from *Fucus*, however, has a blood anticoagulant effect equal to that of heparin.

Antitumoral Effects

Once again, Japanese folklore has long held that sea vegetables are effective in preventing tumors. Recent research has shown the effectiveness of the polysaccharides explained below.

1. Warm-water extracts from such brown algae as *Sargassum confusum* and *Laminaria japonica* and the polysaccharide funoran from the red algae *Gloiopeltis complanata* are effective against sarcoma-180.
2. In tests on the extract fractions of sixty-six green, brown, and red algae from Japanese waters, S. Nakazawa (1974) found that three types of brown algae of the *Sargassum* order (*S. horneri*, *S. hemiphyllum*, and *S. tortile*) prolonged the lives of mice suffering from ascites tumors. Sea vegetables showed tumor-growth inhibiting properties in from 30 to 60 percent of a group of mice suffering from Ehrlich ascites carcinoma and sarcoma-180. Rates of toxicity in the experimental animals, however, were high. Polysaccharide fractions (active ingredients from *S. horneri*) showed complete life-prolonging effects in from 80 to 100 percent of a group of animals given intraperitoneal injections (0.125–0.5 mg per mouse per day for 6 consecutive days) and observed for 60 days.
3. According to S. Nakazawa, the sulfated polysaccharide fraction of the green algae *Codium pugniformis* has the same antitumor effect on cancer-bearing mice as that of *S. horneri*.

Antibiotics

As has already been said, sea vegetables have components that are antibacterial and toxic to fish. This is part of the mutual defense mechanism built into relations among animals, plants, and microorganisms throughout the world. Extensive research conducted since 1950 has shown that the main sea-vegetable components acting as antibiotics against bacteria, fungi, and viruses are fatty acids, terpene, tannin, and bromophenols.

Fatty acids

Numerous studies have shown that fatty-acid-type antibiotics are antibacterial, antifungal, antiviral, anticancerous, and antiprotozoal as well as being highly toxic to animals and plants. Many sea vegetables are fairly strongly antibacterial. Among the brown algae, *Sargassum natans*, and among the red algae, *Chondria littoria*, have fatty acids that are highly antibacterial. Their acids are mainly volatile, have a wide spectrum of antibacterial and antifungal actions, and are toxic to KB tumors.

Acrylic acids

The unicellular alga belonging to Chrysophyta known as *Phaeocystis pouchetii* has a component that is antibacterial to Gram negative and positive bacteria. It is assumed that this component is one of the acrylic acids, which are widely distributed among red, brown, and green algae. Acrylic acid content in dried fronds of *Phaeocystis pouchetii* reaches 8 percent. The food chain is interestingly illustrated by the effect theses acids have on penguins. *Euphausia* eat *Phaeocystis pouchetii*. Penguins in the Antarctic region eat *Euphausia*. And autopsies have shown a lowered number of microorganisms in the stomachs of these penguins as a result of the antibacterial activity of the acrylic acid in the alga.

Acrylic acid, an unsaturated fatty acid, is formed by the decomposition of dimethylpropiotetin, a precursor of dimethyl sulfide, which gives sea vegetables their characteristic flavor. Sea vegetables capable of producing dimethyl sulfide can produce acrylic acid as well. Acrylic acid is thought to account for the strong antibacterial actions of *Enteromorpha* and *Ulva pertusa*.

Bromophenols

The halogens, iodine, and bromine are often bound to phenols in sea vegetables to produce halogenated phenols that have long been recognized as antiseptics and disinfectants. Presumably these substances help account for the antibacterial action of sea vegetables. The bromophenols detected in *Rhodomela larix, Symphyocladia latiuscula, Laminaria angustata,* and *Undaria pinnatifida* inhibit the growth of bacteria. In addition to its antibacterial effects, a crystallized bromophenol isolated from *Symphyocladia latiuscula* is strongly anthelmintic. It is thought that phenols in sea vegetables inhibit growth of epiphytic algae by denaturing and composing proteins in their cells.

Tannins

Tannin, a characteristic plant component, contains polyphenols. Many of the tannin components in brown algae have antibacterial action and protect such sea vegetables as *Sargassum confusum* from alien creatures that might adhere to them. Even if an alien creature does adhere to *Sargassum,* the tannin inhibits its growth.

Terpenes

As has been mentioned, terpenes, present in various types, help account for sea-vegetable flavor. Recent research has detected terpenes with a wide spectrum of antibacterial action in many sea vegetables. Most of these terpenes are toxic to animals. One terpene, extracted from a brown alga, *Dictyopteris latiuscula*, is not antibacterial but is strongly antifungal against ten species of fungus harmful to plants.

Toxic Components

Toxic components in sea vegetables—much smaller a number than in land plants—are shown in Table 25. In Japan and China, *makuri* (*Digenea simplex*) has long been recognized as an anthelmintic.

Table 25 Toxic Components of Seaweeds

	Seaweeds	Action	Toxic Components
Green	*Ulva pertusa*	Hemolytic	Galactolipid, Sulfolipid
	Chaetomorpha	Toxic to fish hemolytic	Long-chain fatty acid
	Caulerpa	Toxic to humans (numbness)	Caulerpicin
	Codium fragile	Anthelmintic (ascaris)	Unclear
Brown	*Sargassum confusum*	Anthelmintic (ascaris)	Sargalin
	Alaria crassifolia, *Cystophyllum hakodatense, Laminaria ochotensis*	Convulsive poison	Crude lipid unsaponifiable matter
	Sargassum thunbergii	Anthelmintic (ascaris)	Unclear
Red	*Phyllophora nervosa*	Lethal (dogs)	Hordenine
	Digenea simplex	Anthelmintic (ascaris)	Kainic acid
	Chondria armata	Anthelmintic (ascaris), insecticide (flies)	Domoic acid

Anthelmintics

Makuri (Digenea simplex): Though they have all but vanished now, until about forty years ago, Japanese—especially children—suffered from diseases caused by such parasites as Trematoda, Cestoda, and Nematoda. The common remedy, inherited from Chinese medicine, was to administer an extract made by boiling the fronds of a seaweed called *Digenea simplex* found in the warm waters of the South China Sea and around Okinawa (it is found in Atlantic waters as well). The dosage, though only a mild anthelmintic because of the presence of kainic acid in the extract, is usually effective for children of less than ten years of age and has no side effects. Santonin, obtained from plants of the aster family, is stronger but has unpleasant side effects. Its strength and the gentler action of *Digenea simplex* are combined in some commercially prepared patent medicines for the treatment of internal parasites. Extract of *Digenea simplex* is stronger when prepared from dried fronds.

The abundance of such epiphytes as coralline algae on Pacific *Digenea simplex* have led to some doubt as to whether these plants or the seaweed itself have the anthelmintic property. But it is scientifically certain that kainic acid—found in *Digenea simplex* and today synthetically produced—is the effective ingredient.

Interestingly, the now protected and rare sea mammal called the dugong (the prototype for the mythical mermaid) lives on such sea grasses as *Halophila*, *Halodula*, *Cymodocea*, and red algae including *Digenea simplex*. The ancient Okinawans, who regarded the dugong as a creature that lives to immense ages, observed its eating habits and consumed a porridge of *Digenea simplex*, which they believed to be the secret of the animal's longevity. They also ate the flesh of the dugong, which is said to resemble pork in flavor.

Digenea simplex is harvested between March and August in the warm waters of the South Pacific, the Indian Ocean, and Australian seas.

Chondria armata: Domoic acid is the effective element producing a still stronger anthelmintic action in the seaweed called *Chondria armata*, which belongs to the *Rhodomela larix* family, as does *Digenea simplex*. It too lives in warm waters. Its insecticidal properties were discovered when it was observed that flies lighting on beach-dried *Chondria armata* died.

Sargassum confusum and Sargassum thunbergii: Both of these brown algae have anthelmintic properties. *S. thunbergii*, found in Japanese waters, has long been a folk remedy for internal parasites. It is extracted by boiling *S. confusum*, which is limited mainly to the Japan Sea and the Tsushima Straits. Its anthelmintic component, known as Sargarin, has been isolated. In a 1.5-percent solution it has a stronger anthelmintic effect than the kainic acid of *Digenea simplex*.

Codium fragile: This green alga is a familiar anthelmintic with the Japanese people. In the past it was eaten as a food too, though today its popularity has dropped.

Anthelmintics in Europe

The red algae *Alsidium helminthocorton*, which grows in the waters off the shores of Corsica, has long been used in medicines for pinworms and roundworms and as a laxative. In addition, it has been used as a treatment for hard fibromas. In Brittany, the red algae, *Corallina officinalis*, *C. squamata*, and *C. rubens*, which have strong catalase action, are used as anthelmintics.

Antihypertensive agents in *Laminaria japonica*

Folk medicine has long employed extracts of root *Laminaria japonica* to reduce tension. Oral administration of an extract of *Laminaria japonica* made by immersing the seaweed in hot water (50°C–60°C) and letting it stand at room temperature for from 5 to 24 hours produces a parallel reduction in both maximum and mininum blood pressures. In 1964, Dr. Takemoto identified the amino acid laminine as the effective hypertensive element in *Laminaria japonica*. Laminine, which occurs in all the Laminariaceae, is most abundant in *L. angustata*. Powdered root *Laminaria* is currently used to treat hypertension.

Medical Uses of Alginate

The industrially valuable polysaccharide alginic acid, which is produced from brown algae, has recently been discovered to have medicinal properties.

(1) Radiography contrast agent

Barium sulfate, the contrast agent in radiography for the early detection of stomach cancer and diagnosis of diseases of the digestive tract, precipitates rapidly since it does not dissolve well in water. The propylene glycol ester of alginic acid effectively ensures uniformity and stability of barium-sulfate suspensions, making the acid useful in x-ray photography.

(2) Calcium alginate wools

Alginic acid is the source of calcium alginate wools, which are used as hemostatic agents in surgery and dentistry. They are easy to sterilize and have no side effects.

(3) Agricultural antiviral agent

Alginic acid (under the brand name *Nomozan*) is marketed for prevention of the tobacco mosaic virus, which greatly reduces tobacco harvests. Alginic-acid spray, both natural and harmless to human beings, is in keeping with the current trend to depreciate agricultural chemicals for the damage they do to the environment.

Folk Medicines

In the Orient, Russia, and Europe, various algae have long been used as cures and treatments for a wide range of sickness and pathological conditions. The following attributes have been assigned to sea vegetables.

	BROWN ALGAE
Laminaria japonica	Effective either charred or pickled, *Laminaria japonica* is believed to be helpful against neuroses and palsy when strips of it are placed in bathwater. It is known to lower hypertension and to be good for edema.
Eisenia bicyclis	Effective against gynecological diseases.
Undaria pinnatifida	Cleanses blood after childbirth.
Nemacystus decipiens	Effective against wens and swellings.

	RED ALGAE
Porphyra sp.	Effective against beriberi and wens.
Digenea simplex	Effective as an anthelmintic.
Chondrus crispus	Irish moss, used by Europeans as a treatment for respiratory ailments from ancient times.

	GREEN ALGAE
Enteromorpha	Effective against wens, hemorrhoids, and stomach diseases.

Thalassotherapy and Algotherapy

In 1867, a French physician named Bonnardiere, coined the word *thalassotherapy* (from the Greek *thalassa* or sea), but the therapy it indicates had been performed in Europe for centuries. It includes seafood and sea-vegetable diets to reduce obesity; drinking of seawater; bathing in hot seawater (38°C); bathing in seawater in which brown algae, in the form of kelp meal, are suspended; kelp-meal and seawater massages, floating in seawater while undergoing mechanical and physical treatment of the muscles; fomentation with bottom mud or radioactive bottom ooze; sand baths on the beach; and sunbathing. Not all of these therapies have medico-scientific substantiation, but custom seems to lend them reliability.

In the many centers established for such therapy in France, West Germany, Belgium, Spain, Italy, Yugoslavia, and the Soviet Black Sea coast, treatment of such problems as chronic rheumatism, gout, neuralgia, asthma, wounds, eczema, hemorrhoids, scrofulosis, neuroses, stress-related diseases, and aging as well as rehabilitation is performed by qualified specialists.

Algotherapy is specifically the use of algae in medical or cosmetic treatment. In Japan, *Eisenia* and *Ecklonia* added to hot bath water are supposed to prevent or cure palsy and hypertension. This kind of treatment is always prescribed for sufferers of caisson disease. In Western Europe, powdered sea vegetables (*Fucus*, *Ascophyllum*, or *Laminaria*) are kneaded into a paste and sometimes combined with other fomentation agents for use as plasters on arthritic joints or used in combination with massage. In some instances, powdered sea vegetables and effervescents are added to the bath water to beautify the skin.

The brown algae are often dried, chopped, worked into colloidal pastes, or combined in a soap that is supposed to promote loss of body weight. Products including alginate from brown algae or carrageenan from red algae are used as beauty aids.

At present the situation regarding scientific verification of thalassotherapy and algotherapy is analogous to that regarding the traditional medicines of the Orient, which, long despised as mere superstition, are now being objectively shown to contain much that is valuable. As our still insufficient knowledge of the marine environment grows, the efficacy of thalassotherapy and algotherapy may be scientifically established. It seems entirely likely that the alginic acid, fucoidan, tanninlike substances, iodine, potassium, calcium, and arsenic in brown algae; the sulfate galactans (agar and carrageenan), bromine, iodine, calcium, and vitamins in red algae; and the enzymes, plant hormones, and antibiotic and antibacterial susbstances in most algae would, either singly or in combination, have some effects. For instance, potassium, sodium, calcium, iodine, and bromine are known to have effects on the permeability and osmotic pressure of cell walls. In 1972, E. Breton used such radioisotopes as ^{131}I, ^{82}Br, ^{42}K, ^{24}Na, and ^{74}As to show that these minerals are absorbed directly from the skin—as they might be from bathing in seawater—and have ion-exchange action within the body. In the beauty departments of some thalassotherapy centers, skin activators made from such polysaccharides as carrageenan and alginates from sea vegetables are combined with sea mud and other substances in skin treatment.

Longevity

In extensive traveling, beginning in 1927, Professor S. Kondō, of Tōhoku University, discovered that geographic region and especially diet play a determining part in life-spans of the Japanese people. In areas where a great deal of rice is eaten, salt intake is high because the Japanese people customarily accompany rice with salty pickles or other foods dipped in soy sauce. The inhabitants of such regions frequently die of cerebral apoplexy, and very long life is rare. On islands and in fishing villages, however, people eat less rice and salty food and more sea vegetables, with the result that they live longer. The village of Oki Island, in Shimane Prefecture, where the people eat plain food and soybeans and sea vegetables—of which they are very fond—has the highest incidence rate of longevity of any other place in the nation. Women who dive in the sea for abalone, sea urchins, and red algae often work vigorously until they are over seventy. They eat sea vegetables—*Undaria pinnatifida*—daily, and this reduces the rate of cerebral hemorrhage among them and apparently contributes to long life.

The people of Okinawa and the other southern islands have always eaten a great deal of sea vegetables, especially *Laminaria*. The menus of the royal Ryukyuan palace always included them from as long ago as the middle ages. Other sea vegetables frequently eaten there include *Eudesme virescens*, *Monostroma nitidum*, *Hypnea charoides*, and agar. Recent statistics show that the people of Okinawa eat somewhat more *Laminaria* than the Japanese average. They prefer it chopped and boiled in soups or fried with pork. The average life-span in Okinawa Prefecture ranks fourth in Japan, but the life-span for women there is the longest in the nation. In spite of a lower (from 20 to 30 percent) caloric intake than the Japanese national average, the Okinawans live long apparently because of their intake of sea vegetables. According to Dr. Kondō, 68 out of every 425 people on Okinawa are still working and healthy after the age of 70. This suggests that simple food; moderate consumption of rice, salt, and proteins; plenty of sea vegetables; and adequate exercise are secrets of longevity.

3. Biology of Algae

Like land plants, algae have photosynthetic pigments and use the sun's rays to photosynthesize organic substance ($C_nH_{2n}O_n$) from inorganic carbon dioxide (CO_2) and water (H_2O). Since animals are incapable of this kind of carbon-dioxide assimilation and must rely on plant-produced organic substances, plants are the primary producers in the food chain. Between land plants and algae, however, there are major morphological differences in both photosynthetic pigment components and methods of reproduction.

Differences

Not strictly taxonomical, traditional classification systems divide plants into Phanerogamae (flowering plants) and Cryptogamae (nonflowering plants) on the basis of reproductive method, or into Columophyta or Tracheophyta (plants differentiated into stems, leaves, and roots) and Thallophyta (plants which are not so differentiated). Algae belong to Cryptogamae, because, though they do not have conspicuous flowers, they do reproduce by spores from minute sporangia, and to Thallophyta, since their bodies are not divided into leaves, stems, and roots. The entire alga-body plant has basically the same form and function. Fungi, bacteria, yeast, and mushrooms have similar morphogeny and reproductive systems. The algae photosynthesize, whereas the fungi do not.

Though generally considered lower plants in contrast to the higher land plants, algae are superior in terms of efficiency of solar-energy utilization. In land plants, only certain parts of the body are usually eaten. Sea vegetables on the other hand can be consumed in their entirety since they are undifferentiated. Furthermore, with the exception of *Caulerpa* sp., which grows in waters near the Philippine Islands, there are no poisonous seaweeds.

Pigment Systems

With some exceptions land-plant foliage is usually green. Algae show greater diversity of color, being classified mainly on the basis of their pigment tone. There are four algae phyla:

Green algae—Chlorophyta
Brown algae—Phaeophyta
Red algae—Rhodophyta
Blue-green algae—Cyanophyta
(For pigment in each phylum and comparisons with land plants see Table 26.)

Table 26. Major Pigments in Algae and Land Plants

Pigments	Blue-green algae	Green algae	Brown algae	Red algae	Land plants
Cholorophylls	a	a, b	a, c	a (d)	a, b
Phycobilins (Biliproteins)	Phycocyanin Phycoerythrin	—	—	Phycoerythrin Phycocyanin	—
Carotenes	β, e	α, β, γ	β	α, β	α, β
Xanthophylls	Zeaxanthin Myxoxanthin Oscillaxanthin Flavacine	Lutein Violaxanthin Neoxanthin Siphonoxanthin Astaxanthin	Lutein Violaxanthin Fucoxanthin Diatoxanthin	Lutein Violaxanthin Zeaxanthin	Lutein Violaxanthin Neoxanthin Zeaxanthin Taraxanthin

Fig. 8

(A)

(B)

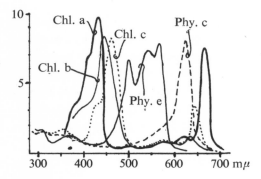

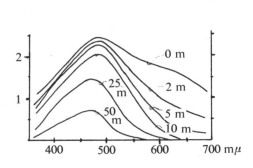

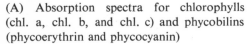

(A) Absorption spectra for chlorophylls (chl. a, chl. b, and chl. c) and phycobilins (phycoerythrin and phycocyanin)

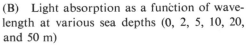

(B) Light absorption as a function of wavelength at various sea depths (0, 2, 5, 10, 20, and 50 m)

(C)

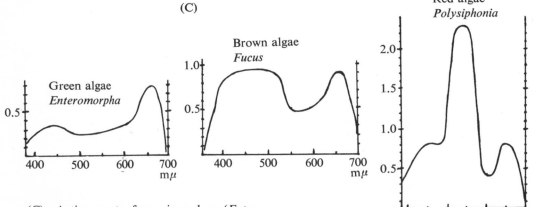

(C) Action spectra for various algae (*Enteromorpha* in green algae, *Fucus* in brown algae, and *Polysiphonia* in red algae)

(B and C by Levring, 1955)

Chlorophyll a is found in all phyla. The other chlorophylls and carotenoids differ in content from phylum to phylum; but they all absorb light energy from the sun, produce photosynthetic products with great efficiency, and assist chlorophyll a in playing the major photosynthesis role. Fig. 8 shows the light-absorption curves of each pigment. Little research has been done to clarify the chemical composition and in-vivo action of a special pigment called phycobilin and found in red and blue-green algae. Algae of different colors can use light of varying intensities and light of varying wavelengths. For instance, brown algae (chlorophyll a+c) and red algae (chlorophyll a and phycobilin) can photosynthesize with less light and with light of shorter wavelengths (for instance green or blue light) than can land plants or green algae (chlorophyll a+b). Evolution of the phyla and environmental adaptation over long periods of time probably account for the differences in pigment content between algae and land plants and among algae.

Quantity of light affects photosynthesis in land plants. But the quantities and qualities of light available to algae in the sea are different from those on land. Obviously, the greater the depth of the sea, the less light penetrates from the sun. In addition to increasing darkness, however, at greater depths the quality of the light alters. At more than ten meters all of the long wavelengths (red light) have been absorbed by the water; and only the short wavelengths (green and blue light) remain. (This accounts for the blue color of the sea.) Green algae grow on the bottom where the sea is shallow. Red algae live at greater depths, and brown algae live somewhere between these other two. Although there are different viewpoints and some questionable points, in general, Th. W. Englemann's chromatic adaptation theory (1883) explains the relation between sea depth and algal color. In some instances, however, seaweeds growing at the same or similar depths are different in pigmentation.

Photosynthetic Products and Storage Substances

Algae are simple in structure. They are undifferentiated and lack the special storage organs found in land plants. It is not known for certain where sugars and polysaccharides produced by photosynthesis and physiological actions are distributed; but the distribution shown in Fig. 9, in spite of differences among phyla, is accepted as probably correct.

Plants produce sugar and oxygen photosynthetically by means of carbon-dioxide assimilation. They also respire in a process in which oxygen dissimilates sugar to form carbon dioxide ($6 CO_2 + 6 H_2O \rightleftharpoons C_6H_{12}O_6 + 6 O_2$). These chemical processes take place inside the plasma membrane (Fig. 9). Under normal living conditions, assimilation is stronger than respiration with the consequence that considerable amounts of sugar are converted and accumulated in the form of storage polysaccharides. Metabolic residual substances are excreted to make up cell-wall contents.

Fig. 9   Diagrammatic Figure of an Algal Cell

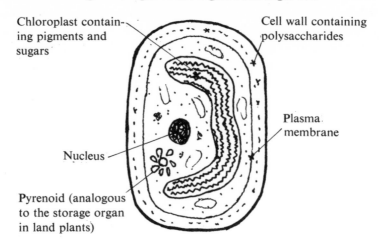

Chloroplast containing pigments and sugars

Cell wall containing polysaccharides

Plasma membrane

Nucleus

Pyrenoid (analogous to the storage organ in land plants)

Table 27.   Sugars and Polysaccharides Present in Sea Vegetables and Land Plants

	Blue-green algae	Green algae	Brown algae	Red algae	Land plants
Sugars forming a major part of poly-saccharides		d-glucose d-galactose d-mannose d-fructose d-xylose l-arabinose l-rhamnose d-glucuronic acid sulfate ester	d-glucose l-fructose d-mannuronic acid l-glucuronic acid mannitol sulfate ester	d-glucose d-galactose d-mannose l-galactose d-xylose sulfate ester	d-glucose d-galactose d-mannose d-fructose d-xylose l-arabinose d-glucuronic acid d-galacturonic acid
Major storage or cell-wall substances	myxophycean starch (X)	starch (X)	laminaran (Y)	floridean starch (X)	starch (X)
	pectin	cellulose	alginic acid fucoidan	floridean mucilage (agar, carrageenan and porphyran) (Z)	cellulose

Note   *Source:* Percival and McDowell, 1967.

(X): α-(1, 4) linked glucan
(Y): β-(1, 3) linked glucan
(Z): galactan

Long study of these processes in land plants (chlorophyll a+b) has made it clear that the sugar produced is glucose, the storage substance is starch, and the cell-wall contents are cellulose. Although research on algae is at a lower level, it has been shown that the storage substances analogous to starch are mainly mannitol and laminaran in brown algae and floridean starch in red algae. Cell walls in red and brown algae contain cellulose. But there are larger amounts of alginic acid and fucoidan in brown algae and carrageenan, agar, and other such galactans as so-called floridean mucilage in red algae. The discrepancies are accounted for by chemical differences among red, brown, and green algae. Some of these variations cause different taste and texture in brown and red algae. For instance, juvenile *Undaria* fronds in which sporangia have not been formed are tastier. *Laminaria* fronds that are two years old taste better than those of one year, even when both are the same size. The galactans that are the major component of some algal polysaccharides produce what is known as floridean mucilage and congeal when extracted from the fronds by boiling and subsequent gradual cooling.

In addition to variations in photosynthetic products and storage or cell-wall structures between sea and land plants and among the algae themselves, mineral contents too vary. For instance, brown algae contain large amounts of iodine and potassium; red algae, on the other hand, contain more bromine and calcium.

Land and Marine Vegetation

The soft bodies of sea vegetation constantly sway with the motion of their watery environment, in contrast to the stiffer forms of most land vegetation, which often has more or less rigid stems. Though some algae are dendroid and have small branches, most of them are thin, flat, and leaflike in shape. Land plants are of three kinds forest (tree), bush, and grassland plants and grow in five zones: tropical, subtropical, temperate, subarctic, and arctic. Each zone has its own characteristic vegetation. Algal vegetation of the sea occurs in three types, the physiognomy of which corresponds to forest, bush, and grassland types. Algae occur in three regions: warm (including tropical and subtropical), temperate, and cold (including subarctic and arctic). Whereas land vegetation in warm zones tends to grow fast and big, algal vegetation in warm zones is smaller (no more than thirty centimeters in length) and usually grassy or bushlike. In the cold seas, however, grow vast forests of dense, luxuriant seaweeds reaching lengths as much as from one to more than ten meters. The physiognomy of the individual plant too is more forestlike than is true in temperate waters. Many of the red algae occur in all three regions. The ratio of green algae to brown algae decreases as the temperature drops. As has been said, the many types of algal vegetation in warm waters are small and tend to be isolated from each other. But in temperate and colder seas, large luxuriant brown algae grow in virtual forests: *Sargassum*, *Ascophyllum*, and *Cystoseira* (all of the Fucales) and *Laminaria*, *Undaria*, *Eisenia*, *Saccorhyza*, *Nereocystis*, and *Macrocystis* (all of the Laminariales). The Fucales dominate in heterogenous forests in the temperate regions, and Laminariales dominate in the monotonous forests of the colder seas. Varieties of edible seaweeds and their quantities are greater in the temperate and colder zones than in the warmer zones.

Rapid motion of seawater and effects of inland rivers on temperatures of the seas around their mouths simplify the regional classifications of algal vegetation from five to three zones by eliminating what would be the subtropical and subarctic. The clas-

Table 28 Representative Algae (by Genus Name) in Intertidal and Sublittoral Zones in Various Areas

	Northern Japan	Temperate Japan	North America, California	Europe
Uppermost tidal zone	*Gloiopeltis* *Porphyra* *Fucus, Pelvetia*	*Gloiopeltis* *Porphyra, Bangia* *Monostroma*	*Pelvetiopsis* *Fucus* *Porphyra*	*Pelvetia, Porphyra* *Fucus spiralis*
Between mean high-tide in neap tides and mean sea level	*Enteromorpha* *Ulva, Chondrus* *Iridophycus*	*Enteromorpha* *Ulva* *Chondrus*	*Gigartina* *Iridophycus* *Ulva, Enteromorpha* *Chondrus*	*Fucus vesiculosus* *Enteromorpha* *Chondrus* *Ascophyllum*
Between mean sea level and mean low-tide in neap tides	*Analipus*	*Gigartina*	*Egregia* *Postelsia*	*Fucus serratus* *Chondrus*
Lowermost tidal zone	*Undaria* *Alaria*	*Endarachne* *Scytosiphon* *Hizikia*		*Laminaria digitata* *Rhodymenia*
Sublittoral zone	*Laminaria* *Cystophyllum* *Cystoseira*	*Codium* *Gracilaria* *Undaria* *Eisenia, Ecklonia* *Sargassum* *Gelidium*	*Codium* *Laminaria* *Nereocystis* *Macrocystis* *Alaria* *Gelidium*	*Rhodymenia* *Lam. cloustonii*

sification presented here pertains to Japanese coastal waters. The waters off the Pacific coast of America, the Atlantic coast of Europe, the southern coasts of Africa, and the coasts of New Zealand and Australia all fall in the cold region, where there is probably a great deal of algal vegetation, though little of it is currently being used.

Life-spans and Seasonality

Perennial land plants display marked seasonal variety in the temperate, subarctic, and arctic regions and much less in the tropical and subtropical zones. Though alive throughout the year, they undergo periods in which they develop foliage, blossom, bear fruit, and lose their foliage. Algae occur in annual and perennial types. Though some perennial algae live for as much as thirty years, most live only a few years. All have reproductive seasons. Annual algae die and disappear after discharge of spores; perennial species decline after spore discharge but later recover and flourish. Seasonal changes, which are remarkable in warm seas and nonexistent in cold ones, are the reverse of those on land; that is, algae grow well in winter and spring and decline in summer and autumn.

Most of the algae living in the littoral or intertidal zone, which are exposed at ebb and submerged at flood tide, are annual since their environment is both unstable and severe. These annual algae occur in winter-spring and spring-summer types. The winter-spring type, found most in temperate and warm seas, cannot survive the summer. It dies, and sprouts of the succeeding generation appear in late autumn or early winter to reach maturity in the winter and spring. The spring-summer type, found in cold regions where the littoral zone freezes, dies in the autumn and winter, and grows during spring and summer. Environmental conditions and habitat strongly influence seasonality of intertidal algal vegetation. Intertidal algae in the cold seas and sublittoral algae—those grown in environments never exposed by the tides—in temperate and cold seas show no marked seasonal changes. It is possible to enable algae to grow year round by artificially eliminating factors conducive to degradation of the vegetation.

Generation Alternations

Like cryptogamic land plants, algae reproduce by sexual or asexual spores and therefore manifest what is called alternation of generations. In simple terms, this means that, when asexual spores germinate they produce gametophytes, or plants that produce sexual spores and female and male gametes. The female and male gametes unite sexually to produce zygotes that develop into sporophytes, which—like the grandparent generation—produce asexual spores. Algae produce both sexual and asexual spores, both of which sometimes coexist, especially in algae demonstrating seasonal growth changes. In some, however only gametophytes or only sporophytes are produced. Because their modes of reproduction differ, as explained below, clarification of life history is one of the most important problems in the biology of algae.

a) In some cases only gametophytes appear, and no alternation of generations is observed.

b) Regular alternation of generations occurs in the following two types:

1. In some, gametophytes and sporophytes are so identical in appearance that differentiation between them is impossible. The only distinguishing feature is the behavior of spores once they are released. This set of circumstances is called isomorphic alternation of generations.

2. Either gametophytes or sporophytes (not both) appear in the sea. The spores they produce grow into minute plants different from the parents. Alternation of generations occurs in macroscopic and microscopic plants in a situation known as anisomorphic or heteromorphic alternation of generations.

c) Gametophytes and sporophytes appear simultaneously. In general, however, only one type predominates in number; and alternation of generations is irregular. Even plants produced in small numbers have strong regenerative capabilities, and growth to the next generation by vegetative propagation is rapid.

Because of the value of such knowledge to the collection, harvesting, and especially the artificial cultivation of sea vegetables, the complex life history will be explained in greater detail later.

At the present stage of human knowlege of marine phenomena, cultivation—in the sense that land plants are cultivated for human use—of sea vegetables is difficult. Different kinds of life histories, described in the preceding section, and the problem of controlling and storing either spores or mother plants complicate techniques involved in preserving, artificially sowing, and artificially controlling spores until germination. In spite of these obstacles, however, along the coasts of Japan, mainland China, and the Philippine Islands, various artificial methods, gauged to the needs of the species, have been successfully used to cultivate *Porphyra*, *Laminaria*, *Undaria*, *Monostroma*, and *Eucheuma*.

Fig. 10   Reproductive Process in Flowering Plants (A) and Algae (B)

(A)   Reproductive process in flowering plants

flower → fertilization → fruit → seed → germination

(B)   Various types of reproductive processes in algae

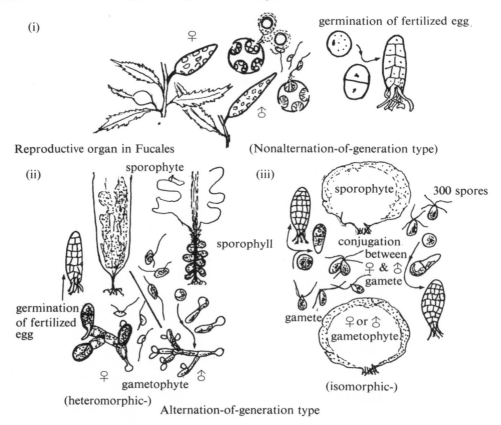

(i)

Reproductive organ in Fucales   (Nonalternation-of-generation type)

(ii)   (iii)

germination of fertilized egg

Alternation-of-generation type

4. Harvesting and Farming

General

Distribution, growing season, and seawater temperature, influence harvest times for sea vegetables. Sea vegetables should be harvested before they are old, since, once spores have formed, the fronds become tough, change color, and lose taste. From the seawater temperatures given in Table 29, it is possible to estimate algal growing seasons and to get an idea of the best times to harvest. It is important to remember that, though some algae flourish in a wide temperature range of from 10°C to 25°C, for the species accustomed to cold climates, from 10°C to 15°C is optimum; and, for warm-water species, from 20°C to 25°C is best.

Sublittoral species—that is algae growing in deep water where they are never exposed by low tides—may be harvested at any time. It is obviously more convenient to harvest intertidal, or littoral algae at ebb tide. Details on ebb and flood tides should be obtained from locally published tide tables. The lowest spring tides, the best time to harvest littoral algae, occur for three or four days when the moon is full or before the new moon appears.

Green Algae

Monostroma and *Enteromorpha*

The three widely utilized green sea vegetables *Monostroma oxyspermum*, *Enteromorpha prolifera*, and *E. linza*, plus *Ulva*, have long been known as *aonori* (green laver) in Japan, and in the past were important diet elements. Today, *Monostroma* alone is popularly eaten; it is artificially cultivated in the same way as *Porphyra*.

The juvenile of the many species of *Monostroma* growing in the cold as well as the temperate and warmer waters around Japan appear first in early October in the upper tidal zone and grow fast as the temperature drops. Winter and spring growth is abundant. Since they are winter-spring annuals, the fronds die out by summer.

Highly adaptible, *Monostroma* grows both in brackish estuary waters and in highly saline, open seas, though the fronds from river mouths, where nutrients are plentiful, grow larger and are tenderer and tastier. *Monostroma* fronds are chopped fine and prepared in paper-thin sheets eaten in Japan in a variety of ways.

Enteromorpha, which grows abundantly near large river mouths or along marshy coasts, is a winter-spring annual that starts growing in late September and thrives from December till May. Fronds harvested between December and February are

Table 29. Monthly Mean Seawater Temperatures along Several Coasts (in °C)

	Jan.	Feb.	Mar.	Apr.	May	Jun.	Jul.	Aug.	Sep.	Oct.	Nov.	Dec.	Mean °C
Pacific													
Seattle	8.6	8.1	8.1	8.9	10.3	11.8	12.9	12.9	13.2	12.9	12.0	11.0	10.6
Los Angeles	13.6	13.8	14.4	15.1	16.1	17.6	18.7	19.3	18.6	16.7	16.1	14.6	16.3
Honolulu	24.2	24.5	24.3	24.6	25.2	25.7	26.3	26.7	26.8	26.7	25.8	25.0	25.4
Nemuro	−1.2	−1.4	−0.7	2.5	7.3	11.0	15.6	17.9	17.3	13.5	7.6	1.3	7.6
Tokyo	7.3	7.0	10.3	15.0	19.2	22.1	25.1	27.7	24.0	18.8	14.9	9.2	16.8
Naha	20.2	20.1	21.5	23.3	26.0	27.7	28.8	28.7	28.1	25.9	23.7	21.4	24.6
Manila	27.0	27.4	28.0	29.0	29.7	29.8	29.1	29.2	29.5	29.4	28.6	27.7	28.7
Atlantic													
Woods Hole	1.8	0.8	2.4	7.2	12.0	16.9	21.3	21.8	19.9	15.6	10.8	5.0	11.3
Richmond	6.4	6.8	8.4	14.7	20.5	24.9	27.1	27.0	23.8	17.9	11.6	5.7	16.2
Miami Beach	21.7	22.0	23.2	25.0	26.9	29.0	29.8	29.0	28.9	26.5	24.3	22.8	25.8
Galveston	13.8	14.9	17.3	21.7	25.9	29.0	30.3	30.5	28.6	24.6	19.2	15.4	22.6
Bermuda Is.	18.8	17.8	18.0	20.5	22.0	24.5	27.5	29.0	27.1	24.2	20.0	18.2	22.3
Plymouth (Eng.)	9.5	6.5	7.6	9.8	10.5	14.5	15.2	18.3	15.4	13.6	11.5	10.0	11.9
Heligoland	3.4	1.5	3.0	5.5	9.9	13.0	15.1	17.5	15.4	12.5	9.9	5.5	9.3
Naples (Ital.)	13.5	10.2	11.0	15.0	18.0	21.0	24.5	25.5	23.3	18.0	15.0	13.8	17.4

Table 30. Monthly Mean Seawater Temperatures in Hokkaidō and Northern Honshū (in °C)

	Jan.	Feb.	Mar.	Apr.	May	Jun.	Jul.	Aug.	Sep.	Oct.	Nov.	Dec.	Mean
Hokkaidō													
Wakkanai	0.7	0.3	1.0	4.5	8.5	12.6	17.0	21.1	19.2	14.6	8.8	3.6	9.3
Erimo Point	0.2	0.5	0.5	3.4	5.7	9.5	13.2	15.9	16.4	12.8	7.8	3.3	7.3
Muroran	3.5	2.3	2.6	4.2	7.0	11.8	16.5	20.0	18.9	15.3	10.2	6.1	9.9
Hakodate	5.2	4.6	5.6	8.3	10.9	14.2	18.9	22.7	21.1	17.0	12.1	8.0	12.4
Esashi	6.0	5.2	6.0	8.5	11.8	16.0	20.4	24.1	21.8	17.0	11.9	7.8	13.0
Northern Honshū													
Hachinohe	5.3	4.4	5.2	7.4	10.7	13.5	17.7	20.9	19.7	16.2	12.2	7.9	11.8
Miyako	7.7	6.1	5.5	7.2	10.4	13.4	17.7	21.0	20.0	17.3	14.1	9.4	12.4
Kinkazan	6.7	4.6	4.0	5.6	8.5	11.8	16.4	19.7	21.9	18.3	14.4	9.7	11.7
Nyudō Point	8.4	7.2	7.4	9.5	13.4	17.8	22.2	25.1	22.7	18.4	14.7	10.8	14.8
Sakata	7.3	6.8	7.1	10.3	14.4	18.7	23.0	26.6	24.3	19.2	14.2	9.6	15.1

Fig. 11 Cultivation of *hitoegusa* (*Monostroma*) green algae.

tenderest and most delicious. Though some artificial cultivation is performed, in general, wild *Enteromorpha* is harvested and air dried to be grilled or powdered for use in a number of dishes.

Brown Algae

Laminariales and *Undaria*

Laminariales (oar weeds or kelp)
Already the most widely used of all sea vegetables, the Laminariales, which include giant north and South American kelps (*Macrocystis* and *Nereocystis*) reaching lengths of from twenty to sixty meters, will probably be even more widely used in the future. They occur in various frond shapes.

According to locale and growing mode, Laminariales may be classified into the following groups.
    A.   Colder seas—*Laminaria, Alaria, Saccorhyza, Macrocystis, Nereocystis, Durvillea, Arthrothamnus, Lessonia, Hedophyllum*, etc.
    B.   Temperate seas—*Undaria, Eisenia, Ecklonia, Eckloniopsis*, etc.

Aside from *Undaria* and *Nereocystis*, most Laminariales are perennial, though they differ from their land counterparts in that almost the entire body grows each year. This is caused by a process called intercalary growth. Whereas in most other plants growth is terminal in the uppermost parts, in Laminariales, the growth point

Fig. 12 Intercalary and Terminal Growth (A and B), and Morphogenesis in the Genus *Eisenia* (C)

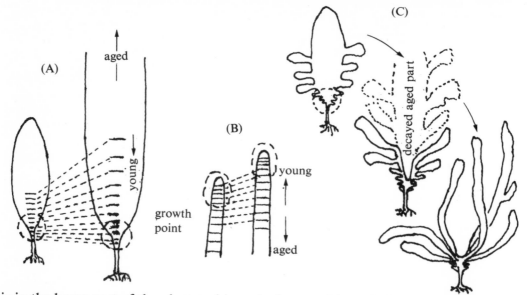

is in the lower part of the plant and is pushed upward by cell division. In all Laminariales except *Macrocystis*, aging occurs in the upper part of the plant. The lower part near the growth point is younger. In other words, various parts of the same blade are of different ages. In summer, when temperatures and sunlight increase, the upper part of the blade weakens and dies. This happens with special speed in waters of more than 20°C. If death proceeds as far as the growth point, the entire plant dies. If it does not, when water temperatures drop and environmental conditions again become favorable, a second-year blade is produced (in *Laminaria*, etc,), ramification occurs, or a blade differently shaped from its predecessor develops (*Eisenia*, *Macrocystis*, *Arthrothamnus*, etc.). (See Fig. 12.)

Differences in distribution and growth modes between *Undaria* and *Laminaria*

Undaria pinnatifida (*wakame*) in the wild is an annual limited to the temperate seas. Juvenile sprouts generally appear in autumn or early winter, when the temperature of the water drops below 20°C. Mature fronds appear in winter and spring, and maximum growth occurs when the temperatures are between 10°C and 15°C. After frond mating, sporophylls appear on the stipe near the boundary of the blade; and spores are produced. Fully ripe spores develop in temperatures between 17°C and 20°C. Above 20°C, the plants degrade. They die at temperatures between 23°C and 25°C. Harvest seasons differ with the region: from February through April in the temperate southwestern region of Japan and July and August in the northeastern temperate region. *Undaria pinnatifida* disappears entirely in September even in northern waters.

Though many species of *Laminaria* (*kombu*) grow in northern Japanese waters, most of them are limited to the Hokkaidō coasts; in other places they cannot survive the summer to reach adulthood of second year. (For instance, *Laminaria* is not a perennial in the warmer waters of the northeastern coast of Honshū.) Along the Hokkaidō coasts, however, the sea temperature rises above 20°C during only a few

Fig. 13 Distribution of Wild Members of Laminariales (Brown Algae) along Japanese Coasts and Areas of Artificial Cultivation of *Laminaria japonica* along Chinese Coasts

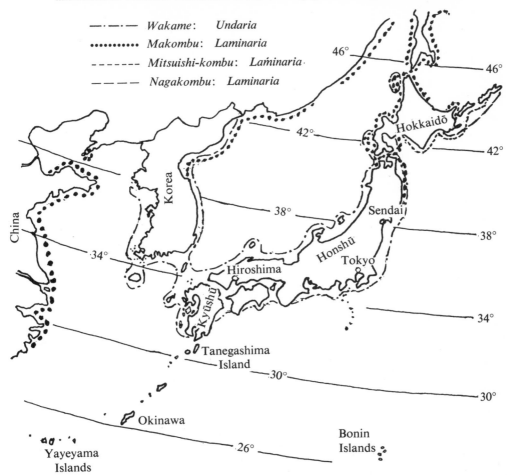

— · — · — *Wakame*: *Undaria*
●●●●●●●● *Makombu*: *Laminaria*
– – – – – *Mitsuishi-kombu*: *Laminaria*
— — — — *Nagakombu*: *Laminaria*

Fig. 14
Kombu growing on the sea floor in the waters off Hokkaidō, Japan.

months and rarely exceeds 25°C. Under these conditions, first-year *Laminaria* blades do not die but continue to grow. Indeed, they sometimes become as large as second-year blades, though they are thinner and less tasty. Generally, only blades in their second or thirds years of growth are used for food.

Undaria and *Laminaria*, both of which grow on rock substrates, tend to weaken in summer in shallow waters where sunlight is strong. Understanding of these conditions of growth and the effects of temperature and location is essential in artificial cultivation. To ensure abundant crops, good growing conditions must be provided by moving substrates as conditions demand (Fig. 13).

Artificial Cultivation

Mass culture of gametophytes in tanks

All Laminariales are sporophytes giving off asexual spores, which soon germinate and develop into tiny (from one to five millimeters) filamentous gametophytes. The female gametophytes form one-cell eggs; the male ones form spermatozoids. The fertilized egg germinates into a macroscopic sporophyte, which grows into the body of the plant. In other words, heteromorphic alternation of generations between microscopic gametophytes and macroscopic sporophytes occurs. Though the gametophyte is the same in all species, zoospore sites and reproduction systems vary.

To collect these zoospores artificially, pieces of mature fronds with spores are placed in a tank of seawater together with convenient plastic filaments, on which the zoospores soon settle. The pieces of frond should be removed in a day since, if left in the water too long, they produce a polluting, brown, mucouslike substance. Developing male and female gametophytes are cultured in mass directly in the tank. At maturity they produce eggs and spermatozoids and ultimately juvenile sporophytes visible to the naked eye. Finally juvenile fronds (from one to two centimeters) appear on the plastic filaments. When they have from two to five fronds at intervals of five centimeters, the filaments with the fronds on them are transplanted to the sea and numerous juvenile fronds appear in about a week. They mature for later harvest (Fig. 15).

Environmental conditions determine the time when juvenile sporophytes may be transplanted into the sea. Water temperature is the most important condition, since the fronds will die at more than 20°C. This means that the optimum time for transplantation is after October along the coasts of Japan (see Tables 29 and 30). Normally, in the case of *Undaria*, mass culture of gametophytes in tanks is begun between April and June. The juvenile fronds appear between May and September when the seawater is warmer than 20°C, or too warm for transplantation. Artificial conditioning of the water in the culture tanks, however, makes possible control of the times at which the fronds appear and permits preserving gametophytes in dormant condition for as long as from one to two years without their forming eggs or spermatozoids. Conditioning can hasten the emergence of juvenile fronds within two weeks after zoospores settle. For best results, either of the following steps is taken to control conditions in the tanks to ensure that the juvenile fronds are ready at the time when sea environmental conditions are optimum.

Fig. 15

(A)

Laminaria   Undaria   Macrocystis

(B) Gametophyte collector for tank culture

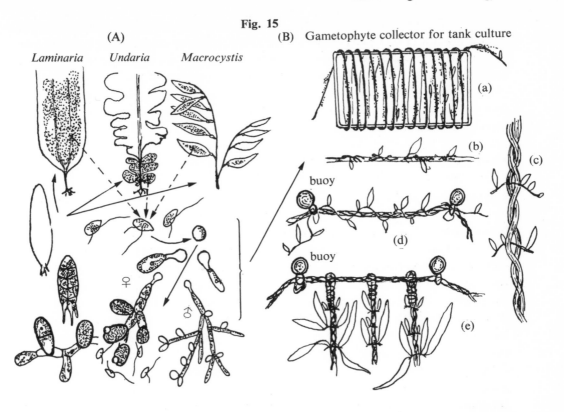

A. Water temperature is controlled at between 5°C and 8°C, and the tanks are shaded and kept dark so that juvenile fronds remain dormant until October.

B. Gametophytes are kept dormant during July and August when the water temperature rises above 25°C and 30°C by keeping the tank dimly lighted. Beginning in September, conditions favorable to the formation of eggs and spermatozoids and for fertilization of eggs are provided.

Since it is somewhat harder to keep the juvenile fronds dormant, the latter method is more practical.

Laminaria releases zoospores in the cool season between October and December, when the water temperature is about 15°C (the same reproductive period applies to many Laminariales species including *Eisenia*, *Ecklonia*, and *Alaria*). In game-tophyte mass-culture tanks, the temperature may easily be kept lower than 20°C; and juvenile fronds will appear in the winter-spring season, when seawater is not too warm. If growth of *Laminaria* juvenile fronds is retarded at temperatures between 5°C and 6°C when they are from 2 to 3 centimeters long, they will grow well when transplanted into the sea. In general, mass artificial cultivation of *Laminaria* is easier than that of *Undaria*.

Practical culture methods in the sea

In some instances, the filaments on which the juvenile fronds have been artificially grown are wrapped around plastic rope (diameter 1.5 centimeters) and stretched in the sea. In others, the filaments are cut into short piece (5 centimeters), which are twisted into plastic rope at intervals of from 10 to 15 centimeters and attached either to floating buoys or to concrete or steel structures fixed to the bottom of the sea.

Though differences occur among species, in both *Undaria* and *Laminaria*, body-growth rate is optimum at a depth of from 2 to 3 meters below the surface. In the case of buoy cultivation, frond lengths differ according to the depth at which the rope to which they are attached hangs (Figs. 15B-d and e). Periodic adjustment of rope lengths ensures maximum harvest.

Laminaria cultivation in China and *Undaria* cultivation in Japan

During World War II, import of *Laminaria* from Japan into China was cut off, causing some hardship to the Chinese, who had long relied on this alga as an iodine supplement in the diet and as a preventative of goiter. In 1944 and 1945, Mr Yōshirō Ōtsuki, who was living in China at the time, instituted a system of artificially cultivating *Laminaria* along the Chinese coast, where it occurs naturally in extremely limited parts. He remained in China until 1953, improving and perfecting this system and spreading its application. According to his method, zoospores settled on cords suspended directly in the sea; and gametophytes survived the summer even in areas where seawater got as warm as 30°C. This seemed to indicate that similar cultivation would be possible in Japanese waters where temperatures rise in summer but never reach 30°C. I pointed out to him, however, decisive differences in the Chinese and Japanese sea environments. In China, river water flowing into the sea causes water-temperatures to drop and water-turbidity to increase and provides abundant nutrients for algae growth. In Japanese waters, the effect of the warm Kuroshio Current is harmful; and the water is generally less rich in nutritious minerals. Only second- and third-year *Laminaria* fronds are used in Japan, and areas permitting artificial cultivation of algae of this age are limited. Taking into consideration Japanese coastal conditions, I made the following suggestion to him.

Undaria (*wakame*), which grows in a natural state in many parts of the Japanese coast, is useful for food within one year. It seemed better to establish sound cultivation for *Undaria* first and then apply information learned in this way to the cultivation of *Laminaria*. When I held my discussion with Mr. Ōtsuki, techniques for the artificial production of the *Conchocelis* stage of *Porphyra* in tanks were almost complete; and studies were under way for the application of these methods to mass culture of *Undaria* and *Laminaria* gametophytes. As a result of the devoted efforts of researchers and culturists throughout Japan, such cultivation is now possible on an industrial scale.

After Mr. Ōtsuki's departure, Chinese researchers continued independent work and developed methods for raising new types of *Laminaria* that will grow even in the temperate and warmer regions of the East China Sea, though only one-year fronds are produced and areas where the algae survive the summer to produce second-year fronds are limited.

Future prospects

Aside from being useful as human food, the Laminariales species, especially where they grow together with the *Sargassum* species, form immense undersea forests

Fig. 16 **Artificial, Large-scale Cultivation of Laminariales (*Macrocystis*, *Laminaria*, *Eisenia*, *Ecklonia*, and so on)**

harboring many useful fishes, shrimps, and crabs and serving as food for such animals as abalone, top-shells, and sea urchins. Since such forests are important in conserving sea resources, some organizations are now planning to produce new ones where there have been no natural ones in the past. These forests, called sea ranches, will employ the cultivation methods used for producing Laminariales artificially. In the United States, giant kelp (*Macrocystis*) is already being cultivated artificially on a large scale as raw material for the production of alginic acid and certain drugs. New developments will be applied to the energy problem by using fermentation products of kelp fronds as fuel. Since sea ranches must be long-term affairs, they require massive steel structures (Fig. 16).

In addition, such brown algae as *Endarachne binghamiae*, *Scytosiphon lomentaria*, and *Analipus japonicus* are harvested in the wild and dried, pulverized, or roasted for foods.

Red Algae

Porphyra

In the wild
The thirty species of the genus *Porphyra*, the most important of all sea vegetables, are annual and grow in the shallow, upper littoral regions of most of the world's seas, though their growing system differs according to region. For instance, in the waters around Japan, *Porphyra* in the cold regions of the western northern Pacific (*P. umbilicalis*, *P. variegata*, *P. tasa*, and *P. amplissima*) grow in summer after the ice of the sea has thawed. Such species are called summer annuals. In the temperate, and warmer regions of the south, *Porphyra* (*P. tenera*, *P. yezoensis*, *P. pseudolinearis*, *P. suborbiculata*, and *P. dentata*) propagate in winter and spring and die in summer and autumn. Such species are called winter-spring annuals. With the exception of those

species native to higher latitudes, the majority of Pacific *Porphyra* are winter-spring annuals. Most of their fronds disappear from July to early October, although in regions where seawater temperatures are below 25°C even in the summer, some plantlets survive into the next growing season.

Growing patterns for *Porphyra* in the eastern part of the Pacific are entirely different, because of variations in environmental conditions. *P. umbilicus*, *P. laciniata*, and *P. amplissima* along the coasts of Alaska, where the sea freezes in winter, are summer annuals. *P. perforata*, *P. variegata*, and *P. nerocystis* (a sublittoral species parasitically attached to fronds of ribbon kelp—*Nereocystis*) in the littoral regions of British Columbia, Washington, Oregon, and California are apparently perennial or winter-spring annuals. The growing seasons of *P. perforata*, which is widely distributed along the North American west coast from north to south, differ according to region: it grows all year on the shores of British Columbia and Washington but is a spring-summer annual along the coast of California. Apparently the following environmental factors largely account for wide diversity in *Porphyra* seasonality.

(1) High water temperatures (more than 25°C) caused by the northward-flowing Kuroshio Current in the western Pacific play a part in the disappearance of *Porphyra* in summertime. (Cold waters from the Oyashio—or Kurile—Current, the Liman Current, and the Yellow Sea cause water temperatures in this same region to drop below 10°C in winter.) In the eastern Pacific, the situation is quite different. The Kuroshio and North Pacific currents prevent the waters of even the northern coasts of North America from dropping below 10°C in winter. But, even in the middle of summer, upwellings from the Humboldt Current, which rises in the Antarctic Ocean, keep sea temperatures low (they rarely exceed 20°C). The smaller range of temperature variation in this part of the Pacific creates good growing conditions for *Porphyra* all year round.

(2) Tide modes too are important in the *Porphyra* growing environment. In the western Pacific, lowest ebbing of the spring tide series occurs at about noon. In other words, *Porphyra* fronds are exposed to the air and sun at the hottest time of day. In the eastern Pacific, on the other hand, lowest ebbs in the spring occur always in early morning or just before sunset. This means that *Porphyra* remain safely submerged during the heat of the day. This protection enables them to survive the summer.

(3) If water temperature and tidal mode were the only elements to be considered, *P. perforata* should be able to grow all year, especially in the winter, along the coasts of California as well as along those of British Columbia and Washington. But another aspect of the California climate makes this impossible. The California rainy season, from October to February, causes dense, daily, morning fogs at the time when *P. perforata* is exposed to the air. The freshwater of the fogs adversely affects the growth of this alga. In Japan, where the rainy season of June-July is followed by a hot, sunny summer period, high water temperatures and strong sunlight accelerate degradation of intertidal vegetation (Fig. 17).

Few ecological reports have been published on *Porphyra* spp. on the east coast of North America, on the west coast of Europe, in the British Isles, and in Iceland, where these algae are known to grow. In these areas, most *Porphyra* grow the year round without remarkable degradation in summer. But it seems likely that harvest

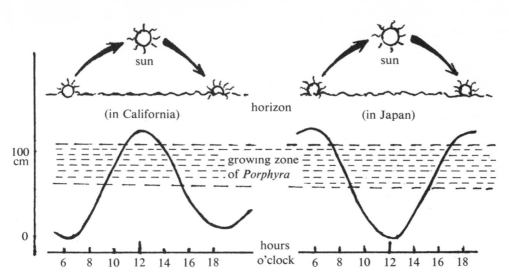

Fig. 17 Diagram Illustrating Differences in Tide Phases between the
California and Japanese Coasts

times would be limited, since such food values as taste and tenderness vary in *Porphyra* from these regions according to season. Most of the *Porphyra* in the warm seas around India, Thailand, Vietnam, the Philippine Islands, and South China are sublittoral and are winter annual in growing mode, although variable currents between monsoon and nonmonsoon seasons result in some spring-summer species in Indian waters.

Since it is largely tropical, the South China Sea should not be a place where *Porphyra* spp. grow; but cold waters from rivers taking their sources in the inland mountains of China and the cold waters of the Kuroshio countercurrent flowing along the coast and through the Straits of Taiwan probably create temperature conditions close enough to those of temperate seas to enable the algae to survive. *P. crispata* and *P. suborbiculata* grow there and have been eaten by the Chinese for centuries under the name *zicai*, or purple vegetable.

Artificial cultivation

As has already been explained, *Porphyra* spp., especially *Porphyra tenera*, are among the most nutritious and popular of all algae eaten in Japan. From ancient times, artificial cultivation has been essential since naturally produced algae could not meet the great demand for this popular food. The method devised for such cultivation was to construct an artificial substratum by setting bamboo branches and nets fiber in the littoral areas near river mouths at about the end of September or the beginning of October. From somewhere, no one knows precisely where, *Porphyra* spores settled on these poles and began to grow, juvenile fronds appearing after two or three weeks. During the winter and spring the fronds grew, to be nipped off for processing into food when they reached about fifteen centimeters in length. From ten to twelve harvests could be made each year. To make paper-thin sheets of *Asakusa-nori* from them, the fronds were thoroughly washed in freshwater, chopped fine, and while wet spread thin on reed screens to dry.

The old system of using bamboo or tree branches and trunks went out of use as time passed because material limitations forbade cultivation of *Porphyra* in water more than five meters deep. The only part of even the longest bamboo branches to which *Porphyra* fronds attached themselves were the upper one meter, which corresponds to the intertidal level. Finally, once put in place, these branches and trunks are difficult to move. At a later time, bamboo branches or plastic poles were set up and nets of palm-fiber yarn or synthetic fiber were hung on them. This produced a horizontal substrate on which frondlets could grow. This system became popular about fifty years ago. About ten years ago, further improvement occurred in the form of floats for the nets instead of poles. Technical advances gradually increased the sea depths that can be used for *Porphyra* farms (Fig. 18). But the cultivation season remains largely unaltered. The substrates are set in place from late September to mid-October, when the water temperature is between 20°C and 22°C. Harvests are made until the end of March. Though fronds continue to develop into April, they are too short to be suitable for production of sheet *nori*. The substrates are removed either then or at the end of the cultivation period. A few *Porphyra* fronds continue to grow on natural substrates near the beach until the middle of June. But, for all practical purposes, except when sea temperatures remain low, *Porphyra* disappears in the summer.

For a long time the summer behavior of *Porphyra* and the origin of the spores that settle on the artificial substrates in the autumn remained a mystery. The complicated life cycle of the plant has helped solve the mystery, and this in turn has led to the possibility of wide-scale artificial cultivation. *Porphyra* fronds produce two kinds of spores: carpospores and monospores. Tests with these spores, germinated on glass slides, have shown that monospores undergo bipolar germination to produce normal

Fig. 18

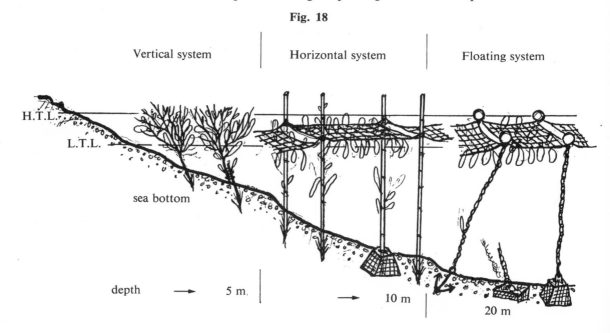

Vertical system   Horizontal system   Floating system

H.T.L.

L.T.L.

sea bottom

depth ⟶ 5 m.   ⟶   10 m

20 m

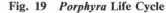

Fig. 19 *Porphyra* Life Cycle

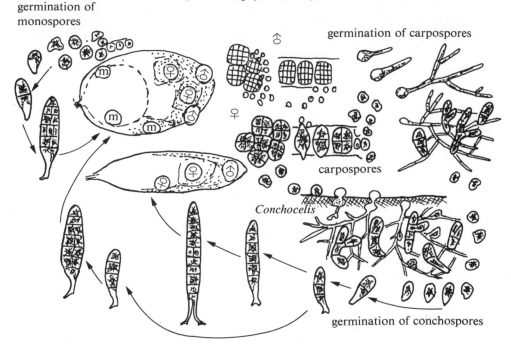

Porphyra fronds. Carpospores, on the other hand, produce germ tubes that develop into branched filaments without ever becoming normal *Porphyra* fronds. Some races of fronds produce monospores; others do not. When the fronds produce no monospores, they generate male and female cells and carpospores at the same time. When they are produced, monospores are released first; then the same fronds produce male and female cells and carpospores. Both races of fronds exist side by side on *Porphyra* farms. From December to early February, they produce both monospores and carpospores; but in February and March, only carpospores appear.

As has been said, carpospores produce filaments, not fronds, and cannot therefore be related to the *Porphyra* fronds appearing in September. Much research was devoted to discovering what the carpospores actually do in the summertime. In 1949, in England, Dr. Drew Baker made the important discovery that carpospores of *P. umbilicalis* bore into the shells of certain mollusks to develop into the filamentous *Conchocelis rosea*. She further learned that *Porphyra* fronds develop from *Conchocelis* spores (conchospores). This information provided the missing link in the life cycle of *Porphyra* fronds (Fig. 19).

On the basis of Dr. Drew's work, Japanese researchers discovered that *P. tenera* carpospores boring into oyster shells produce *Conchocelis* fronds, which generate conchospores that can be sown to produce *Porphyra* fronds. Conchospores have been discovered on free-living *Conchocelis*, too, though the ones grown inside oyster shells resist unfavorable summer conditions better. Three or four years after a cooperative effort was made by Japanese biologists and *Porphyra* farmers, an efficient system of mass culture of *Conchocelis* in tanks for later production of *Porphyra* was established. The technique is explained in the following section.

Mass culture of *Conchocelis*

1. In February or March, mature *Porphyra* fronds producing carpospores are placed in tanks filled with seawater together with oyster shells.
2. Growth of *Conchocelis* is stimulated by sufficient sunlight and fertilizers as long as the tank-water temperature is lower than 15°C. Water is kept circulating all the time.
3. Tanks are shaded when the water temperature exceeds 20°C. Light is reduced to about 150 lux at the peak of summer, when water temperatures rise to between 25°C and 30°C. This keeps *Conchocelis* dormant. At this time, conchospores begin to appear; but the high temperatures prevent the growth of filaments.
4. When water temperatures drop to about 25°C, 8 or 10 hours of sunlight a day (short-day treatment) are permitted so as to allow conchospores to grow to maturity.
5. Microscopic examinations have shown that, in September or October, when the water temperature drops below 25°C and especially when it is between 20°C and 22°C, conchospores in oyster shells grow vigorously. At this time, artificial sowing for the production of *Porphyra* fronds is performed in either of the two following ways.
    A. Large numbers of the conchospore-producing oyster shells are placed in net bags or other openwork containers among the artificial substrates (net farms) directly in the sea.
    B. The conchospore-producing oyster shells and the substrate nets are placed together in large tanks containing constantly circulating seawater.

The oyster shells producing the conchospores can be easily stored and transmitted, making possible introduction of new varieties of *Porphyra* into regions where they have not previously grown. For instance, formerly only *P. tenera* was artificially cultivated; but now *P. yezoensis* and *P. pseudolinearis* too are used, with no major alteration in the taste and quality of the finished dried *nori*. By means of this method, which has been in use for about twenty years, it is possible to store crop seeds for sea vegetables in a way not unlike that in which mankind has stored land-crop seeds for thousands of years.

Weedlike pests, in the forms of unwanted sea-vegetable fronds, pose a problem similar to that of land weeds. Though they cannot be as easily removed as their terrestrial counterparts, these unwanted fronds can be controlled by adjusting the time of sowing to one at which *Porphyra* thrives and the others do not or by altering the heights of substrates to expose the algae to the air for more time than fronds other than *Porphyra* cannot tolerate. The substrates can be removed entirely from the sea for about twenty-four hours to rid them of unwanted varieties of about one centimeter in length. This much exposure will not damage *Porphyra*. If they are larger, they can eliminated by being removed from the sea, drained for two or three hours, and then quick frozen at minus 25°C or minus 30°C. The *Porphyra* will be made dormant by this treatment but will begin growing again when returned to the sea. The unwanted sea vegetables, however, will have died.

Diseases wreaking havoc among *Porphyra* fronds and leaving other sea vegetables undamaged are not infrequent. The Phycomycetes fungus *Pythium* parasite causes an

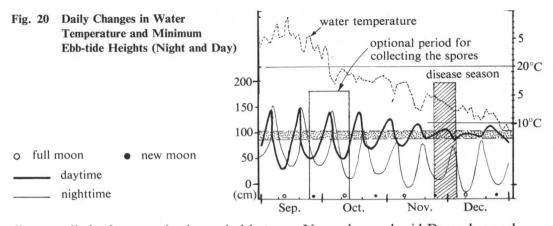

Fig. 20   Daily Changes in Water Temperature and Minimum Ebb-tide Heights (Night and Day)

o   full moon   ● new moon

———— daytime

———— nighttime

ailment called *Akagusare* in the period between November and mid-December each year. The occurrence of this disease at regular times is related to tides. For best *Porphyra* growth, substrates must be set at a height that allows from three to four hours of emergence from the sea and partial drainage daily. But, in Japan, during the period from the vernal to the autumnal equinox each year, tides are lower during the day than at night. The opposite is true during the rest of the year; that is, low tides are not as low during the day as they are at night. This is apparently a phenomenon peculiar to the Pacific coast of Japan. Tides that do not fall sufficiently deprive *Porphyra* of emergence from the water (from the middle of November to the middle of December) and the fronds weaken. At water temperatures of between 10°C and 15°C, the *Pythium* fungus grows and reproduces with astounding speed with the result that the disease spreads rapidly among the weakened *Porphyra* fronds. The *Pythium* mycelium produces sporangiophores in large numbers. Each sporangiophore produces from sixteen to forty zoospores on its tips. Zoospores invade healthy *Porphyra* fronds. Then the mycelium reaches maturity and produces spores of its own by the next day. When the temperature drops below 10°C, *Pythium* ceases growth and zoospore production. Then sexual reproduction (oogonium and antheridium) take place. But the fungus remains dormant only to burst into activity again when the temperature rises. When this happens, *Porphyra* harvesting comes to an end. Regulation of substrate heights effectively controls damage caused by the *Akagusare* disease. Damage reaches a maximum from the middle of November through December. Setting the substrates from thirty to fifty centimeters higher than normal at this time to accord with tidal phases and water temperatures protects the algae from fungal attacks. In late December, the substrates should be returned to their normal heights or lower.

Eucheuma and *Gelidium*

Most of the red algae are perennials and flourish in temperate and warmer sea regions in spring, summer, and autumn (Fig. 21). Harvest is generally in the spring and summer, though a few species are harvested in the winter and spring.

    There is great color variation in these plants. As has been said, chlorophyll a and phycobilin are their two main pigments. Kept in dark, dry places after harvest, some

Fig. 21   Distribution of Important Red Algae in the Far East

A—*Ahnfeltia*
G—*Gelidium*
 g—*Gracilaria*
D—*Digenea*
E—*Eucheuma*
C—*Campylaephora* and *Ceranium*

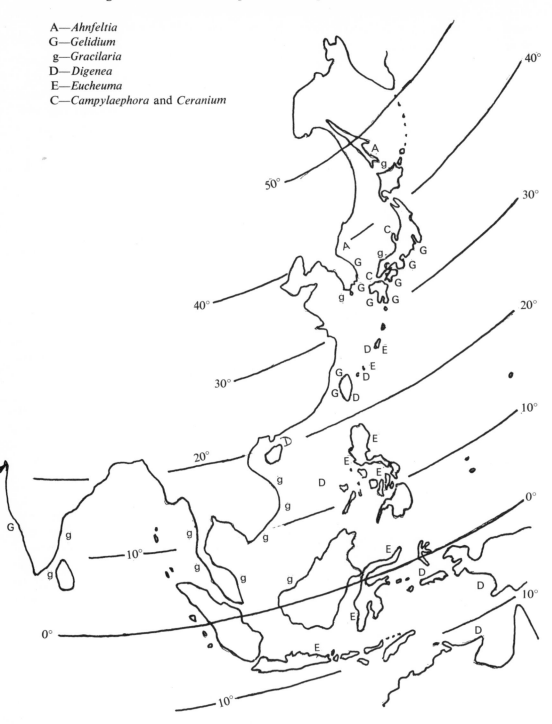

fronds preserve their original colors for a long time. Exposed to sunlight and humidity, however, they turn rosy. Soaking in water bleaches them white. Alkali treatment (sprinkling of wood ash) followed by brief steaming or boiling turns them a beautiful bluish-green.

Perennial red algae, which, aside from *Porphyra*, are used less for food than *Laminaria* and *Monostroma*, do not grow very fast. They are harvested in the wild and used mainly in salads with very little preliminary processing. Some of the ones used for food are *Palmaria* (dulse), *Asparagopsis* (*limu*), *Gracilaria* (*ogo*), *Meristotheca* (*tosakanori*), and *Eucheuma* (*kirinsai*). In some cases, such red algae as *Chondrus* and *Eucheuma*, raw materials for carrageen, and *Gelidium*, *Gracilaria*, and *Campylaephora*, raw materials for agar, are cultivated artificially. The first to be raised in this way was *Eucheuma* (Fig. 22).

Fig. 22 Cutting to Stimulate Regeneration of Lost Parts of the Body by Cutting (a) and (b) in *Eucheuma* and the Practical Artificial Cultivation of *Eucheuma* (B) and *Gracilaria* (C)

(A)   Regeneration in *Eucheuma*

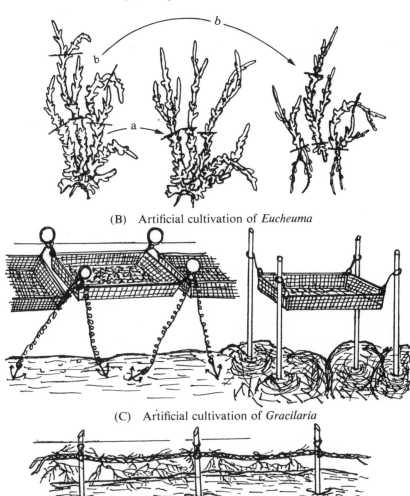

(B)   Artificial cultivation of *Eucheuma*

(C)   Artificial cultivation of *Gracilaria*

Eucheuma

Artificial cultivation of tropical *Eucheuma* has been successful along the coasts of Mindanao in the Philippine Islands and in Indonesia. Because of their remarkable powers of regeneration, red algae are most easily cultivated by the simple method of being chopped into small pieces and hung in net containers in the sea at a depth of about 1 meter or more below the sulface (Fig. 22). They, of course, reproduce by spores as well; and artificial cultivation of the kind used with *Porphyra*, *Laminaria*, and *Undaria* is possible but takes much longer than the regeneration method. Though attempts to cultivate *Gracilaria* and *Gelidium* have been made in Japan, the results have not been as good as they have been with *Eucheuma*.

Gelidium

The most important of the red algae, *Gelidium*, which is used in the production of agar and congealed foods, grows at depths of from 5 to 20 meters and is harvested, in Japan by women divers. Though it occurs in both cold and warm seas, only the species in temperate zones are industrially useful. In the southern regions, for instance the lower tip of Kyūshū and still farther, *Gelidium* species are too small for use. Effects of cold river water create conditions suitable to growth of usable *Gelidium* species around Taiwan and in the Hawaiian Islands. In short, environmental conditions are more important than geographic region in the growth of these sea vegetables.

Freshwater Algae

Green *Prasiola* (*kawanori*) and blue-green *Nostoc* spp., though occurring in smaller quantities than marine algae, are high in protein content and promise to be useful to man.

Prasiola: Though most *Prasiola* species are too small for eating, *P. japonica* and *P. mexicana* (northern parts of South America) are larger. Thin and thallic, they resemble *Ulva* and *Monostroma* (sea lettuce) among the marine algae. They usually grow on the bottoms of fast-flowing, inland rivers. In Japan, *P. japonica* is limited to rivers where water temperatures are lower than 14°C. It is harvested, prepared into thin dried sheets, and eaten in the same way as *Asakusa-nori*, which it resembles in taste. *P. mexicana* could probably be eaten in the same way.

Nostoc and other blue-green algae: Some of the many species in the *Nostoc* genus in Japan grow in water. Others are found at the roots of plants in fields or riverbeds where the environment is sometimes dry and sometimes wet. They prefer the tropical and subtropical regions. In temperate zones, they remain dormant, covered with a thick galactan cover during autumn and winter or the dry season but grow rapidly during the warm, humid spring and summer. Nonnucleated or procaryotic organisms, algae of the *Nostoc* genus are extremely small, unicellular organisms (diameter of 10μ) that propagate asexually only by cell-division. These minute organisms form colonies that link together into irregular chains. Their thick galactan cover has great

Fig. 23 Microscopic Views of Inner Structure of Some *Nostoc* Algae

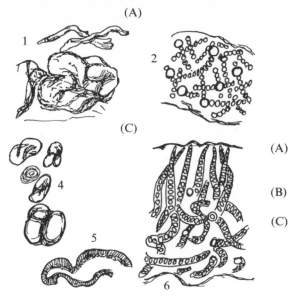

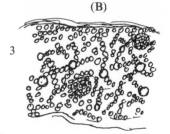

(A) *Nostoc verrucosa*
  1. General view of body
  2. Microscopic view of inner structure
(B) *N. commune*
  3. Microscopic view of inner structure
(C) *Brachytrichia quoyi*
  4. General view of bodies
  5. Longitudinal section of body
  6. Microscopic view of inner structure

moisture-absorption characteristics. It dries out and looks dead in arid weather but swells to become soft and gelatinous when placed in water. Under unfavorable conditions, in the dry state, it will remain dormant for two or three years only to grow again when the environment improves.

Certain species of *Nostoc* algae are eaten in Japan (so-called *Suizenji-nori, jusentai,* and *kawatake-nori,* products of northern Kyūshū). Today these species are cultivated only on the gravel-covered bottoms of small, flowing, clear rivers near the city of Amagi, in Fukuoka Prefecture. Perennials, they grow near grass roots and flourish throughout the year. Other varieties of *Nostoc* algae—*ashitsuki* (*Phragmites communis*), which was found attached to the basal parts of water plants, and *Anegawa-kurage*—were eaten in Japan in the past. They grew in riverbeds or in marshes. But today both the algae and the custom of eating them have died out. A *Nostoc* growing in fields is eaten—often fried with pork—in Okinawa. This variety has a high vitamin B_1 content. Though *Nostoc* algae are plentiful throughout Asia, they are rarely eaten. Since some of them fix mineral nitrogen contained in air, they could be grown in paddy fields as living fertilizer. It would be better, however, to concentrate first on their use as food sources.

On Taiwan an algae called *Brachytrichia quoyi,* which resembles *Nostoc,* has long been eaten. Chinese restaurants—especially those specializing in the South China cuisine—serve an expensive sweet dessert soup called *Fa-cai* or *Ko-xian-mi* containing a species of the *Nostoc* genus, *N. commune* (or *Nematonostoc flagelliforme*). When dried, *Fa-cai* occurs in thin, short, hairlike threads. Its high water-absorbing capacity causes it to swell to more than ten times its original diameter when it is soaked or cooked. The soft, slippery sensation produced by drinking soup containing it is oddly exciting. *Ko-xian-mi* seems to be the alga called *ashitsuki* in Japan.

5. Processing and Preserving

General

After harvesting, sea vegetables discolor and deteriorate faster and to a greater extent than land plants, though there is considerable variation in their rate or spoilage depending on classification and on location of cultivation. The following three things must be done to all sea vegetables to keep them in good shape for a maximum period.

1. Wash them immediately in freshwater to desalt them.
2. Dry them fast in the shade.
3. Store them in dark, dry places.

It is probably alteration in the physical properties of cell walls, which are different from those of land plants, that facilitates water permeability when sea vegetables are dried and thus accelerates degradation of pigments (especially the chlorophylls). Salt on the fronds absorbs water—especially in humid conditions—and speeds up discoloration. Exposure to sunlight results in photodegradation of pigments and causes algae to discolor.

When algae are to be used as raw materials in colorless agar and carrageenan, as *Gelidium*, *Eucheuma*, and Irish moss are, loss of color is an asset. In these instances, therefore, the fronds are exposed to the sun deliberately and are sprayed with freshwater to hasten decoloration. Sometimes, under exceptional circumstances, chemical bleaching agents, like chlorine compounds, may be used to whiten algae.

Processing for food depends on the kind of algae involved and the nature of the food.

Amanori and *Aonori*

In Japan, *amanori* (purple laver, *Porphyra* sp.) and *aonori* (green laver, *Monostroma*, *Ulva*, *Enteromorpha*, and *Prasiola*) are dried and pressed into paper-thin sheets for a variety of culinary purposes. In the past, sun and wind were the forces harnessed for the task. Today, the fronds of these algae are mechanically shredded and dried in blowers that are well ventilated and kept at a temperature of from 35°C to 45°C for from 2 to 2-1/2 hours. After drying, their water content is as low as 5 percent.

But, since humidity destroys both the color and flavor of these products, storage has often presented great difficulties. Modern methods of air-tight packing have to some extent—though not entirely—solved to problem. *Amanori*—or *Asakusa-nori*, to use the name of the most representative variety—deteriorates in color and quality much worse than *aonori*. *Asakusa-nori* is a glossy, purplish black when fresh but, if improperly stored, turns rosy pink and loses flavor. Degradation of chlorophyll a

Fig. 24 A widely popular Japanese confection called *kakimochi*. The upper pieces are wrapped in what is called dragon-skin *kombu*. The lower ones are wrapped in dried *nori*.

and the persistence of phycobilins unchanged probably account for the rose-pink color. The bluish green of toasted or boiled *Asakusa-nori*, on the other hand, is evidence of undegraded chlorophyll a. The process of chlorophyll-a disintegration involves complex enzyme action. To counter this, dealers in such edible seaweeds employ an added heat treatment (*hi-ire*), in which completely dried *Asakusa-nori* is stored at 60°C for from two days to a week. This system has the double advantage of further reducing moisture content and of killing the enzymes playing an important part in the disintegration of chlorophyll a. Seaweed dealers in Japan are traditionally tea dealers as well, and this *hi-ire* method may have been inspired by the toasting process used in preparing some kinds of tea.

Freezing as a method of preserving is unsuited to algae of the *nori* category. Even though after thawing they seem to be in their original condition, they soon exude a pink fluid, indicating that they are no longer fit to be eaten.

Green Algae

Caulerpa (Sea Grapes)

Of the great many varieties of the genus *Caulerpa* occurring widely in the warm parts of the Pacific, Atlantic, and Indian oceans a few—notably *C. racemosa* and its relations—are both edible and delicious. Called sea grapes because of their shape, they are harvested in autumn and spring and either eaten immediately or preserved in salt or brine. Salting deflates them. To prepare salted sea grapes for food, they should be inflated and desalinated by means of soaking in freshwater. Familiar in the South Pacific and Caribbean islands, sea grapes taste like fresh lettuce.

Brown Algae

Brown algae—*Undaria* (*wakame*), *Laminaria* (*kombu*), *Eisenia* (*arame*), and *Hizikia* (*hijiki*). These thicker, more durable algae have strong cell walls; and less care is required in their preservation than is needed for the storage of the more fragile algae of the *nori* category. They practically never fade or discolor because, in addition to chlorophyll a and chlorophyll c, they include a variety of carotenoids and dark-brown, tannin like substances. Alginic acids and fucoidan present in large amounts in the cell walls protect them from bacteria and fungi. Indeed it is wise to store *Laminaria* in slightly moist places to promote the growth of harmless bacteria and fungi, which soften cell walls and make the algae more palatable and tender. In recent years, amylase and other digestive enzymes have been used to soften brown-algae cell walls and make them easier to digest.

Wakame

Wakame (*Undaria*), considered a necessity to the traditional Japanese diet, was formerly gathered from the seabed by boat-born fishermen using scythes attached to long poles. Today, though wild *wakame* is still gathered, the alga is extensively cultivated in all parts of the country. Once only the soft upper parts were eaten; and the lower hard parts and the stipe, which puts forth sporophylls, were either discarded or left undisturbed in the sea. Today, however, treatment with enzymes renders the tougher parts edible. After being harvested, *Undaria* blades are cut down the middle at the rib and hung out to dry, much like laundry on a clothesline. They may or may not be washed in freshwater first. Variations of the drying process

Fig. 25 *Wakame* powdered for use in a popular rice-and-broth dish called *chazuke*.

include the production of thick sheets by pressing the *Undaria* blades on the ground and leaving them to dry in the sun and shredding already halved blades and twisting them into cords before drying.

Naruto-wakame is especially popular because it retains color even better than other kinds of *Undaria*. The secret of its durability is a soaking in an ash solution prior to drying. This method originated with a probably accidentally discovered primitive custom of sprinkling ashes on algae. The alkaline (ash) solution possibly stimulates changes in the polysaccharides in the frond cell walls. It is known that an alkali bath prevents both disintegration and decomposition of chlorophylls and the transformation of chlorophyll a into phaeophytin a. Taking a hint from the alkali bath, modern cultivators soak *Undaria* fronds in chemicals and keep them in cold storage for both prolonged preservation of fresh fronds and increased food value.

Though they look alike, there are subtle differences between wild and cultivated *Undaria* fronds. Wild fronds are called hard and retain their crispness in hot liquids. Cultivated ones turn mushy. Probably this results from environmentally created variations in the polysaccharide contents of cell walls in *Undaria* farms. The roughness or calmness of the water apparently plays an important role.

Often encountered in expensive restaurants, the delicacy called *komochi wakame* (*Undaria* with herring roe attached) is not *Undaria* at all but dried *Laminaria* or *Alaria*. It is usually imported from Alaska or the Scandinavian countries, where it was highly prized until environmentalists and conservationists began objecting to its use from the standpoint of protection of wild species; that is, of the herring that lay the roe.

Kombu

Though it went out of fashion in the West long ago, the ancient custom of eating *kombu* (*Laminaria*) persists in Japan. *Laminaria* is used as a source of alginates in other nations, but the Japanese prefer to eat it and use cheap brown algae for alginate or import raw materials from abroad. The more than ten species of Japanese *Laminaria*—*L. japonica* (*ma-kombu*), *L. ochotensis* (*rishiri-kombu*), *L. angustata* (*Mitsuishi-kombu*), *L. diabolica* (*oni-kombu*), *L. religiosa* (*hosome-kombu*), and so on— grow in the cold seas, especially in the vicinity of the island Hokkaidō. Because of limitations in geographical areas producing wild *Laminaria*, the alga is cultivated artificially, though the results are inferior in yield and commodity value. For the soup bases and soy-sauce boiled foods the Japanese make of *Laminaria*, blades of more than one year's growth are preferred. Older plants are difficult to raise artificially. The fronds are harvested by means of long poles with hooks or forks on the ends in the period between July and September and are spread on the ground to dry. The configuration of the ground determines the success of the dried product. Fronds gathered from the sea while alive are superior to those that have been washed up on shore.

The dried fronds are folded and bundled according to standard methods and marketed. Commercial names for *Laminaria* products vary with the place of origin, the use for which the alga is intended, or even the way the product is bundled. *Lami-*

Fig. 26   Outer Appearance (A) and Vertical Section of a *Laminaria* Blade (B)

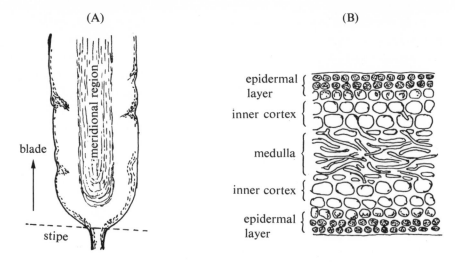

(A)   (B)

naria species bearing the same taxonomical names are often marked under different commercial names. But all of these dried brown algae are stored in dark, dry places for two or three years.

Thick-blade *Laminaria* is sold in Japan in a wide range of guises. It may be softened in vinegar, dried, then shaved (*oboro-* or *tororo-kombu*); stewed in a strongly flavored soy-sauce mixture (*tsukudani-kombu*); and prepared into an infusion known as *kombu* tea. *Laminaria* is sometimes divided into an epidermal layer containing chloroplasts (*kuro-tororo*) and a cortex and medulla layer without chloroplasts (*shiro-tororo*). This latter is used in a famous Ōsaka sushi dish of pressed mackerel and vinegared rice (*battera*).

Chopped *Laminaria* is fried in oil and eaten by the Japanese and by the Chinese, who have long imported this alga from Japan as a curative for goiter. As is explained elsewhere, after World War II, the Chinese began cultivating their own *Laminaria*.

In 1908, the late Dr. Kikunaye Ikeda discovered that the substance making the flavor of *Laminaria* popular with the Japanese is an amino acid called glutaminic acid. He succeeded in isolating it from other plants and thus paved the way for the production of the modern chemical seasoning called monosodium glutamate, which is used in many parts of the world.

Arame and *Hijikı*

Eisenia (*arame*), which is another member of the Laminariales order, is harvested wild and wind dried. It may be preboiled. It is preserved in its original form or shredded into something resembling shredded *Laminaria*. *Eisenia bicyclis*, which is produced in Japan on the Pacific northeast coast and the Izu Peninsula, is eaten as food only when fronds are young. It is tougher, less sticky, and lighter than *Undaria* and *Laminaria* and is considered more delicious by some people when fried in oil.

E. arborea, which grows on the Pacific Coast of North and South America may be eaten when fronds are young or after they have reached adulthood. It is considered superior. It grows in Japan too, and there is little difference in taste between the American and the Japanese products.

Like *Fucus, Plevetia, Cystoseira, Sargassum*, and *Durvillea, Hizikia* (*hijiki*) belongs to the order Fucales. It too is wind dried after harvesting, but preboiling eliminates unpleasant astringency by stimulating the excretion of blackish-brown, tanninlike substances. *Analipus* (*matsumo*) too is preboiled before drying for the same reason.

Though in its natural state *Hizikia* is dendroid, when dried, its leaflike parts fall away, producing dark-brown, stringlike pieces. The boiling step of processing preserves the color for a long time.

Mozuku

The Japanese refer to the edible species of the order Heterochordariales as *mozuku*, of which there are four kinds: *Nemacystus decipiens* (*mozuku*), *Tinocladia crassa* (*futo-mozuku*), *Eudesme virescens* or *Cladosiphon virescens* (*Okinawa-mozuku*), and the different *Sphaerotrichia divaricata* (*ishi-mozuku*). All *mozuku* are branched and filamentous with extremely soft, fine branchlets. Annuals living in temperate or warm seas, they flourish and are harvested in spring and early summer. Only *futo-mozuku* and *Okinawa-mozuku* are cultivated artificially, along the coasts of southern Kyūshū and Okinawa. To prevent the harvested fronds from adhering to each other and thus becoming unusable for food, *mozuku* is preserved in condensed brine. Flavored with combinations of either soy sauce and vinegar alone or soy sauce, vinegar, and sugar, *mozuku* is served as an appetizer with sakè.

Red Algae

Red algae—*Gracilaria* (*ogonori*), *Meristotheca* (*tosakanori*), *Grateloupia* (*mukade-nori*), *Gloiopeltis* (*funori*), *Chondrus* (*tsunomata*), *Eucheuma* (*kirinsai*), and so on—which contain large quantities of floridean mucilage in their cell walls—are, as has been explained, used in the manufacture of agar or carrageenan. They may be used as foods as well. Usually, after harvest, they are simply dried for preservation or are treated with ash or quicklime. Commercial use is made of the changes occurring in coloration in these algae owing to the chlorophyll a and phycobilins they contain.
1. Heating, steaming, or boiling turns them bluish green as long as chlorophyll a is still present.
2. Exposure to sunlight and storage in damp places turn them rosy pink as chlorophyll a degrades and only the phycobilins remain.
3. Soaking in freshwater or in a bleaching agent turns them white.

These various colors are used in the manufacture of food products that look different though they are actually all prepared from the same algae.

Fine filamentous *ogonori*, thicker *funori*, and still tougher and wider *tsunomata*, turned bluish green by exposure to heat, often accompany the Japanese delicacy called sashimi (sliced raw fish). *Ogonori* (*Gracilaria*) has an unpleasant dirty appearance in its natural state but can be turned an appetizing bluish green by steaming or soaking in hot water. In all cases, the care exercised during processing determines whether or not the resulting color is clear and bright or dull and unappealing.

Nostoc Freshwater Algae

The most famous of these freshwater algae is *Suizenji-nori*, which grows only submerged in clear, flowing water and is so troublesome to preserve that it is an expensive delicacy. The traditional way of preserving *Suizenji-nori* is to spread it on unglazed ceramic plates with a spatula. The material dries to form fairly thick sheets that are later cut for use in soups and other foods. A simpler method is to store it in a concentrated solution of sugar and salt. Other *Nostoc* vegetables—*ashitsuki* in Japan, *Kon-zao-mi* and *Fa-cai* in China—growing in different environments have large amounts of galactan mucoids in cell walls protecting colonies of unicellular bodies. The fronds may be easily cleaned and dried for extended preservation as long as they are not exposed to direct sunlight.

Domestic Algae

The history of agar production and methods and problems connected with its industrialization are covered in other parts of the book (p. 36). Here a few words are said about producing agar as a food in the home. Although there are many agarophytes among the algae, the one that responds best to simple processing is *Gelidium*. After harvesting *Gelidium* is dried. Freshwater is sprinkled on it before the drying process to bleach it. It is then chopped and boiled in an acidic solution (acetic or dilute sulfuric acid) water to produce the required extraction. The hot extract is filtered through cotton cloth to remove a residue of chopped algal bodies. The filtrated mucoids are neutralized by means of an alkali (baking soda). They begin to congeal when their temperature drops below 40°C. The result is a crude agar called *tokoroten* in Japanese. This jelly has a slight color and a tinge of seaweed flavor. When these traits are considered undesirable, further purification can be performed by freezing the substance in a home freezer, thawing it, then dehydrating it. If carried out once or twice, this process produces colorless, flavorless agar.

A crude agar (*okyūto*) produced in Fukuoka, Kyūshū, from *Campylaephora hypnaeoides* (*egonori*), is gray and has a faint seaweed odor. Served with vinegar sauces, it is less sticky than *tokoroten*.

Fig. 27 *Okyūto* raw agar, especially made from *Campylaephora* red algae.

6. Illustrations of Major Sea Vegetables

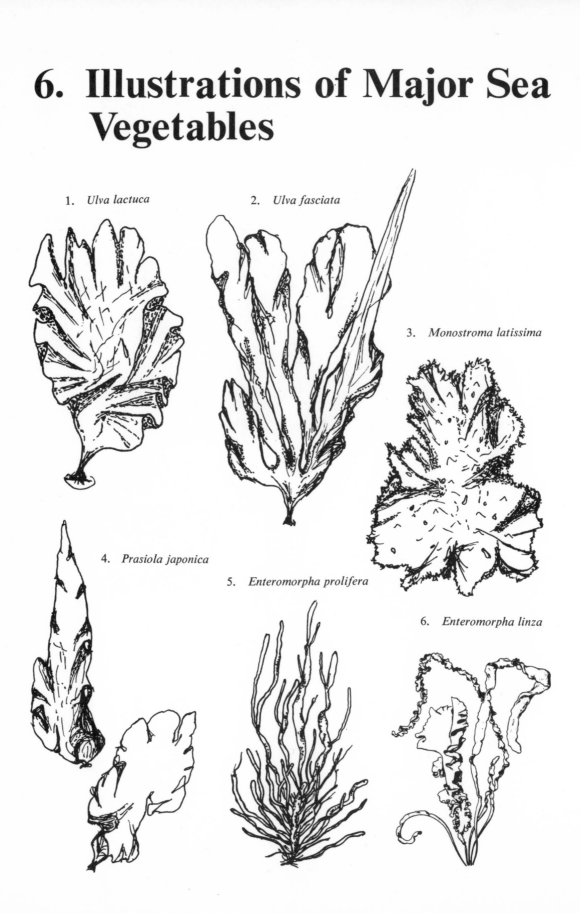

1. *Ulva lactuca*

2. *Ulva fasciata*

3. *Monostroma latissima*

4. *Prasiola japonica*

5. *Enteromorpha prolifera*

6. *Enteromorpha linza*

7. *Codium fragile*   8. *Codium edule*

9. *Codium reediae*

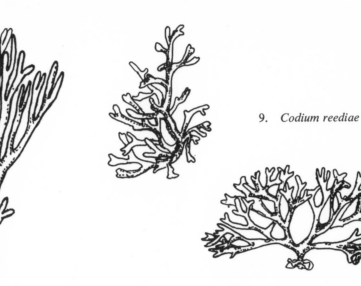

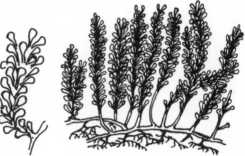

10. *Caulerpa okamurai*   11. *Caulerpa racemosa*

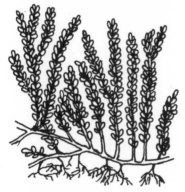

Cross Section of the Thallus

Ulva (2 layers)

Enteromorpha
(tubelike)

Monostroma
or
Prasiola
(1 layer)

Green Algae (Chlorophyta)

Species	Characteristics	Size	Distribution	Main Application	Common Names
1. *Ulva lactuca* Linnaeus	Green, wide, leaflike fronds; green, flatly expanded thallus.	10–50 cm	Worldwide, common in temperate and colder seas	Fodder	Sea lettuce *Aosa* (Japanese) Green laver
2. *Ulva fasciata* Delile	Edges are irregularly split to form several leaves with many variations in shape.	10–50 cm, max. 1.0 m or over	Common in temperate and warmer seas in Pacific, Atlantic, and Indian oceans.	Fodder	Sea lettuce *Pahapaha* or *Limu pahapaha* (Hawaiian)
3. *Monostroma latissima*, Wittr. (*M. oxispermum*)	Light-green, tender, thin, leaflike fronds.	10–30 cm	In the temperate coastal waters of northwestern Pacific.	Food: paste	*Aonori, hitoegusa* (Japanese) *Hai-cai* (sea vegetable, Chinese)
4. *Prasiola japonica* Yatabe	Grows in rapidly flowing rivers in mountainous regions. Resembles *Monostroma* and has tender, thin, leaflike fronds.	10–20 cm	Japan, in highlands; closely resembles *P. mexicana* grown in South America.		*Kawanori* (Japanese)
5. *Enteromorpha prolifera* J. Agardh	Thin, long, multibranched, tubular fronds.	30–150 cm, max. 2.0–3.0 m	Asia, South America, in estuaries.	Fish meal; spicelike pleasant aroma	Green laver *Suji-aonori* (Japanese) *Limu-ele'ele* (Hawaiian) *Tai-tiao* (Chinese)
6. *Enteromorpha linza* J. Ag.	Leaflike fronds with few branches, closely resembling *Ulva* but differentiated by thin, tubular roots.	10–30 cm	Worldwide.	Fish meal; spicelike aroma	*Usuba-aonori* (Japanese) *Hai-cai* (Chinese)
7. *Codium fragile* Harvey	Deep-green, dichotomously branching, cylindrical, forming	8–30 cm	Worldwide in temperate seas.	Food in southern Japan and Indonesia	*Miru* (Japanese) Sea staghorn

	Characteristics	Size	Distribution	Main Application	Common Names
	large clusters, feltlike and water-impregnated.				
8. *Codium edule*	Plants creep over coral forming mats, firm but spongy.	5–10 cm	Hawaiian Islands, warmer regions in the Pacific Islands.	Food in Hawaii	*Limu, Wawaeiole,* or *Alaula* (Hawaiian) *Miru* (Japanese)
9. *Codium reediae*	Closely resembles the two preceding types, though somewhat smaller.	5–10 cm	Hawaiian Islands.	Same as for the two preceding types	*Limu-aalaulaa* (Hawaiian)
10. *Caulerpa okamurai* W. van Bosse	Stems grow on rocks like ivy; erect branches resembling bunches of grapes. Light green, tender, and juicy.	5–10 cm	Temperate and warmer waters of Japan.	Food locally; only erect parts eaten; taste is faint.	*Fusa-iwazuta* or *umibudo* (Japanese) Sea grapes
11. *Caulerpa racemosa* W. van Bosse	Light green; stems grow on rocky bottom and produce erect grapelike branches. Shape of branches different from that of preceding types.	5–10 cm	Grows on coral rocks and pebbles in warmer seas in southern Japan, East Asian islands, Southern Pacific, east coast of Northern America and West Indies.	Only erect branches eaten; tender and juicy. Said to be toxic, though this is doubtful.	Sea grapes *Lelatu* (Indonesian) *Araucip* (Philippine) *Limu eka* (Cook Islands)

Brown Algae (Phaeophyta)

Species	Characteristics	Size	Distribution	Main Application	Common Names
12. *Endarachne binghamiae* J. Ag.	Dark-brown, long, slightly hard, flat, leaflike fronds.	5–10 cm	Temperate and warmer-regions on both sides of the Pacific, Japan, Hong Kong, and southern California.	Food; dried material ground into fine powder; pleasant aroma	*Habanori* (Japanese)

Species	Characteristics	Size	Distribution	Main Application	Common Names
13. *Scytosiphon lomentaria* J. Ag.	Dark-brown, long, thin, tubular fronds. One type has clearly constricted joints; the other does not.	10–30 cm	Temperate and colder-regions on both sides of the Pacific along Japanese coast, through the Bering Sea to Baja California and Australia.	Food; dried material, similar to preceding type	Leather tube *Kayamonori* (Japanese)
14. *Nemacystus decipiens* Kuckuck	Dark-brown, thin, multiple, sticky, thread-like branches forming bunches. Grows twisted around fronds of *Sargassum* sp.	Forms loose bunches with stems of about 10–20 cm	Temperate region around Japan and the coast of Qingdao in northern China.	Food; preserved with brine and eaten as an appetizer in Japan	*Mozuku* (Japanese)
15. *Heterochordaria abietina* Setch. et Gard. (*Analipus japonicus* Wynne)	Main erect axes rise from prostrate base and are surrounded by numerous branchlets.	5–30 cm	Colder region on both sides of the Pacific, Japan, and from Alaska to the middle of California.	Food	Far needle *Matsumo* (Japanese)
16. *Dictyopteris plagigramma* Vickers (*D. australis*)	Repeated dichotomous branches. Fronds have thin winglike membranes along the midrib.	5–10 cm	Hawaii, warmer-sea species occurring in the West Indies, Bermuda, and the Atlantic.	Food	*Limu-lipoa* (Hawaiian) Net wing
17. *Hizikia fusiforme* Okam.	Clear, erect, main branches surrounded by numerous, small, cylindrical branchlets.	40–100 cm	Temperate Japan and from Guang dong to Hong Kong Bay along the coast of China.	Food	*Hijiki* (Japanese)
18. *Sargassum echinocarpum* Greville (*S. coriifolium* J. Agardh)	Stems and leaves clearly differentiated; small serrations around the edges of the leaves.	20–60 cm	Hawaiian Islands, north-west coast of Australia, Taiwan, and the Indian Ocean.	Food; juvenile fronds are tender and delicious.	*Limu-kala* (Hawaiian)

12. *Endarachne binghamiae*   13. *Scytosiphon lomentaria*   14. *Nemacystus decipiens*

15. *Analipus japonicus*

16. *Dictyopteris plagigramma*

17. *Hizikia fusiforme*

18. *Sargassum echinocarpum*

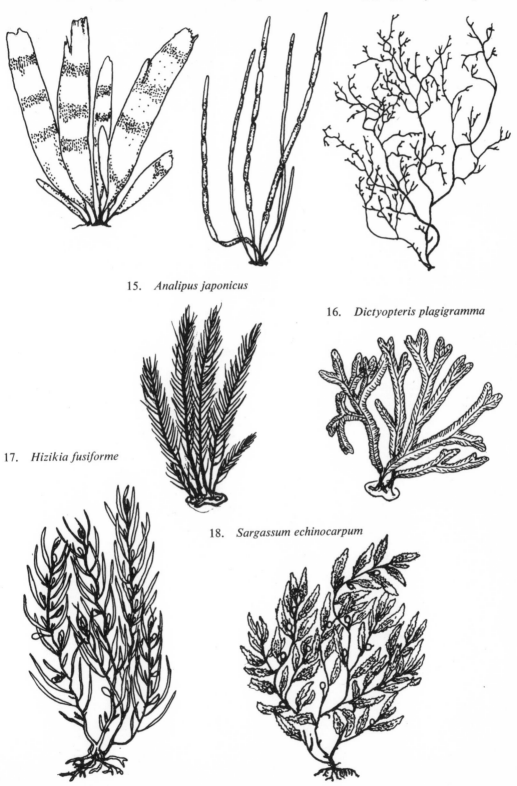

Species	Characteristics	Size	Distribution	Main Application	Common Names
19. *Sargassum fulvellum* C. Ag.	Dendroid with stems and leaves. Lower leaves large; those in upper parts thin, long, and small. Many air bladders. Annual.	30–150 cm	Temperate coasts of Japan and Korea.	Juvenile plants eaten only locally; algin.	*Hondawara* (Japanese)
20. *Ascophyllum nodosum* Le Joll.	Long, tough, leathery fronds; compressed, irregularly dichotomous; conspicuous air bladders.	30–150 cm	Colder regions on both sides of the Atlantic.	Algin	Knotted wrack Knobbed wrack
21. *Durvillea antarctica* Hariot	Dark-brown, long, thin cylindrical fronds with dichotomous branches; often mistaken for sea snakes when drifting along the sea bottom.	5–15 m	Antarctic Ocean, Chile Terra del Fuego, Patagonia, Falkland. Georgia St., New Zealand, Cape Horn.	Algin	Bull kelp
22. *Laminaria japonica* Areschoug	Blackish-brown with wide, thick, leaflike fronds.	1–3 m	Southern Hokkaidō.	Food, especially soup or boiled with soy sauce; the best of the *Laminaria sp.* produced in Japan.	*Ma-kombu* (Japanese) *Hai Tai* (sea sack, Chinese)
23. *Laminaria sinclairii* Farlow	Numerous distinctive rhysomes and roots at the basal part.	Up to 1 m	Endemic on Pacific coasts of North America from British Columbia to San Francisco.		Kelp
24. *Laminaria saccharina* Lamouroux	Wide, long, bandlike, wrinkled fronds. Uneven in the center and moiré in form.	90–120 cm (3–4 feet)	5–10 fathoms deep, common and abundant on both sides of the Atlantic. Horses are said to be fond of its sugary fronds.	Algin and food	Sugar wrack Sea belt Poor man's weather glass

19. *Sargassum fulvellum*

20. *Ascophyllum nodosum*

21. *Durvillea antarctica*

22. *Laminaria japonica*

23. *Laminaria sinclairii*

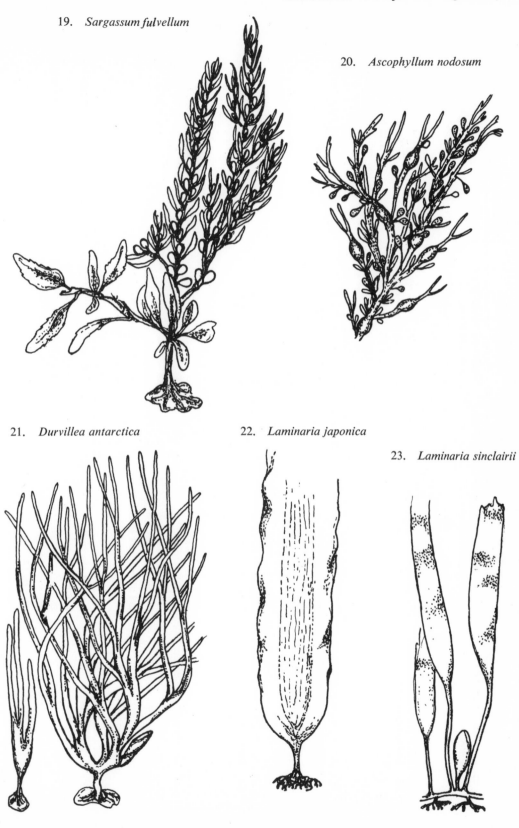

Species	Characteristics	Size	Distribution	Main Application	Common Names
25. *Laminaria cloustonii* Edmondston (*L. hyperborea* Foslie)	Mucilage glands scattered on surfaces of blades.	60–360 cm	Grows on rocks at low water levels in colder regions on both sides of the Atlantic.		Cuvie Tangle Split whip wrack
26. *Laminaria digitata* Lamouroux	No mucilage glands.	130–400 cm	Low water mark 15 fathoms; widely distributed along both coasts of the Atlantic.		Oar weed Tangle, sea tangle, fingered tangle, horsetail tangle Sea girdle
27. *Postelsia palmaeformis* Ruprecht	As the common name suggests, resembles a land palm.	60 cm long	Endemic on Pacific coast of North America from British Columbia to Central California; on rocks of rough shores.	Algin	Sea palm
28. *Nereocystis luetkeana* Post et Rupr.	Despite its size, the plant is annual or persisting up to 18 months, usually from February to December.	12 m long (of which 11 m is stipe)	Endemic on Pacific coast of North America.	Algin	Giant bull kelp Ribbon kelp
29. *Ecklonia cava* Kjellm.	Closely resembles *Eisenia*, except that is has one unwrinkled blade in the upper part of the stipe.	0.5–3 m	*E. cava* endemic in Japan, but *Ecklonia* occurs in South Africa, Australia, and New Zealand. South African species reaches 10 m.	Algin; juvenile fronds can be used as food	*Kajime* (Japanese) Paddle weed
30. *Eisenia arborea* Areschoug	Closely resembles *Ecklonia*, except that (a) there are two apparent branches on the upper part of the stipe and (b) blade surface is wrinkled.	0.5–3 m	Both coasts of the Pacific, in North America, South America (Peru), and Japan.	Algin, food	*Arame* (Japanese) Sea oak Southern sea palm

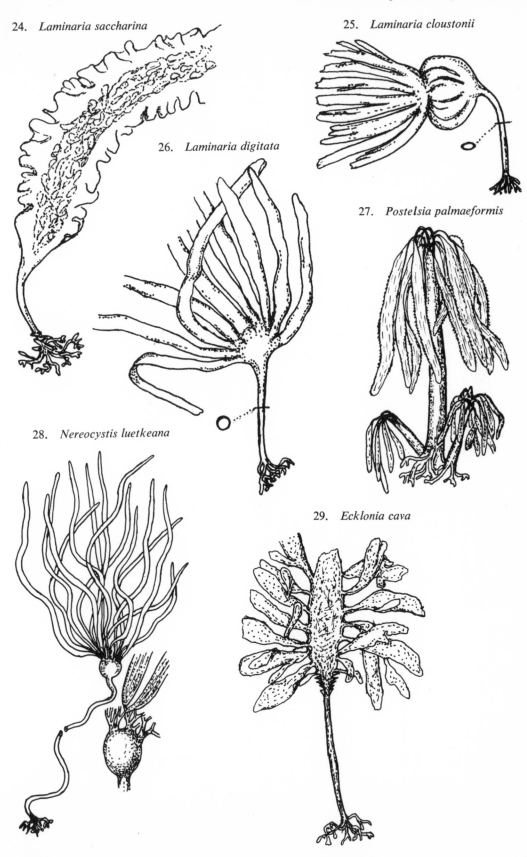

24. *Laminaria saccharina*

25. *Laminaria cloustonii*

26. *Laminaria digitata*

27. *Postelsia palmaeformis*

28. *Nereocystis luetkeana*

29. *Ecklonia cava*

Species	Characteristics	Size	Distribution	Main Application	Common Names
31. *Lessonia flavicans* Bory	Many dichotomous branchlets on the long stipe with blades attached at the end of the branchlets.	4 m	The chief center of distribution is in the colder region of the Southern Atlantic and Antarctic Oceans*.	Algin	
32. *Arthrothamnus bifidus* J. Agardh	Dichotomous branching rhysomes and thick, bandlike blades.	2–4 m	Colder sea regions of the Northern Pacific, Kamchatka, Aleutian Islands, Alaska, and eastern part of Hokkaidō.	Food and algin	*Nekoashi-kombu* (Japanese)
33. *Macrocystis pyrifera* C. Agardh	The largest of all seaweeds, with total lengths reaching 60 m. Many large leaves at the ends of long, thin, branching stems. Air bladders at stem—thallus junctures keep the kelp afloat. Perennial.	20–40 m	In cold seas, along the coast of North and South America, Australia, New Zealand, and South Africa.	Algin and food	Giant kelp Giant bladder kelp
34. *Saccorhyza polyschides* Batters (*Sacchos*—sack; *rhyza*—root)	Blades on upper parts of the stipe are split into more than 10 parts. In adult stage, sporophylls appear on both sides of the stem and the basal parts inflate like a sack.	Up to 3–5 m	Colder waters on both sides of the Atlantic, Europe, and North America.	Food and algin	Furbelows
35. *Undaria pinnatifida* Suringar	Upper parts of stipe develop into midribs along the center of the blades. In the adult stage, there are undulated or twisted sporo-	1–2 m	Temperate waters along the coast of Japan, Korea, and China.	Food	*Wakame* (Japanese)

* Only *Lessoniopsis* genus with short stems grows along the Pacific coast of North America.

30. *Eisenia arborea*

31. *Lessonia flavicans*

32. *Arthrothamnus bifidus*
(young plant)

33. *Macrocystis pyrifera*

34. *Saccorhyza polyschides*

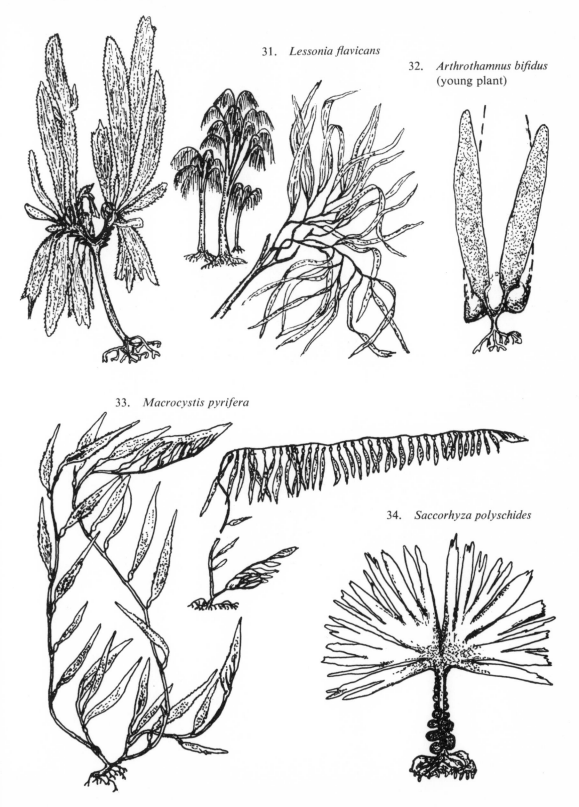

Species	Characteristics	Size	Distribution	Main Application	Common Names
	phylls on both sides of the stipe. Annual. A speciality of Japan.				
36. *Undaria peterseniana* Okamura	Wide bandlike fronds appear similar to those of *Laminaria* but can be differentiated by the red color of the midribs and growth in temperate waters at depths of 5–10 m. Annual.	2–4 m	Temperate waters along the coast of Japan.	Food	*Ao-wakame* (Japanese)
37. *Alaria esculenta* Greville	Upper parts of stipe develop into midribs along the centers of the blades. Many sporophylls are attached to both sides of the stipe. Tougher than *Undaria*.	2–4 m	Colder waters on both coasts of the Atlantic and Pacific. Succulent midribs of young plants are eaten in parts of Scotland and Ireland.	Algin and food	Honey ware Wing kelp Dabberlocks Stringy kelp Murlins *Chigaiso* (Japanese)
38. *Egregia laevigata* Areschoug	Many side branches and air bladders on both sides of a single central axis, suggesting the form of a large centipede.	5–15 m, up to 20 m long	Pacific coast of North America from British Columbia to the middle of California.	Algin; little used	Feather boa Feather-boa kelp
39. *Fucus evanescens* C. Agardh	Repeated dichotomous branching and flat fronds. Ends of the branches often expand to form air bladders.	10–25 m	Widely distributed in cold waters along both the Atlantic and Pacific coasts, but species differ in each area. *F. evanescens* is common in Japan, *F. disticus* in North America, and various kinds of *F. disticus* in Europe.		Rock weed Popping wrack Bladder wrack Black wrack *Hibamata* (Japanese)

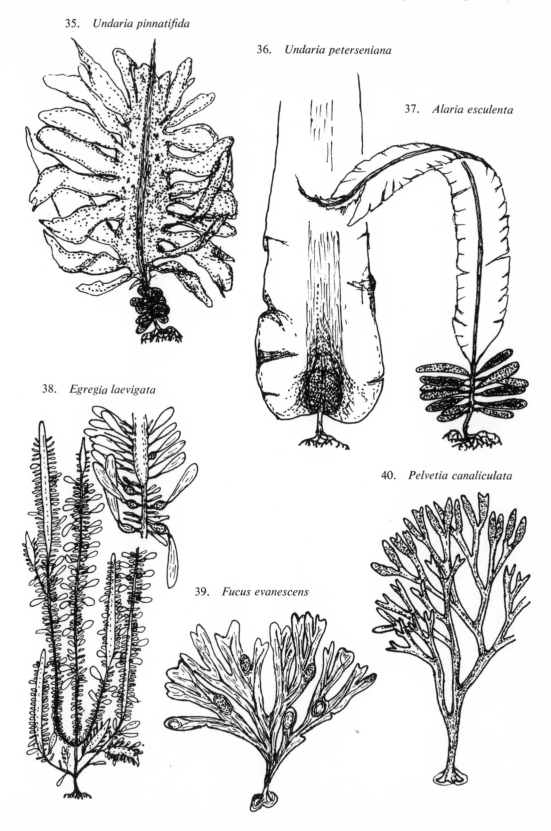

35. *Undaria pinnatifida*

36. *Undaria peterseniana*

37. *Alaria esculenta*

38. *Egregia laevigata*

40. *Pelvetia canaliculata*

39. *Fucus evanescens*

Species	Characteristics	Size	Distribution	Main Application	Common Names
40. *Pelvetia canaliculata* De Toni	Resembles *Fucus* but is more slender and tender.	Up to 1 m	*Pelvetia* genus is widely distributed in the cold seas on the Pacific and Atlantic coasts, but species differ regionally. *P. fastigiata* is widely distributed on the Pacific coast of North America from British Columbia to Baja California.		
41. *Cystoseira osmundacea* C. Ag.	Branched trunk and branches form a chain; prominent air bladders.	Up to 8 m tall	From Oregon to Baja California in North America, frequently mingled with *Macrocystis*.		Woody chain bladder (sea oak)

Size Comparisons Among Several Brown Algae
(modified from Stephenson and Chapman)

a.	*Macrocystis* of North America	about 25 m
		46 m up to 60 m
b.	*Macrocystis* of South Africa	about 10 m
c.	*Ecklonia* of South Africa	about 11 m
d.	*Nereocystis* of North America	40 m
e.	*Laminaria* of South Africa	10 m
f.	*Laminaria longissima* of Japan	20 m
g.	*Durvillea* of south New Zealand	25 m
h.	*Sargassum* of Japan	max. 5 m
i.	*Eisenia* of Japan	5 m
j.	*Ulva*	1 m
k.	*Porphyra*	0.5 m

41. *Cystoseira osmundacea*

42. *Porphyra suborbiculata*

43. *Porphyra crispata*

44. *Porphyra dentata*

45. *Porphyra tenera*

46. *Porphyra pseudolinearis*

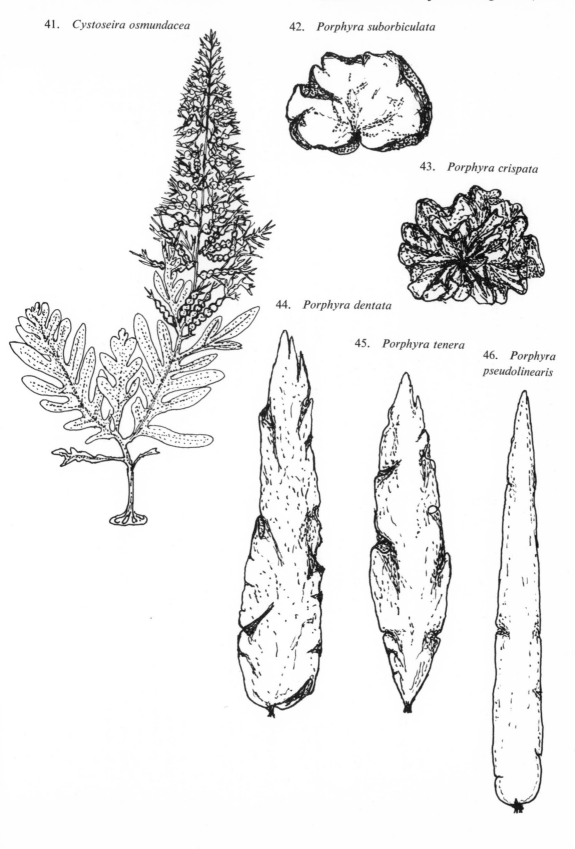

Red Algae (Rhodophyta) *Porphyra*

Species	Characteristics	Size	Distribution	Main Application	Common Names
42. *Porphyra suborbiculata* Kjellman	Circular, thin, flat, leaf-like fronds with folded edges.	3–6 cm	Widely distributed on the temperate coasts of Japan, Korea, and China, growing on rocky shores falling into rough, open sea.	Food	*Maruba-amanori, iwanori* (Japanese) *Zi-cai* (purple vegetable, Chinese)
43. *Porphyra crispata* Kjellman	Circular, leaflike, folded fronds with a crumpled shape.	3–5 cm	Warmer regions from southern Japan to southern China, and Indochina; rough rocky shores.	Food	*Tsukushi-amanori* (Japanese) *Zi-cai* (purple vegetable, Chinese)
44. *Porphyra dentata* Kjellman	Long, leaflike, thin, bandlike fronds.	10–30 cm	Middle Japan, temperate species.	Food	*Oni-amanori* (Japanese)
45. *Porphyra tenera* Kjellman	*Tenera* means soft. The most delicious of all *Porphyra*.	10–30 cm	Widely distributed along the temperate coasts of Japan. Cultivated.	Food	*Asakusa-nori* (Japanese)
46. *Porphyra pseudolinearis* Ueda et Okamura	Very slender, long, leafy fronds.	20–40 cm	Along the coast of Japan and Korea facing the Japan Sea.	Food	*Uppurui-nori* (Japanese)
47. *Porphyra yezoensis* Ueda	Large, round, leaflike fronds. Cultivated recently.	10–15 cm	Temperate and colder waters in Japan.	Food	*Susabi-nori* (Japanese)
48. *Porphyra umbilicalis* J. G. Agardh	Leaflike fronds with wrinkled edges.	5–20 cm	Colder waters along the coasts on both sides of the Pacific and Atlantic.	Food	Purple laver *Chishima-kuronori* (Japanese)
49. *Porphyra perforata* J. G. Agardh	Perforated fronds.	20–30 cm, max. up to 150 cm	Common on rocks from Alaska to southern California along the North American coast.		Red laver

47. *Porphyra yezoensis*

48. *Porphyra umbilicalis*

49. *Porphyra perforata*

50. *Porphyra nereocystis*
grown on *Nereocystis* fronds

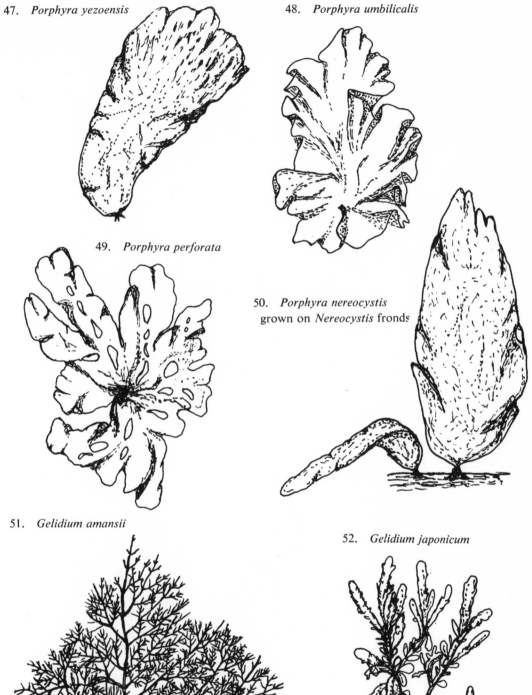

51. *Gelidium amansii*

52. *Gelidium japonicum*

53. *Gelidium subcostatum*

54. *Gelidium pacificum*

55. *Gelidium latifolium*

56. *Gelidium arborescens*

57. *Gelidium cartilagineum*

58. *Pterocladia americana*

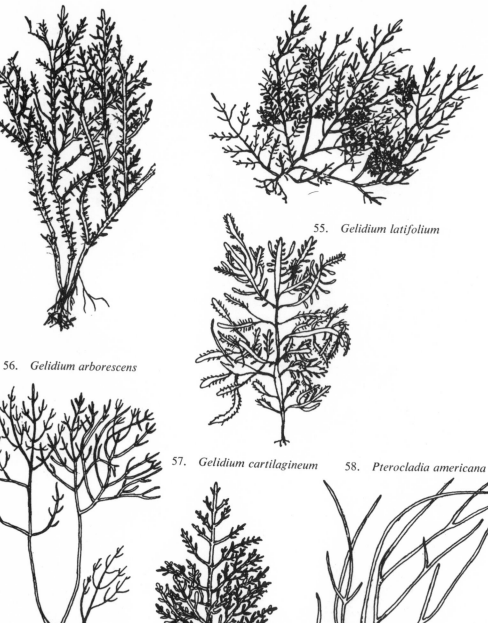

59. *Pterocladia pyramidale*

60. *Pterocladia capillacea*

61. *Acanthopeltis japonica*

62. *Gracilaria verrucosa*

63. *Ceramium boydenii*

64. *Campylaephora hypnaeoides*

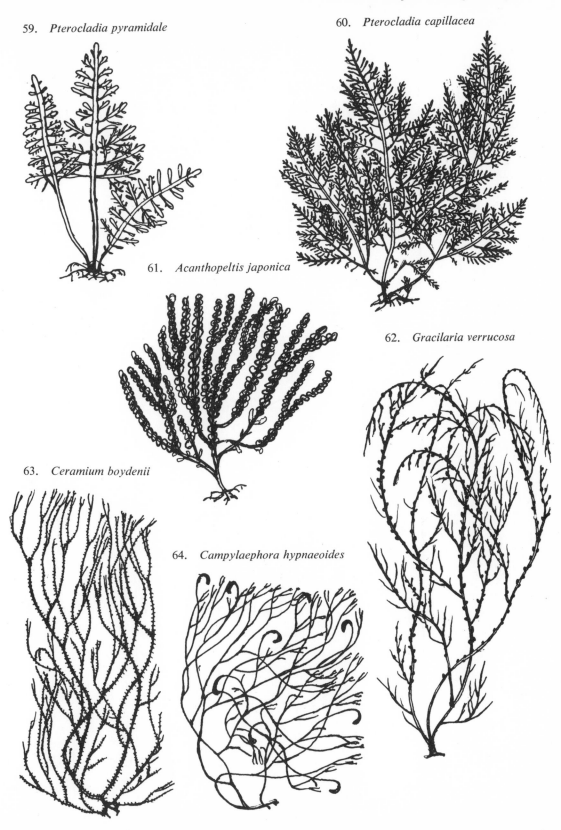

Species	Characteristics	Size	Distribution	Main Application	Common Names
50. *Porphyra nereocystis* Anderson	Epiphytic on stipes of *Nereocystis*.	25–90 cm, max. up to 300 cm	North America from Alaska to southern California; annual. Found during the period from November to June.		

Red Algae–Gelidium*

Species	Characteristics	Size	Distribution	Main Application	Common Names
51. *Gelidium amansii* Lamouroux	Dendroid fronds with repeated branching. Cartilaginous branches slender and dark red with many variations in color and shape.	10–30 cm	Temperate waters of Japan.	Main raw material for the manufacture of agar; grows at a depth of 5–15 m on the sea bottom.	*Tengusa, makusa* (Japanese)
52. *Gelidium japonicum* Okamura	Rather large, tough leaves on stems with little branching. Grows on rocks in rough seas and is often covered with coralline algae.	10–20 cm	Temperate and warmer water of Japan.	Agar raw material	*Onikusa* (Japanese)
53. *Gelidium subcostatum* Okamura	Main branches are flat, wide, and quite long.	10–40 cm, up to 1 m	Temperate and warmer waters of Japan, growing on the bottom 10–20 m in depth.	Agar raw material	*Hirakusa* (Japanese)
54. *Gelidium pacificum* Okamura	Resembles *G. amansii*; can be differentiated because reproductive branches are more closely grouped.	10–30 cm	Temperate waters of Japan. Narrow distribution.	Agar raw material, high quality.	*Ōbusa* (Japanese)

Species	Characteristics	Size	Distribution	Main Application	Common Names
55. Gelidium latifolium Bornet et Thuret (G. corneum Var. latifolium Grev.) (latus—bread; folium—leaf)	Broad fronds that become gelatinous upon boiling or maceration.	10–15 cm	Along both sides of the Atlantic.	Agar	
56. Gelidium arborescens Gardner	Erect shoots with alternately placed branchlets of 4–5 orders.	8–25 cm	Central California.	Agar	
57. Gelidium cartilagineum Harvey	Various erect shoots with mutual branches.	10–30 cm	Along Atlantic coast and from British Columbia to Baja California along Pacific coast.	Agar	

* Main source of agar.

Red Algae—Agarophytes*

Species	Characteristics	Size	Distribution	Main Application	Common Names
58. Pterocladia americana Taylor	Main axes difficult to determine, branching sparce.	6 cm	Warmer waters of North America, West coast of Florida, and Bermuda.	Agar	
59. Pterocladia pyramidale Dawson	Resembles Gelidium but base of branches is slender.	10–15 cm	East side of the Pacific, southern California, Central gulf of California, Galapagos Archipelago, and Ecuador.	Agar	
60. Pterocladia capillacea Bornet et Thuret (P. pinnata, P. corneum)	Resembles the preceding type but more branches and many variations in shape.	10–25 cm	Widely distributed in the Atlantic and Pacific, especially abundant around New Zealand.	Agar	Obakusa (Japanese)
61. Acanthopeltis japonica Okamura	Circular, thorny leaves wrapped around the trunk stem.	10–15 cm	Only in temperate waters of Japan.	Agar	Toriashi, Yuikiri (Japanese)

* Secondary sources of agar.

Species	Characteristics	Size	Distribution	Main Application	Common Names
62. *Gracilaria verrucosa* Papenfuss (*G. confervoides* Grev.)	Dark-red, cartilaginous, multibranched fronds. Many cystocarps on branches in adult stage.	30–50 cm	Worldwide; abundant in shallow marshes and estuaries.	Food and agar	*Ogonori* (Japanese) Sewing thread *Ogo* (Hawaiian)
63. *Ceramium boydenii* Gepp	Dark-red, slender, intertwined, threadlike branches with many small thorns. Attached to *Sargassum* sp.	Clumps of 20–40 cm	Temperate and colder waters along Western Coast of North Pacific, Japan, Korea, and China.	Agar	*Amikusa* (Japanese)
64. *Campylaephora hypnaeoides* J. Agardh	Brownish-red, fine, threadlike, multibranched intertwined, hooklike shapes at the ends of the branches. Intertwined with *Sargassum*.	Clumps of 20–40 cm	Temperate and colder waters in Western North Pacific, Japan, Korea, and Sakhalin.	Agar and food	*Egonori* (Japanese)
65. *Gracilaria textorii* Suringar	Purplish-red, tough, leathery, flat, leaflike fronds. Many small warts on surfaces.	5–15 cm	Temperate and warmer waters in Japan, Java, and Indonesia.	Food and agar	*Kabanori* (Japanese)
66. *Gracilaria follifera* Boergesen	Size, manner of branching, and color extremely variable.	Up to 30 cm	Common on the American coast along the Gulf of Mexico.	Food	
67. *Gracilaria coronopifolia* J. Agardh	Form variable, usually with decumbent axes or branches.	10–15 cm tall	Hawaiian Islands, southern China, and east Asian islands.	Food	*Limu-Manauea, Ogo* (Hawaiian)
68. *Gracilaria crassa* Harv.	Greenish-red, tough, gnarled, cylindrical branches that creep on coralline rocks.	5–10 cm	Warmer waters on the western side of the Pacific, Okinawa, Taiwan, and Sri Lanka.	Food and agar	*Taiwan-ogonori* (Japanese)

65. *Graciliaria textorii*

66. *Graciliaria follifera*

67. *Graciliaria coronopifolia*

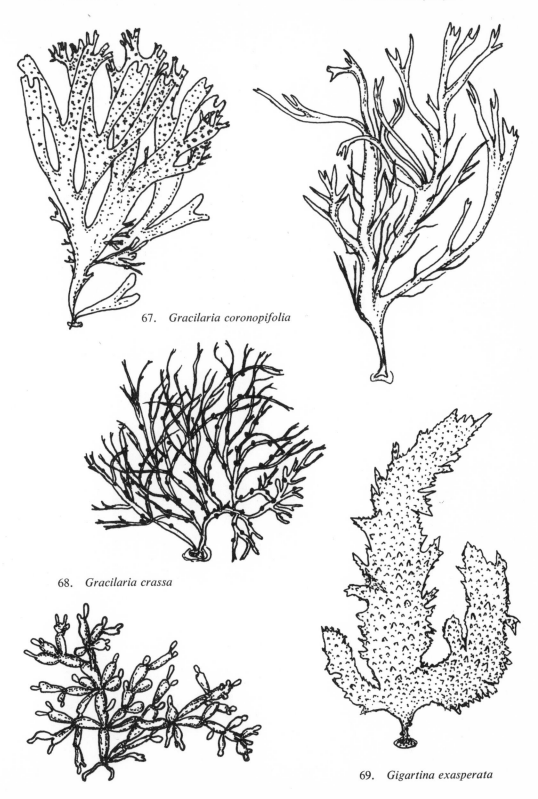

68. *Graciliaria crassa*

69. *Gigartina exasperata*

Species	Characteristics	Size	Distribution	Main Application	Common Names
69. *Gigartina exasperata* Harvey et Baily	Deep-brownish-red, flat, irregularly shaped blade with uniform outgrowths on the surfaces.	30–50 cm	Colder waters from Southern British Columbia to North California along Pacific coast of North America.	Carrageen and food. New uses of *Gigartina* are being developed.	Turkish towel

Red Algae—Main Source of Carrageen

Species	Characteristics	Size	Distribution	Main Application	Common Names
70. *Eucheuma nudum* J. Agardh (*E. isiforme, E. acanthocladum*)	Usually procumbent. Main axes devoid of whorls, spines, or nodules.	30–50 cm	West coast of Florida and Bermuda in waters of 5–30 m deep.		
71. *Eucheuma muricatum* Weber van Bosse (*E. spinosum*)	Axes branched irregularly and covered with numerous spines or nodules.	10–20 cm	Warmer waters in southern Japan, New Holland, Papua New Guinea, Indonesia and Philippines, and the Indian Ocean.	Food and carrageen	*Kirinsai, Ryukyu-tsunomata* (Japanese)
72. *Eucheuma gelatinae* J. Agardh	Axes with irregular branchlets; decumbent, creeping on the coralline bottom.	8–15 cm	Warmer waters of southern Japan, New Holland, New Caledonia, and Indian Ocean.	Food and carrageen	*Katamen-kirinsai* (Japanese)
73. *Chondrus elatus* Okamura	Long, thin, flat axes with 2–3 dichotomous branches on the tops.	10–25 cm	Temperate waters in middle Japan; low production.	Carrageen	*Kotoji-tsunomata* (Japanese)
74. *Chondrus crispus* Stackhouse	Dichotomously branched, flat, leaflike fronds with many variations in shape, size, and color.	5–10 cm	Colder waters on both sides of the Atlantic.	Carrageen	Irish moss

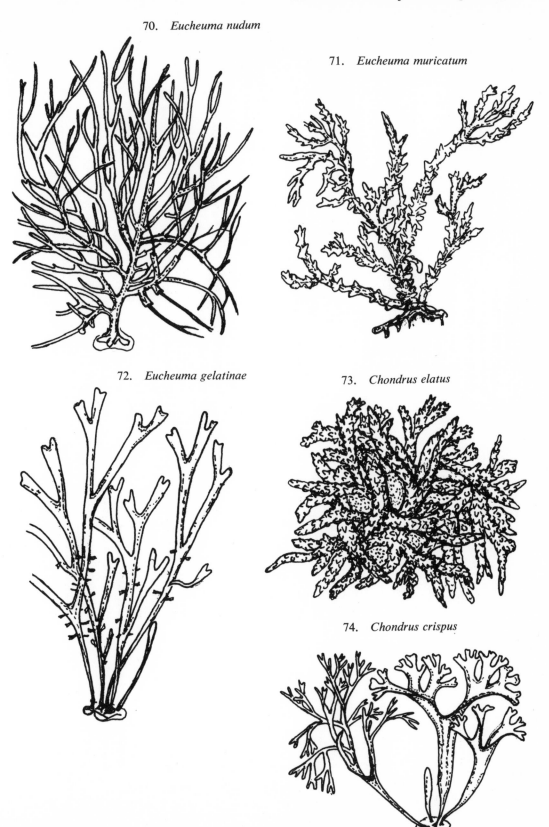

70. *Eucheuma nudum*

71. *Eucheuma muricatum*

72. *Eucheuma gelatinae*

73. *Chondrus elatus*

74. *Chondrus crispus*

Red Algae with Miscellaneous Applications

Species	Characteristics	Size	Distribution	Main Application	Common Names
75. *Chondrus ocellatus* Holmes	Highly variable in form, color, and size but commonly has numerous round, peacock-feather marks, scattered on the blade surface.	3–20 cm	Temperate waters of Japan.	Adhesive paste and food	*Tsunomata* (Japanese)
76. *Chondrus yendoi* Mikami (*Iridophycus cornucopiae*)	Resembles the preceding genus.	5–10 cm	Endemic to the colder seas of Japan.	Adhesive paste	*Ezo-tsunomata*, *kuroha-ginnanso* (Japanese)
77. *Asparagopsis taxiformis* Collins et Harvey	Hairlike branches formed on rather large trunks. Tender and juicy.	10–20 cm	Temperate and warmer seas on both sides of the Pacific Ocean and Bermuda.	Food. Highly rated for *linin* salad in Hawaii.	*Kagikenori* (Japanese) *Limu-kohu* (Hawaiian)
78. *Ahnfeltia plicata* Fries	Highly variable in form with rigid, often dense, tufts.	5–15 cm	In colder areas in both Atlantic and Pacific oceans.	Agar; excellent bacteriological agar.	Bushy Ahnfelt's seaweed *Itanigusa* (Japanese)
79. *Ahnfeltia gigartinoides* J. Agardh	Dense branching near the tops of the plants.	10–25 cm high	Mexico, Hawaiian Islands, and along the North American coast.	Food and agar	*Limu-'aki'aki* (Hawaiian)
80. *Ahnfeltia paradoxa* Okamura	Very variable in form and size.	15–80 cm	Along the temperate coast of Japan.	Agar	*Harigane* (Japanese)
81. *Meristotheca papulosa* J. Agardh	Pure-red, flat, tender, irregularly formed, leaflike fronds. Small, crestlike protrusions on the edges of the leaves.	15–30 cm	Temperate and warmer waters of Japan and Taiwan.	Food; widely used in large quantities in Japan and China.	*Tosakanori, keikansai* (Japanese)

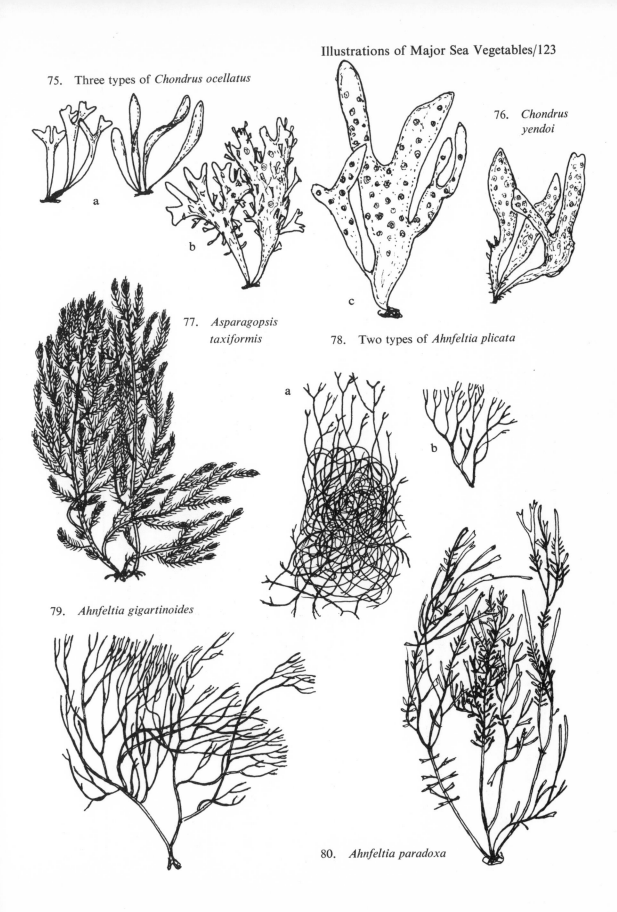

75. Three types of *Chondrus ocellatus*

a

b

76. *Chondrus yendoi*

c

77. *Asparagopsis taxiformis*

78. Two types of *Ahnfeltia plicata*

a

b

79. *Ahnfeltia gigartinoides*

80. *Ahnfeltia paradoxa*

Red Algae: Used for Food

Species	Characteristics	Size	Distribution	Main Application	Common Names
82. *Palmaria palmata* Greville (*Rhodymenia palmata*)	Purplish-red, usually tufted perennial; form variable.	15–30 cm	Colder waters of both Pacific and Atlantic.	Food, eaten widely in Europe and North America.	Dulse *Soul-söll* (Norwegian)
83. *Gloiopeltis furcata* Postels et Ruprecht	Purplish-red, tubelike stem branches dichotomously 2 or 3 times.	3–10 cm up to 15 cm	Widely distributed from colder waters to warmer waters along the Japanese, Korean, and Chinese coasts; grows in the uppermost intertidal zone.	Food; soup stock or garnish for sashimi	*Fukuro-funori* (Japanese)
84. *Grateloupia filicina* C. Agardh	Many branches on both sides of the main stock; centipedelike form; very sticky.	15–40 cm	Worldwide.	Used, though rarely, for food.	*Mukade-nori* (Japanese) *Limu Huluhu-luwaena* (Hawaiian)
85. *Grateloupia doryphora* Howe (*G. californica*)	Wide variations in shape and color. Flat, leaflike, soft, gelatinous fronds. Considerable confusion among names of species.	Up to 2 m long	Along Pacific coast of North America and South America from British Columbia to Peru.		
86. *Digenea simplex* C. Agardh	Hairlike branchlets cover entire surfaces of tough, cylindrical axes shaped like foxtails. Small coralline algae often grow on the surface.	5–15 cm	Warmer waters of the Pacific and Atlantic.	Anthelmintic for ascarid agar, and food.	*Makuri* or *Kaijinso* (Japanese)

81. *Meristotheca papulosa*

82. *Palmaria palmata*

83. *Gloiopeltis furcata*

84. *Grateloupia filicina*

85. *Grateloupia doryphora*

86. *Digenea simplex*

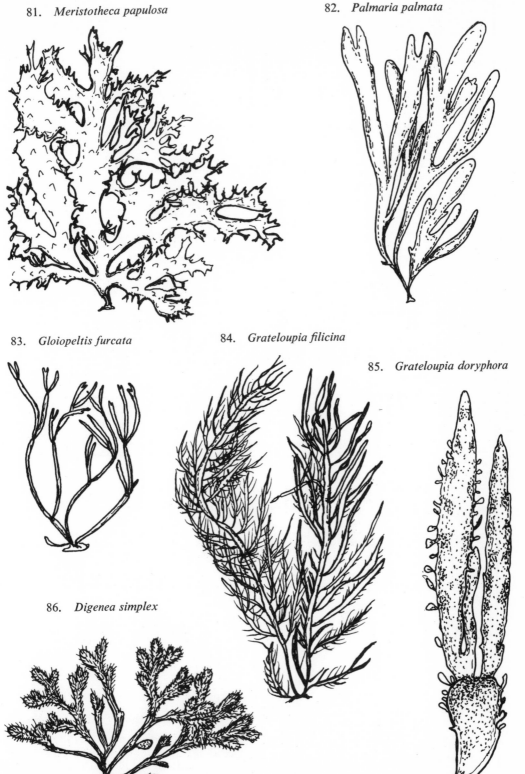

Chemical Compositions (%)

Contents in 100 g	Water (g)	Crude Protein (g)	Fat (g)	Carbohydrates (g) Sugar	Carbohydrates (g) Fiber	Ash (g)	Minerals (mg) Ca	Minerals (mg) Fe	Minerals (mg) P	Minerals (mg) K	Minerals (mg) J	Vitamins (mg) A (iu)	Vitamins (mg) B_1	Vitamins (mg) B_2	Vitamins (mg) C	Vitamins (mg) Niacin
Ulva pertusa	15.2	23.8	0.6	42.1	4.6	13.7	730	87	230			500	0.04	0.52	10	10.0
Ulva fasciata	18.7	14.9	0.04	50.7	0.2	15.6										
Enteromorpha sp.	3.7	20.7	0.3	61.5	7.2	6.6	600	106	220			960	0.06	0.30	10	8.0
E. compressa	13.6	12.4	1.7	53.0	10.6	10.4										
E. linza	13.6	19.4		46.2		19.2										
Monostroma sp.	10.0	14.4	0.2	59.8	4.8	10.8	890	10	550							
Nori-tsukudani	69.3	4.7	0.5	12.4	0.3	12.8	1,400	29	56			10	0.07	0.16	0	1.6
Prasiola japonica	14.8	35.8	1.5	39.1	4.8	4.0	880	99	600			80	0.44	0.32	0	1.5
Nemacystus decipiens	73.9	0.7	0.4	0.6	—	24.4	190	4	44			30	0.04	0.04	0	2.0
Scytosiphon lomentaria	—	23.6	3.3	21.9	20.7	27.0	—		—	4,670	20					
Analipus japonicus	13.1	19.4	4.4	40.3	5.5	17.3	890	10	550	—	—	60	—	—		3.3
Hizikia (a)	16.8	5.6	0.8	29.8	13.0	34.0	1,400	29	59	14,700	40	150	0.01	0.20	0	4.6
Hizikia (b)	16.4	8.5	—	41.9	17.1	16.2	—	—	—	—	—					
Hizikia fusiforme	—	10.1	0.8	30.6	16.7	39.3	—		—	14,860	40					
Sargassum ringgoldianum	—	6.3	1.3	44.7	16.7	19.1	—		—	4,440	10					
Pelvetia wrightii	—	10.5	2.6	38.5	17.1	19.8	—		—	4,670	20					
Laminaria japonica	14.3	7.3	1.1	51.9	3.0	22.0	800		150	5,800	170	430	0.08	0.32	11	1.8
L. ochotensis	13.1	6.9	1.7	46.9	4.7	21.7	750	10	170	5,020	440	320	0.06	0.08	1.5	2.0
L. longissima	15.8	6.9	1.3	38.0	10.8	27.2				7,900	280	250	0.08	0.40		1.8
L. angustata	18.0	6.7	1.6	49.1	5.4	19.2	850	10	180	3,700	340	360	0.02	0.20		2.0
L. religiosa	16.3	6.0	0.3	41.5	6.7	29.2	1,200	10	280	9,600	190	130	0.03	0.19		3.5
Tororo-kombu	28.5	5.2	0.7	40.3	9.5	15.8	740	5	150			10	0.04	0.14		2.3
Kobu-tsukudani	60.4	6.3	0.9	15.5	1.7	15.1	420	14	270			10	0.07	0.16	0	0.2
Kobu-maki	59.1	2.8	1.5	29.7	1.2	5.7	115	8	55				0.07	0.10	0	0.7
Eisenia	19.3	7.5	0.1	50.8	9.8	12.5	1,170		150	3,900	260	50	0.02	0.20	0	2.6
Laminaria saccharina		6.4	0.7	59.4	3.3	16.7										
L. agardhiana		13.1	1.9			27.2										
Arthrothamnus bifidus		6.8	0.8	45.6	7.5	20.7										
Eisenia bicyclis		12.1	1.3	44.7	7.1	16.8				3,860	260					

Eisenia arborea	16.0	9.9	2.1	44.1	10.8	24.4				6,160	390					
Wakame (a)	18.0	12.7	1.5	47.8	3.6	18.4	1,300	13	260	6,800	30	140	0.11	0.14	15	10.0
Wakame (b)		11.6	0.3	37.8		31.4										
Alaria esculenta		16.7	2.8	35.0	10.6	29.2			0.4	4,840	50					
Fucus evanescens		12.0	2.1	22.8	13.9	39.3			0.3	6,780	40					
F. vesiculosus		10.8	0.4			21.5			0.2							
Ascophyllum nodosum		11.0	2.5			19.8			0.2							
Seaweed meal (A)		5.6	0.4	35.3	3.5	10.7										
Seaweed meal (B)		13.1	4.4	61.4	10.6	38.5										
Asakusa-nori (a)	11.4	35.6	0.7	39.6	4.7	8.0	260	12	510			11,000	0.25	1.24	20	10.0
Porphyra tenera (b)	11.1	34.0	0.7	40.5	4.8	8.7	470	23	380			10,000	0.21	1.00	20	3.0
Porphyra tenera (c)	13.4	29.0	0.6	39.1	7.0	10.0	510	36	280			5,600	0.21	0.89	20	3.0
P. suborbiculata	19.3	23.4	0.6	45.9	2.5	8.3	220	16	180			25,000	0.07	1.36	0	0.5
Gelidium jelly	99.0	0.1	0	0.8	0	0.1	2	1	4	16						
Agar	20.1	2.3	0.1	74.6	0	2.9	400	5	8							
Seaweed gelatin (a)	22.8	11.7		62.1		3.4										
Seaweed gelatin (b)	22.3	6.9		60.3	6.7	3.8										
Gracilaria verrucosa	83.5	2.3	0.2	11.0	0.5	2.5	510	56	12			260	0	0.03	0	0.5
Gracilaria sp.	12.9	7.9	0.05	58.4	3.0	17.8										
G. confervoides		4.3		24.3	4.3	3.6										
Campylaephora hypnaeoides		13.7		32.2	12.3	3.0										
Ahnfeltia concinna	20.2	5.6	0.07	55.0	2.7	16.6										
Irish moss (Chondrus crispus)	18.8	9.4	—	55.4	2.2	14.2										

From food analysis tables.

Note: Main cell-wall polysaccharides are cellulose in Ulva and Enteromorpha, mannan in Codium, and xylan in Caulerpa.

Digestibility of Polysaccharides Extracted from Sea Vegetables
(Utilization: %)

	Sea vegetable	dogs	humans	
Pentosan	Ulva	—	34	Green algae
	Enteromorpha	35	9	,,
	Haliseris paralis	16	—	Brown algae
	Dulse (Palmaria palmata)	73	100	Red algae
Galactan	Irish moss (Chondrus crispus)	33	6	Red algae
	Gracilaria coronopifolia	33	30	,,
	Ahnfeltia concinna	—	60	,,
	Hypnea nidifica	56	10	,,

Source: Swartz, 1914.

Ascorbic Acid (Vitamin C) Contents of Sea Vegetables

	Sea vegetable	Ascorbic acid in 100 gr. (mg)
Green algae	Ulva lactuca	27—28
Brown algae	Laminaria digitata	3—15
	L. cloustonii	10—47
	L. saccharina	4—24
	Alaria esculenta	11—29—45
	Fucus serratus	11—48
	Fucus vesiculosus	13—77
	Himanthalia sp.	28—59
	Ascophyllum nodosum	11—30—62
Red algae	Porphyra umbilicalis	44—83
	Palmaria palmata	17—24—49
	Gigartina mamillosa	26—63

Source: Lunde & Lie, 1938.

Distribution Map of Some Important Seaweeds Used in Industry or as Food

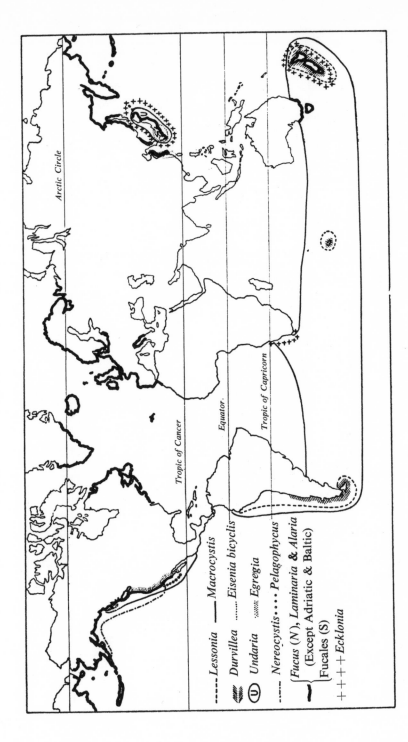

Lessonia —— *Macrocystis*

Durvillea ...... *Eisenia bicyclis*

Ⓤ *Undaria* ⦂⦂⦂⦂ *Egregia*

Nereocystis•••• *Pelagophycus*

⎰*Fucus (N)*, *Laminaria & Alaria* ⎰
⎱(Except Adriatic & Baltic)⎱
⎰*Fucales (S)*⎱

+ + + + *Ecklonia*

Map Showing Locations of the Main Seaweed-utilization Centers

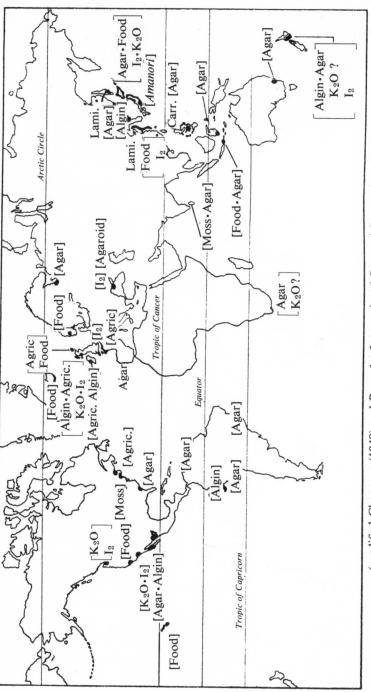

(modified Chapman (1949) and Proc. 1st International Seaweed Symposium (1952)

Part **2** | # Cooking with Sea Vegetables

The preceding chapter explained the biology and cultivation of sea vegetables and showed how, though eaten in many parts of the world by primitive peoples, these algae are now consumed in large quantities mainly in Japan. As a matter of fact, the Japanese Ministry of Health and Welfare reported, in 1971, that, whereas the average Japanese eats about 4.3 grams of dried algae daily, from the nutritional standpoint, half this amount would be sufficient. Nonetheless, modern food shortages in underdeveloped nations and the desire for nutritional, low-calorie foods in the industrialized nations suggest that sea vegetables can play a much greater role in the diets of many peoples. Mildly flavored, they can be included in meals regularly without palling on diners' palates. Since their fibers are softer than those of land plants, they have excellent intestinal regulatory effects.

It is not surprising that, since the Japanese are their most enthusiastic fans, almost all recipes for sea vegetables are designed to suit the traditional Japanese diet, which centers on rice and fish. Many old ways of preparing sea vegetables are refreshingly delicious. Such varieties as *Meristotheca papulosa (tosakanori)*, *Gracilaria verrucosa (ogonori)*, *Nemacystis decipiens (mozuku)*, and *Undaria pinnatifida (wakame)* lend themselves to use raw in salads, vinegared dishes, and garnishes for sashimi. *Laminaria japonica (kombu)*, *Undaria pinnatifida (wakame)*, *Analipus japonicus (matsumo)* and *Porphyra tenera (Asakusa-nori)* are suitable for soups. In addition, *Asakusa-nori* is considered essential to the preparation of sushi. *Laminaria japonica (Kombu)*, *Hizikia fusiforme (hijiki)*, and *Eisenia bicyclis (arame)* are good boiled and delicious sautéed, and the highly viscous agar obtained from *Gelidium* sp. *(tengusa)* is an excellent replacement for gelatin as a thickener in jellies.

It is hoped that the reader will try and learn to enjoy many of these traditional Japanese ways of eating sea vegetables. But perhaps more important still is the hope that peoples everywhere will come to know and understand these potentially valuable foods and learn to adjust their preparations to local customs and needs.

Kombu (*Laminaria*)

Broths and stocks are highly important to the traditional Japanese cuisine; and *Laminaria*, or *kombu*, and dried bonito shaved into fine flakes (*katsuo-bushi*) are the two sources from which these stocks are generally prepared. In 1908, Dr. Kikunae Ikeda discovered that monosodium glutamate is the source of the pleasing flavor of *kombu*. Forty years later, it was found that 5′-inosinic acid is the secret of dried bonito's taste. Today these substances, artificially produced, are popular chemical seasonings in most Japanese homes. Good restaurants and some gourmets, however, still make their own stocks from natural ingredients.

Kombu is featured in a wider variety of Japanese foods than any other sea vegetables. Long an essential treat in the imperial court, it was the only source of stock available in the diet of Buddhist priests who were forbidden to eat flesh, including fish, and could not, therefore, use dried bonito in soups. Stock was and remains the most important of all the uses to which *kombu* is put.

Kombu Stock (*Kombu Dashi-jiru*)

In general from 20 to 50 g (3/4 to 1-3/4 oz) of dried *kombu* are needed to prepare 1 liter of stock. The quantities and proportions may be varied according to the need of the moment.

Clean and wash *kombu* thoroughly, taking care to remove all sand and grit. Let it stand from 30 to 60 minutes in a saucepan containing from 10 to 20 percent more water than the desired amount of stock. Slowly heat the water. Just before the boiling point is reached, remove the *kombu*. *Kombu* must not be allowed to boil in stock preparation since the higher temperatures release unpleasant flavors and dissolve polysaccharides thus making the soup sticky.

Kombu-and-bonito Stock (*Kombu-katsuo Dashi-jiru*)

To 1 liter of water, 20 g (3/4 oz) of *kombu* and from 10 to 30 g (1/3–1 oz) of dried bonito flakes are needed. Clean the *kombu* thoroughly and, after allowing it to stand in water as in the preceding recipe, slowly bring the contents of the pot to a boil. Just before the boiling point is reached, remove the *kombu*. Add the bonito flakes and bring to a boil. Turn off the heat and strain through a cloth at once. This is called first stock and, because it is the best, it is used for soups and broths. But the *kombu* and bonito need not to be discarded yet. They can be reheated in freshwater to produce a less flavorsome second broth. The *kombu* can be further cooked with soy sauce and sugar to produce a strongly flavored preserved product called *kombu Tsukudani*, which is delicious with boiled rice.

In all the recipes given below, unless special mention is made of the need for something else, broth or stock means the basic *kombu* or *kombu*-and-bonito stocks explained here. Water seasoned with artificial flavoring (monosodium glutamate, or instant *katsuo-dashi*) may be substituted.

Powdered-*kombu* Stock

This is a simple easy-to-prepare drink that makes possible quick, economical use of *kombu*'s vitamins and minerals, the iodine it contains to combat goiter, and the laminine it contains for treatment of hypertension. For one serving, dissolve one teaspoon of powdered *kombu* in one cup of hot water.

Another popular drink made with this sea vegetables called *kombu* tea is prepared with hot water and salted powdered *kombu*. The name *kombu* is pronounced *kobu* as well; and, because of the similarity between this and the verb to be happy (*yorokobu*), this drink is served on felicitious occasions, notably weddings in Japan.

Aside from stock and drinks, *kombu* occurs in many other dishes, marinated, boiled, roasted, and fried as well as in such preserved foods as pickles and *Tsukudani*. Dating as far back as the eighth century, rolled *kombu* and *Tsukudani* are still great favorites prepared in distinctive ways in various localities. Most of the recipes for *kombu* dishes given below are about five centuries old and have preserved their popularity and preparation methods largely unaltered to the present.

Soups

Conger-eel Broth

> 2 oz (60 g) conger eel (or white-fleshed fish)
> 12 snow peas
> 12 stalks (1 oz or 24 g) trefoil
> 1/2 oz (12 g) *tororo* (white) *kombu*
> cornstarch
> 9 cups stock
> 3 tsp salt
> 1/2 tsp soy sauce

1. Clean the eel and, without boning, cut it into six pieces. Lightly salt and dust with cornstarch. Dip very briefly in boiling water then in freshwater. Remove and drain.
2. Lightly parboil snow peas.
3. Cut trefoil in 1-in (3-cm) lengths.
4. Cut *tororo kombu* into six strips, one for each soup bowl.
5. Arrange eel, snow peas, trefoil, and *kombu* in the bottoms of individual soup bowls.
6. Prepare hot stock. Season to taste with salt and soy sauce.
7. Pour servings of hot stock over the ingredients in the soup bowls and serve at once. Fine julienne strips of *yuzu* citron peel or young leaves of the prickly ash

(*kinome*) are an excellent garnish for this light soup.

Serves six.

Egg and Bean-paste Soup

> 1/8 oz or 2-1/2 g *tororo kombu*
> 1 egg
> 1 stalk (1/3 oz or 10 g) edible chrysanthemum leaves (*shungiku*)
> 1-1/2 cups stock
> 1 Tbsp bean paste

1. Heat stock and dissolve bean paste in it.
2. When the stock is at the boiling point, drop in the raw egg.
3. Shred chrysanthemum leaves. Add them to the hot soup and turn off heat.
4. The soup is done when the outer parts of the egg are white. The secret of success is to avoid overcooking.

Serves one.

Kombu and Sparerib Soup

> 14 oz (400 g) spareribs
> 1 strip *kombu* 12 in (30 cm) long or 2 oz (60 g) in weight
> 14 oz (400 g) *daikon* radish or turnip
> 9 cups water
> 2 Tbsp grated fresh ginger root
> 5 tsp salt
> 1/2 Tbsp soy sauce
> 1/2 cup sakè or dry sherry

1. Moisten *kombu*. Cut into 4-in (10-cm) strips and tie in attractive knots.
2. Chop spareribs into 2-1/2-in (6-cm) pieces. Dip in boiling water. Remove and drain.
3. Cut *daikon* radish into rounds 2 in (5 cm) thick then cut the rounds into quarter sections.
4. Heat stock in a saucepan. Add the other ingredients except ginger root and simmer till all are nearly tender. (This may be done in a pressure cooker.)
5. Season to taste with salt. Lower the heat and simmer for an additional thirty minutes. Add soy sance.
6. Arrange spareribs, radish, and *kombu* in the bottoms of individual soup bowls. Pour in soup from the pan and top with small servings of grated fresh ginger root.

Serves six.

Consommè Printanier Japonais

2 (2 oz or 60 g) turnips
1-1/2 oz (40 g) carrots
3/4 oz (20 g) fresh green peas
6 tsp *kombu* powder
9 cups water
4 consommé cubes
1/2 tsp salt
1/2 tsp pepper
1 tsp chopped parsley

1.   Cut turnips and carrots into thin rounds and trim into floral shapes. Shell peas. Parboil all these ingredients till barely tender.

2.   Combine water, consommé cubes, and 6 tsp *kombu* powder in a saucepan and bring to the boiling point. Season to taste with salt and pepper. Add vegetables.

3.   Put a little chopped parsley in the bottom of each of six soup plates. Add hot soup and vegetables. Serve at once. Do not boil the soup too long after adding the *kombu* powder.

Serves six.

Chicken Broth

13 oz (360 g) unboned chicken
1/2 (4 oz or 120 g) onion
1 oz (30 g) carrot
1/2 stalk (2 oz or 60 g) celery
1/5 cup uncooked rice
1/4 oz (20 g) butter
6 cups water
6 tsp *kombu* powder
3 tsp salt
1/2 tsp pepper

1.   Combine water and chicken in a saucepan and bring to a boil, removing scum that floats to the surface.

2.   Coarsely chop all vegetables and sauté them in butter.

3.   Wash rice thoroughly. Combine rice and vegetables with chicken and stock. Cook till tender.

4.   Remove chicken and bone it. Chop flesh and return it to the pot. Bring to the boil again.

5.   When the boiling point has just been reached, add *kombu* powder, salt, and pepper to taste. Serve hot.

Serves six.

Marinated Dishes and Sashimi

Tricolor Vinegared Vegetables

> 11 oz (300 g) *daikon* radish
> 2 oz (60 g) carrot
> 1 strip dried *kombu* 3 in (8 cm) long or 1 oz (30 g) in weight
> 3 tsp salt
> 3 Tbsp rice vinegar
> 3 Tbsp sugar

1. Peel the *daikon* radish and carrot. Cut into julienne strips 1-1/2 in (4 cm) long. Sprinkle with 1 tsp salt, mix well, and allow to stand for 10 minutes. When the carrot and *daikon* are limp, wash them in freshwater and squeeze out as much moisture as possible.
2. Cut *kombu* into slender julienne strips 3/4 in (2 cm) long.
3. Combine vinegar, sugar, and 2 tsp salt. Mix well, pour over vegetables and *kombu* and marinate till needed.

This refreshing dish, served often at Japanese New Year, will keep for days.

Serves six.

White Fish and *Tororo Kombu*

> 8-1/2 oz (240 g) sliced white-fleshed fish
> 2 oz (60 g) *tororo* (white) *kombu* flakes
> 6 sprigs *bōfu* (*Siler divaricatum*) or parsley or watercress
> 1 tsp salt
> 3 Tbsp rice vinegar
> 2 Tbsp soy sauce
> 2 Tbsp stock or water

1. Cut the fish into thin slanting slices. Lightly salt it and allow it to stand for twenty or thirty minutes.
2. Wipe away moisture that has formed on the fish.
3. Sprinkle the fish thoroughly with *tororo kombu* flakes.
4. Combine vinegar, soy sauce, and stock.
5. Arrange slices of fish in individual serving dishes. Decorate with *bōfu*, parsley, or watercress, and top with the vinegar sauce.

Serves six.

Marinated Horse Mackerel with Julienne *Kombu*

> **4 horse mackerel (*aji*)**
> **1-1/2 oz (40 g) shredded (*ito*) *kombu***
> **1 cup rice vinegar**
> **3 Tbsp sugar**
> **1 tsp salt**
> **oil for frying**

1. Medium horse mackerel are best for this dish. Scale and clean them. Lightly salt them and dry them in the sun for half a day.
2. Deep-fry the mackerel.
3. Combine vinegar, sugar and salt in a saucepan. Bring to the boil and remove from the heat.
4. Arrange the fried fish in the bottom of a deep container. Top with shredded *kombu*. Then pour on the vinegar sauce. Allow to stand for two or three days. This convenient, long-lasting dish can be made from other kinds of mackerel, sea bream, or other white-fleshed fish.

Serves four.

Kombu-firmed Fish

Wrapping cleaned, raw fish in *kombu* and allowing it to stand weighted for an hour in a cold place firms and imparts a delicate flavor to the flesh, making it an excellent accompaniment for sakè. Any fish suitable for use as *sashimi* can be prepared in this way. In addition, *kombu* is sometimes used to firm squid or even a gelatinous product called devil's tongue jelly (*konnyaku*).

1. Fillet the fish. Small fish (sillago, for example) can be used whole. Large fish should be cut into slanting slices.
2. With a damp cloth, wipe two full strips of *kombu*.
3. Spread one strip of *kombu* on a working surface and align the whole or sliced fish on it. Sprinkle with salt. Thinly sliced cucumbers may be added on top of the fish if desired.
4. Top with the remaining strip of *kombu* and allow to stand, weighted, for an hour. Refrigerated, this fish will keep well for two or three days and may be used in a variety of ways, some of which are explained below.

Sillago and Snake-belly Cucumbers

> **6 (13 oz or 360 g) sillago**
> **2 cucumbers**
> **2 strips *kombu* 8 in (20 cm) long**
> **red *shiso* (perilla) sprouts (optional)**
> **salt**
> **1/2 cup of a combination of rice vinegar and soy sauce in proportions of 6 to 4**

1. Fillet the sillago and remove heads and tails. Salt lightly, allow to stand a while, then rinse in freshwater.
2. Wipe *kombu* strips with a damp cloth.
3. Putting one strip of *kombu* on a working surface, align the sillago fillets on top. Cover this with the remaining strip of *kombu* and allow the fish to stand weighted for an hour.
4. While the fish are being firmed, salt the cucumbers. Roll them on a wooden chopping board to soften their skins. Dip them briefly in boiling water. Cut into segments and then make incisions crosswise, but not all the way through, in each segment to produce what is called the snake-belly cut.
5. Prepare a sauce by combining vinegar and soy sauce in proportions of 6 to 4.
6. Remove the *kombu* from the fish. Cut the fillets into diagonal slices.
7. Arrange a piece of cucumber and a few slices of sillago in each individual serving dish. Garnish with red perilla sprouts and top with the vinegar sauce.

Serves four.

Sea Bream and Sea Urchin

> 11 oz (320 g) sliced sea bream (*tai*) fillet
> 2 strips *kombu* 8 in (20 cm) long
> 2 Tbsp sea-urchin paste
> 6 sprigs *bōfu* (*Siler divaricatum*) or parsley or watercress

1. Prepare the fish as explained in the preceding recipe.
2. Arrange slices in individual serving dishes. Garnish with *bōfu* and dabs of sea-urchin paste.

Serves four.

Baked, Fried, Simmered, and Steamed Dishes

Kombu Grill (*Matsumae-yaki*)

This dish is a speciality of Hokkaidō, where the best Japanese *kombu* is grown. Using freshest, most recently caught seafoods, diners spread strips of *kombu* on a wire grill over an open fire. On top of the *kombu* they roast fish, shellfish, and vegetables, which they eat with a mixture of soy sauce and citrus juice called *pon-zu*. Thick *kombu* (*Laminaria japonica*) is best for this dish. The *kombu* imparts a delicate flavor to the roasted ingredients.

> 2-3/4 lb (1200 g) fish and shellfish including oysters, salmon, cod, scallops, and so on
> 18 fresh *shiitake* mushrooms
> 1 onion

> 36 stalks (3 oz or 80 g) trefoil
> 4 or 5 strips *kombu* 8 in (20 cm) long
> salt
> sakè

Dipping sauce (*pon-zu*):
> 1/3 cup bitter orange or lemon juice
> 1/4 cup soy sauce

Condiments:
> 6 Tbsp grated *daikon* radish
> 6 Tbsp chopped scallion
> red chili pepper (optional)

1. Clean the *kombu* strips and wipe them with a damp cloth. Spread them on a cookie sheet. On top of them arrange the seafood ingredients. Lightly salt them, sprinkle them with sakè, and allow them to stand for from twenty to thirty minutes. The seafood should be cut in bite-size pieces.

2. Cut vegetables in bite-size pieces.

3. Combine bitter-orange or lemon juice and soy sauce. Divide it into individual serving cups.

4. Arrange all ingredients except the *kombu* in serving dishes. Spread the strips of *kombu*, one for each diner, on wire grills over open fires. If this is impractical, an electric table grill will serve.

5. Each diner roasts his own seafood and vegetables on the hot *kombu* strips. To his individual bowl of *pon-zu* sauce, each may add grated *daikon*, chopped scallion, and red chili pepper to suit his taste. The roasted vegetables and seafood are dipped in this sauce before being eaten.

Serves six.

Kombu, Oysters, and Bean-curd Boats

The *kombu* is formed into something like a pot. Seafood and bean curd are then cooked in this *kombu* vessel, which greatly enhances their flavor.

> 1/2 cake bean curd (*tōfu*)
> 12 oysters
> 8 small shrimps
> 4 fresh *shiitake* mushrooms
> 24 stalks (2 oz or 60 g) trefoil
> 4 strips broth *kombu* 7 in (18 cm) long
> 8 Tbsp sakè

Dipping sauce:
> juice of one bitter orange or lemon
> 2 Tbsp rice vinegar
> 4 Tbsp soy sauce

Condiments:
> chopped scallion

grated *daikon* **radish**
1 red chili pepper

1. Shell the oysters. Lightly salt them. Mix gently, rinse in cold water, and drain.
2. Shell, devein, and wash shrimps.
3. Cut the bean curd into four equal blocks.
4. Clean *shiitake* mushrooms. Remove and discard stems. Cut caps in half.
5. Wash trefoil and cut into 1-1/2-in (4-cm) lengths.
6. Wipe strips of *kombu* with a damp cloth. Tie each end together on both sides to make a boat-shaped vessel. Prepare four of these.
7. Fill the boats with oysters, shrimps, mushrooms, and bean curd. Sprinkle them with sakè. They may be cooked in various ways. They may be placed in a low flat pan and cooked in a medium oven for ten minutes. They may be cooked in the same kind of pan for two minutes in an electronic range. Or they may be stood on an electric table grill and cooked until the ingredients reach the desired degree of doneness.
8. When the ingredients are done, the *kombu* boats are placed on serving dishes.
9. Dipping sauce is prepared by combining the juice of one bitter orange or lemon with vinegar and soy sauce and is served in individual bowls. Condiments include chopped scallion that has been soaked in cold water then lightly squeezed dry and *daikon* radish grated together with a seeded red chili pepper.
10. Diners add condiments to their sauce cups and dip the seafoods, vegetables, and bean curd in the mixture before eating.

Serves four.

Steamed Fish and Bean Curd

1/2 cake bean curd
1 slice (3-1/2 oz or 100 g) boned fish (flounder, cod, sea bream)
1 strip *kombu* **2 in (5 cm) long**
aonori **or crushed laver (***Asakusa-nori***)**
1 Tbsp soy sauce
1 Tbsp *yuzu* **citron or lemon juice**
julienne sliced citron or lemon peel

1. Spread *kombu* in the bottom of a deep, heatproof bowl. Arrange fish and bean curd on top, and steam in an oriental steamer, or on a rack in a deep pot partly filled with boiling water and tightly covered, for about fifteen minutes.
2. Arrange fish and bean curd in serving plates and top with citron peel and crushed *aonori*.
3. Combine citron or lemon juice and soy sauce. Pour over fish and bean curd. Serve hot.

Serves one.

Fried *Kombu*

Fried *kombu* is an excellent snack with sakè. It requires *kombu* that has been dried in the shade.

> **5 oz (150 g) *kombu***
> **5 oz (150 g) white *shiraita kombu***
> **3 sheets *Asakusa-nori***
> **18 gingko nuts**
> **oil for frying**
> **salt**

1.   Wipe the *kombu* with a dry cloth to remove sand or grit. Cut into strips 2-3/4 by 3/4 in (7×2 cm). Dampen slightly. Put one slice on top of another and make a slit 3/4 in (2 cm) long in the center. Bring the left end of the strip through the hole in the center (Fig. a). Or cut as shown in Fig. b or tie in a knot as in Fig. c. In addition, *kombu* can be folded into basketlike shapes that serve as edible containers.
2.   Cut each sheet of *Asakusa-nori* into eighths.
3.   Shell the gingko nuts. Boil in slightly salted water. Remove the thin inner membrane.
4.   Heat fresh cooking oil to from 160°C to 170°C (310°F–330°F) in a fairly shallow pan. Fry the *Asakusa-nori* quickly.
5.   Fry the *kombu*. Drain and salt it lightly.
6.   Fry the gingko nuts and skewer them, two or three together, on toothpicks or, for greater elegance, pine needles.
7.   Combine fried *kombu* and gingko nuts with *nori* strips on serving plates. Potato chips may be substituted for gingko nuts.

Serves six.

a

b

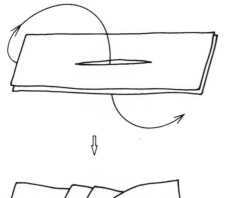

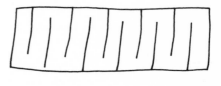

c

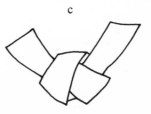

Kombu Rolls

Dried fish, most often herring, wrapped in *kombu* and simmered slowly for a long time is an ancient Japanese favorite that keeps well. *Laminaria angustata* cooks faster and tastes better than other varieties of *kombu* in this dish.

Herring rolls

> 6 strips (6 in or 15 cm long) *kombu*
> 3 dried herring
> 6 strips dried *kampyō* gourd (4 in or 10 cm long)
> 3 cups stocks or water
> 1/2 cup *mirin* or sweet sherry
> 1/2 cup soy sauce
> 3 Tbsp rice vinegar

1. Soak herring overnight in water in which rice has been washed. If no rice has been washed to provide this water, substitute an equal amount of water to which has been added 1 Tbsp of raw rice or flour. If even this method is unacceptable, the fish may be soaked in water overnight, heated in water to about 90°C (194°F), and then washed in freshwater to remove astringency or other undesirable tastes.

Remove and scrub thoroughly with a stiff brush. Cut each fish in half. If they are thick, they may be split down the center.

2. Using thin fronds that will cook quickly, soak *kombu* in water till soft. Wrap one piece of herring in each strip of *kombu* and tie with a strip of *kampyō* gourd. Secure the ends by folding them in.

3. Arrange the *kombu* rolls in a saucepan, add stock, *mirin*, soy sauce, and rice vinegar. Simmer over a low heat until the *kombu* is tender.

Serves six.

Pond-smelt rolls

The same *kombu* rolls may be made with smelt. If the fish are fresh, not dried, lightly salt and roast them. Then roll them in *kombu*. Otherwise the preparation is the same as for herring rolls.

Serves six.

Sweetfish Rolls

When *kombu* rolls are made with very fresh sweetfish and cooked for several hours the result is a lightly flavored delicacy that is especially popular in certain parts of Japan.

Soybeans and *Kombu*

Kombu, as has been explained, is the source of an excellent stock and may be used in many other foods. In addition, cooked with tough or hard ingredients, it has the property of softening their fibers and making them more palatable and easier to digest. *Kombu* simmered with soybeans and dried cod is another ancient Japanese favorite.

> **1-1/2 cups soybeans**
> **6 cups water**
> **1 strip *kombu* 20 in (50 cm) long**
> **1 cup sugar**
> **1/2 tsp salt**
> **3 Tbsp soy sauce**

1.   Allow the beans to stand overnight in 4 cups water. In this same water, bring the beans to a boil. Remove scum and add 2 more cups water. Simmer over a low heat.

2.   Cut the *kombu* in fine strips, which may or may not be tied in bows. Add them to the pot and pour in enough water to cover all ingredients. Simmer until beans and *kombu* are tender.

3.   Add 2/3 cup sugar and salt. Simmer for ten minutes. Add remaining sugar and 3 Tsp soy sauce. Simmer until almost all liquid has evaporated.
Serves six.

Kombu and Dried Cod

> **1 strip *kombu* 20 in (50 cm) long**
> **6 cod halves**
> **3 cups stock**
> **3 Tbsp soy sauce**
> **3 Tbsp sakè**

1.   Soak cod in water for a day or two. Cut in pieces 1 in or 3 cm long.

2.   Cut *kombu* in strips 1 in (3 cm) wide and 6 in (15 cm) long and tie each into a bow.

3.   Combine cod and *kombu* in a deep saucepan. Add stock and sakè. Slowly simmer until *kombu* is tender. Add soy sauce and continue simmering until all liquid has evaporated.

Serves six.

Kombu and Herring

> **7 oz (200 g) *kombu***
> **6 dried herring**
> **5 cups water**
> **1 cup sakè**
> **2 Tbsp rice vinegar**
> **1/2 cup sugar**
> **1/2 cup soy sauce**
> **3 Tbsp *sanshō* berries prepared in the *Tsukudani* fashion (optional)**

1. Prepare herring as for herring *kombu* rolls (see p. 144), except that each should be cut in three equal pieces. Cut *kombu* into strips 1 in (3 cm) long.

2. Starting with *kombu*, make alternating layers of herring and *kombu* in a saucepan. Add 5 cups water, 1 cup sakè, and 2 Tbsp rice vinegar. Bring to a boil over a high heat. Reduce the heat to low and simmer for one hour. If the liquid evaporates during this time, add water. When the *kombu* is tender, add 1/2 cup sugar, 1/2 cup soy sauce, and *sanshō* berries. Cook over a high heat till the liquid evaporates.

Serves six.

Pickles

Quick Cucumber and *Kombu* Pickles

> 3 or 4 cucumbers
> 1/2 in or 4 cm long (1/4 oz or 8 g) *kombu* for stock
> 1 red chili pepper
> 2 cups soy sauce
> salt

1. Wipe the *kombu* and, using scissors, cut into fine strips.

2. Salt cucumbers and roll them on a cutting board to soften the skins. Allow them to stand for a while. Wash in freshwater and chop coarse.

3. Deseed and chop the red chili pepper.

4. Combine *kombu*, cucumbers, and pepper in a bowl. Pour soy sauce over these ingredients. Marinate for about twelve hours, stirring from time to time.

Serves six.

Light Cucumber Pickles

> 10 (3-1/2 oz or 100 g) medium cucumbers
> 1 strip *kombu* 2 in (5 cm) long
> 3 Tbsp salt
> 3 red chili peppers

1. Salt cucumbers. Roll them on a chopping board to soften their skins. Dip them briefly into boiling water then plunge them into cold water at once. Drain.

2. Arrange in a deep jar with a lid. Sprinkle with salt. Julienne cut the *kombu* and chop the peppers (after deseeding). Sprinkle these two ingredients over the salted cucumbers. Weight with a stone and allow to stand for two or three days.

Serves six.

Quick Eggplant and Green-pepper Pickles

     5 green peppers
     2 small eggplants
     1 strip *kombu* 1/2 in (1 cm) long
     3 Tbsp soy sauce
     1-1/2 Tbsp *mirin* or sweet sherry
     salt

1.   Remove stalks and seeds from green peppers. Cut them in half and then into slender strips.

2.   Remove caps from eggplants. Cut each in half and soak in salted water for a while. Then cut into thin strips.

3.   Wipe the *kombu* with a damp cloth. Julienne cut it with scissors.

4.   Lightly salt and rub both the eggplant and green peppers till they are pliant. Squeeze them in a cloth to remove as much moisture as possible.

5.   Combine soy sauce and *mirin*. Marinate the green peppers and eggplants in this mixture for about thirty minutes. The pickles will then be ready to eat.

Serves four.

Kombu and Rice

Mackerel Sushi

     6 cups rice prepared for sushi (see p. 171)
     1/2 large mackerel
     2 strips ordinary *kombu* (8 in or 20 cm long)
     2 strips white *kombu*
     1 Tbsp prepared mustard (oriental style)
     1 aspidistra leaf
     2 Tbsp red pickled ginger (*beni-shōga*)
     1 oz (30 g) red pickled ginger (*beni-shōga*)

This kind of sushi is called *battera* (Portuguese for boat) because of its shape. The fish must be fresh. Horse mackerel may be used in place of mackerel.

1.   Leaving the skin intact, fillet the fish and salt it generously. In summer allow it to firm for from three to four hours; for from five to six hours in winter. Plenty of salt is essential to remove the strong odor of the fish.

2.   Wash the fish and pat it dry. Sandwich the fish between two strips of *kombu*. Place it in a container and pour over it a mixture of 1/2 cup vinegar, 1/5 cup soy sauce, 1 Tbsp sugar, and 1 tsp salt. This mixture, called *sanbai-zu*, is widely used in Japanese cooking. Though the quantities of the ingredients may be increased or decreased, these proportions should be preserved. Allow this to stand for from thirty to forty minutes.

3.   Remove the thin epidermal covering by pulling it from the head end toward the tail. Remove any small bones that remain and, holding a sharp knife on a slant, cut the strips into three thin slices. The first slice, which must be the cleanest, should appear on the top of the finished sushi. Cut skinless slices into two vertical strips.

4.   Boil white *kombu* in a mixture of vinegar, soy sauce, sugar, and salt (see step 2 above) for two minutes. Let it stand in this marinade until needed.

5.   Spread a damp cloth on a bamboo sushi-rolling mat. On top of this arrange half of the slices of mackerel, skin side down. They should form a rectangle 2-1/2 in or 6 cm wide.

6.   Make a streak of mustard down the center of the fish. Divide half the sushi rice into half again and form each portion into a small ball. Place two balls on top of the fish. Bring cloth and rolling mat over it. Press and adjust the shape to form a rectangular bar. Remove the mat. Wrap the *battera* bar in a sheet of white *kombu*. Repeat with the remaining ingredients.

7.   Cut each *battera* bar into 1-in (2-1/2 cm) pieces and serve decorated with fancy cut aspidistra leaves and red pickled ginger.

Serves four (two bars).

Sea Bream and *Sanshō* Sushi

> 7 oz (200 g) fresh sea bream
> 6 cups rice prepared for sushi (see p. 171)
> 24 fresh green *sanshō* leaves
> 1 strip *kombu* 8 in (20 cm) square
> 1-1/2 cups of a mixture of soy sauce, vinegar, sugar and salt
>   (see step 2 in the preceding recipe)
> 1 aspidistra leaf
> red pickled ginger (*beni-shōga*)

1.   Salt the fish and allow it to stand for an hour. Wash it. Pat it dry, wrap with *kombu*, and let it stand weighted with a stone or brick for another hour in a mixture of soy sauce, vinegar, sugar, and salt.

2.   Skin and cut the fish into the thinnest possible slanting slices.

3.   This kind of sushi requires a wooden sushi mold (3×6×1-1/2 in or 8-1/2× 15×3-1/2 cm). Wet the mold thoroughly. Cut the aspidistra leaf into two rectangles. Line the bottom of the wet mold with one piece of aspidistra.

4.   Spread a layer of sliced sea bream over the bottom of the mold. Top this with a few *sanshō* leaves, upper sides down. Put half of the sushi rice on top of this and top the whole thing with another sheet of aspidistra leaf.

5.   Holding the outer part of the mold in both hands, press the inner board with both thumbs. Turn and press again. Remove the outer form.

6.   Cut into bite-size pieces and garnish with red pickled ginger.

Serves four.

Note: If a stone is not used in marinating the fish, shorten the time to thirty minutes. When putting the fish into the mold, place the most attractively cut surfaces down since the part that is in the bottom of the mold will become the top of the finished sushi. A little extra rice in the corners will ensure better shape when the form is removed.

Oboro-kombu Sushi

> 2 slices (7 oz or 200 g) salt salmon
> 1/2 cup vinegar
> 2 cucumbers
> 1 Tbsp salt
> 1-3/4 oz (50 g) *oboro kombu*
> 2 cups rice prepared for sushi (see p. 171)
> white sesame seeds

1. Cut lightly salted salmon into 1/2-in (1-cm) cubes, sprinkle with vinegar, and allow to marinate for twenty minutes.
2. Cut each cucumber vertically in quarters. Lightly salt and allow to stand for ten minutes.
3. On a bamboo sushi rolling mat, spread *oboro kombu* evenly. On this spread an even layer of sushi rice. Down the center of this arrange a strip of salmon and cucumbers. Using the mat, roll this into a cylinder. Make another cylinder with the remaining ingredients. Cut each into four or five pieces.

Serves two.

Rice Balls with *Tororo Kombu*

> 1 cup rice
> 1 salt plum (*umeboshi*) or a few slices of vinegared ginger
> 1/8 oz (4 g) *tororo kombu*
> 1 tsp salt

1. Steam the rice in 1-1/5 cups of water.
2. Prepare a bowl of lightly salted water in which to dip your hands before squeezing the rice into generous balls. In the center of each ball put either a salt plum or few slices of vinegared ginger.
3. Press a piece of *tororo kombu* on each rice ball.

These balls remain delicious all day. In place of the salt plum or vinegared ginger slices, you can put salt *kombu* or salt salmon in the middle of each ball.

Serves two.

Wakame (*Undaria pinnatifida*) and *Matsumo* (*Analipus japonicus*)

Undaria (*wakame*) is a popular food gathered for centuries from practically all Japanese coasts. It is dried, salted, treated with ash, and processed in other ways for the sake of preservation. The midribs (*kuki-wakame*) of *Undaria* and the sporophylls (*mekabu*) near the rootlike base are prized as delicacies.

Since it can be quickly restored to tenderness and handsome green color by soaking in water, dried *Undaria* is widely used in a variety of soups, marinated dishes, and even Western-style salads. Like *kombu*, *Undaria* (*wakame*) has the property of softening the tough fibers of other foods—bamboo shoot for example—cooked with it.

Kuki-wakame is salted, vinegared, or served in other ways. *Undaria* has long been an important source of calcium in the Japanese diet.

Restorable to a lovely green color in hot water, *matsumo* (*Analypus japonicus*) is a product of the northeast of the main Japanese island, Honshū. It is sold dried and in sheets and used crumbled in soups, in marinated dishes, toasted, or sprinkled on rice. In marinated dishes it combines the flavor of the sea with deep green of pine needles. It is highly nutritious because of its protein, vitamin, and mineral (especially calcium) content. Since the laminine it contains prevents aging of the arteries, it is an effective preventative of hypertension and other ailments that plague modern man. No recipes for *matsumo* are given here since this sea vegetable is prepared almost exactly as is *wakame*.

Soups

Wakame and Shrimp Soup

> 4 oz (120 g) salt *wakame*
> 6 (8 oz or 240 g) shrimp
> 9 cups stock
> 3 tsp salt
> 1/2 tsp soy sauce
> 18 stalks (1-1/2 oz or 40 g) trefoil
> julienne-cut lemon peel

1. Soak the *wakame* in cold water. Wash it thoroughly and cut it into 1-in (3-cm) lengths.
2. Shell and devein the shrimp.
3. Bring the stock to a boil. Add the *wakame*. When the boiling point is reached again, add the shrimp. Season first with salt then with soy sauce.

4. Cut the trefoil into 2-in (5-cm) lengths. Put some in the bottom of individual soup bowls. Pour in the soup, dividing shrimp and *wakame* equally. Add a small piece of lemon peel to each bowl.

Serves six.

Wakame and Bamboo-shoot Soup

> 8 oz (240 g) *wakame* soaked in water
> 5 oz (150 g) bamboo shoot
> 9 cups stock
> 2 tsp salt
> 1 tsp soy sauce
> 6 *sanshō* leaves (optional)

1. Cut the bamboo shoot in thin slices and wash carefully, removing all of the white substance inside the compartments of the stalk.
2. Cut the *wakame* into 1-in (3-cm) lengths.
3. Bring the stock to a boil. Add the *wakame* and bamboo shoot. Simmer for two or three minutes. Season first with salt then with soy sauce. Serve in individual bowls garnished with *sanshō* leaves.

Serves six.

Bean-paste Soup with *Wakame* and Bean Curd

> 8 oz (240 g) *wakame* soaked in water
> 1/2 cake bean curd
> 9 cups stock
> 3 Tbsp bean paste (combination of 2 Tbsp of red bean paste with 1 Tbsp of white
>   bean paste)
> 1/2 cup chopped scallion

1. Cut the bean curd into 1/2-in (1-cm) cubes. Cut the *wakame* into 1/2-in (1-cm) lengths.
2. Bring stock to a boil. Add the bean paste and stir till it is completely dissolved.
3. Add bean curd and *wakame*. When the mixture comes to a boil again sprinkle in chopped scallion and remove from the heat.

Serves six.

Korean-style *Wakame* and Beef Soup

> 7 oz (200 g) *wakame* soaked in water
> 3-1/2 oz (100 g) beef
> 1 scallion

1 tsp white sesame seeds (optional)
9 cups water
2 tsp salt
1-1/2 tsp soy sauce
1 Tbsp sakè
black pepper

1. After cleaning the *wakame* and discarding the hard stalks, cut it into 1-in (2-1/2-cm) lengths.
2. Cut the beef in thin strips.
3. Chop the scallion.
4. Toast then chop the sesame seeds.
5. Combine beef and 9 cups water in a saucepan. Bring to a boil. Remove scum that surfaces. Simmer over a moderate heat for about ten minutes then add the *wakame*. Season with salt and soy sauce. Then add 1 Tbsp sakè and black pepper to taste. Immediately before removing from the heat, add chopped scallion. Serve with a sprinkling of toasted, chopped sesame seeds.

Serves six.

Bouillabaisse with *Wakame*

This is a slightly different version of the nourishing, easy-to-make Marseilles speciality with an addition of fresh *wakame*.

1-3/4 lb (800 g) fresh white-flesh fish (cod, sea bream, flounder, sillago, or flathead)
4 prawns
12 fresh oysters
3/4 oz (80 g) *wakame*
1 tomato
1 potato
1-1/2 onions
5 cups water
6 bay leaves
1/4 oz (20 g) parsley
3 peppercorns
8 dried saffron stigmas
4 slices bread
1/3 Tbsp salt
salad oil
pepper

1. Clean and scale the fish. Reserve head and bones. Leaving the skin on, cut fish into convenient pieces. Shell, devein, and wash the prawns. Cut them into two or three pieces each. Wash the oysters in lightly salted water and drain in a colander.
2. Wash *wakame* and cut it into 1-1/2-in (4-cm) pieces. Peel and slice (1/2 in or 4 mm thick) both tomato and potato.

3.   Prepare stock in the following way. In a deep pot combine 5 cups water, 1/3 Tbsp salt, 1/3 onion, 3 peppercorns, 3 parsley leaves, and 3 bay leaves. Bring to a boil over a high heat. Add fish head and bones. Simmer for twenty minutes, removing scum that surfaces. Strain through cloth. If speed is important, substitute 4 cups of light stock for this fish broth.

4.   Chop onion. Heat salad oil in a deep pan. Sauté onion until golden brown. Add tomato, potato, and a bouquet garni made by tying together bay leaves, saffron, and parsley. Continue sautéeing briefly then add fish stock and bring to a boil over a high heat. Just before the potatoes are done, remove and discard the bouquet garni. Then add fish, prawns, oysters, and *wakame*. When the fish is done, season to taste with salt and pepper.

5.   Make croutons by removing the crust from bread, cutting it into small dice, and deep-frying it in salad oil. Drain on paper towels.

6.   Put a serving of croutons in the bottom of each individual soup plate and pour the bouillabaisse over it. Serve at once.

Serves four.

Salads

Marinated *Wakame* and Cucumbers

> 3 medium (11 oz or 300 g) cucumbers
> 1-1/2 oz (40 g) dried *wakame*
> 1/2 cup vinegar
> 1/5 cup soy sauce
> 1 Tbsp sugar
> 1 tsp salt

1.   Slice cucumbers thin (if Japanese cucumbers are being used, peeling is unnecessary). Salt them, rub the slices lightly between the fingers, allow to drain.

2.   Soften the *wakame* in water. Dip briefly in boiling water. Cool and cut into 1/2-in (1-cm) pieces. Allow to drain.

3.   Combine vinegar, soy sauce, sugar, and salt to make a marinade.

4.   Combine *wakame* and cucumbers and top with the vinegar sauce.

Serves six.

Wakame and Cucumber in Sesame-mayonnaise

> 3 medium cucumbers
> 1-1/2 oz (40 g) dried *wakame*
> 1 tsp white sesame seeds
> 6 Tbsp mayonnaise
> vinegar

1. Prepare the cucumbers and *wakame* as in the preceding recipe.
2. Toast the sesame seeds and grind them in a mortar or blender. Combine with mayonnaise and vinegar to taste.
3. Combine cucumbers, *wakame*, and sesame-mayonnaise sauce.

Serves six.

Wakame Salad

2 oz (60 g) dried *wakame*
3 medium cucumbers
6 radishes
1 stalk celery
3 leaves cabbage
lettuce
9 Tbsp French dressing

1. Soften the *wakame* in water. Dip it briefly into boiling water. Cool and cut into 1/2-in (1-cm) pieces. Drain.
2. Slice cucumbers into thin rounds. Lightly salt. Wash in freshwater and drain.
3. Slice radishes into thin rounds. Soak in cold water then drain.
4. Cut the celery and cabbage in coarse julienne strips. Lightly salt, wash in cold water, and drain.
5. Spread lettuce leaves in the bottom of individual salad bowls. Heap the *wakame* and vegetables on it and top with French dressing.

Serves six.

Variety Dishes

Bean Curd with Chicken and *Wakame*

8 oz (240 g) boned chicken thigh
2 cakes lightly toasted bean curd (*yakidōfu*)
1-1/2 oz (40 g) dried *wakame*
4 oz (120 g) carrot
2 cups stock
5 Tbsp soy sauce
5 Tbsp *mirin*
5 Tbsp sugar
***wasabi* horseradish**
flour

1. Cut each cake of bean curd into three equal pieces.
2. Soften the *wakame* in water and cut into bite-size pieces.

3. Slice chicken meat in diagonal pieces and flour lightly.
4. Cut carrot into coarse julienne strips.
5. Bring stock to a boil and season with soy sauce, *mirin*, and sugar. Add bean curd, *wakame*, and carrot. Reduce heat to medium. Add chicken slices from the side of the pot and simmer till ingredients are done.
6. Arrange servings in individual bowls. Add a small amount of the broth. Top with a dab of grated *wasabi* horseradish.

Serves six.

Wakame and Young Horsebeans or Broad Beans

> 3 cups hulled fresh green young horsebeans (*sora-mame*)
> 2 oz (60 g) dried *wakame*
> 3 cups stock or water
> 1 tsp salt
> 3 Tbsp sugar
> 2 Tbsp soy sauce

1. Soak hulled beans in water.
2. Soften *wakame* in water and cut into 3/4-in (2-cm) pieces.
3. Combine beans and *wakame* with 3 cups stock or water in a deep pan. Add 1 tsp salt. Simmer over a low heat till the beans are tender. Add sugar and soy sauce to taste.

Serves six.

Wakame and Bamboo Shoots

> 2 oz (60 g) dried *wakame*
> 1-1/3 lb (600 g) bamboo shoots
> 3 cups stock
> 1 Tbsp sugar
> 2 Tbsp and 1 tsp soy sauce
> 1 Tbsp *mirin*
> 6 young *sanshō* pepper leaves (optional)

1. Soften *wakame* in water and cut into 3/4-in (2-cm) pieces.
2. Purchase preboiled bamboo shoots. Wash them thoroughly removing all the white sediment in the individual compartments and slice thin. If you are using fresh bamboo shoots, they must be boiled in the husks until tender in water to which a small amount of rice bran has been added. They are then removed from the water husked, and sliced.
3. Combine stock, *wakame*, and bamboo shoots in a saucepan over a medium heat. Add sugar, soy sauce, and *mirin* and simmer till most of the liquid has evaporated. Add one more teaspoon of soy sauce.

4.   Arrange in individual serving dishes and garnish each with a fresh young *sanshō* pepper leaf.

Serves six.

Variation
Follow the recipe as outlined above; but, when the bamboo shoots are tender, add a small amount of bean paste in place of the final 1 tsp soy sauce for a more full-bodied flavor.

Sautéed Liver with Stalk *Wakame* (*Kuki-wakame*)

> 8 oz (240 g) salted *kuki-wakame*
> 11 oz (300 g) chicken livers
> 10 small garlic cloves
> 2-in (5-cm) length of scallion
> sakè
> 2 Tbsp soy sauce
> 1 Tbsp sugar
> 1 tsp sesame oil
> oil for frying

1.   Wash *kuki-wakame* in water. Allow to stand to soften and desalt. Drain and cut in 3-in (8-cm) lengths.
2.   Thoroughly clean chicken livers, removing any discolored areas. Cut each into four equal pieces and blanch well in cold water. Then drain.
3.   Heat oil for frying to 140°C or 380°F. Slice garlic buds thin and deep fry.
4.   In the same oil, but at a higher heat, quickly deep fry well-drained chicken livers.
5.   Chop the scallion.
6.   In a saucepan combine *kuki-wakame* and enough water to cover. Simmer for a few minutes or until the *kuki-wakame* is tender. Add livers, garlic, sakè, soy sauce, and sugar. Simmer till almost all the liquid has evaporated. Add sesame oil, sprinkle on chopped scallion, and serve.

Serves six.

Rice with *Wakame* and Green Peas

> 6 cups uncooked rice
> 2 oz (60 g) sheet *wakame*
> 1 cup green peas
> 6-2/3 cups water
> 1-1/2 tsp salt
> 1 Tbsp sakè

1.   After washing the rice until the wash water runs perfectly clear, combine it with water, 1 tsp salt, and sakè in a heavy lidded pot or rice cooker and steam in the ordinary fashion.

2.   Boil green peas in salted water till tender.

3.   When the rice is done, spread the green peas on top of it evenly, cover again, remove from heat, and allow to steam for fifteen minutes.

4.   Toast the sheet *wakame* over an open fire, in an oven, or in a toaster for a few minutes. Crush it coarsely in the hands.

5.   Add the *wakame* to the rice. Mix and serve in individual bowls.

Serves six.

Hijiki (*Hizikia fusiforme*)

Hizikia fusiforme or *hijiki* is especially rich in such important and usually insufficiently provided diet elements as iodine, iron, and calcium. Popular with the Japanese from ancient times, *hijiki* was eaten regularly on certain days once or twice a month by many families in commercial business until recently. This was not because such people understood the science of *hijiki's* nutritional values, but probably because, through instinct and experience, they found out that this alga is beneficial to health. It is still widely eaten today and is valuable because nutritious yet low-calorie.

It is important to remember that soaking dried *hijiki* in water immensely increases their bulk (five or more times). Since it harmonizes well with oil, *hijiki* is good sautéed. The Japanese are fond of *hijiki* that, after having been sautéed, is simmered in a liquid flavored with soy sauce and sugar. Incidentally, this dish can be prepared in large quantites for use over a long period since it keeps very well.

Hijiki in Bean-curd Sauce

> **1/2 oz (15 g) dried *hijiki***
> **1/4 cake bean curd**
> **1-1/2 oz (40 g) carrot**
> **1 fried bean-curd bag (*abura-agè*)**
> **1-1/2 Tbsp white sesame seeds (or walnuts or peanuts)**
> **1/2 cup stock**
> **1-1/2 Tbsp sugar**
> **1 tsp salt**
> **2 tsp soy sauce**

1. Soften the *hijiki* in water and cut it in 1-in (3-cm) lengths. Simmer till tender.
2. Cut the carrot into coarse julienne strips 1 in (3 cm) long. Julienne cut the *abura-agè* bag.
3. Combine 1/2 cup stock, *hijiki*, carrot, *abura-agè* bag, 2 tsp sugar, and 1 tsp soy sauce in a saucepan and simmer till all ingredients are well flavored.
4. Dip bean curd in hot water. Lift out and squeeze in a towel to remove as much moisture as possible.
5. Toast the sesame seeds and crush in a mortar or in a blender, adding stock or water if necessary. Combine this with the bean curd and blend thoroughly. Flavor this with the remaining sugar, salt, and soy sauce. Add the *hijiki*, carrot, and *abura-agè* and mix well to coat. Serve it in individual dishes well coated with the bean-curd sauce.

Serves four.

Hijiki Sautéed with Ground Chicken

       1/2 oz (15 g) dried *hijiki*
       7 oz (200 g) ground chicken meat
       1-3/4 oz (50 g) ginger root
       3 Tbsp oil
       2 Tbsp sakè
       2 Tbsp soy sauce
       2 Tbsp sugar

1.   Soften the *hijiki* in water. Sauté it in 2 Tbsp oil over a high heat. Remove and set aside. In the same pan, add 1 Tbsp oil and sauté the chicken meat. Add 2 Tbsp sakè, 2 Tbsp soy sauce, 1 cup water, and the *hijiki*. Simmer for ten minutes.

2.   Peel and julienne cut the ginger. Soak it in water.

3.   Add ginger and sugar to the *hijiki* mixture and simmer till almost all the liquid has evaporated.

Serves four.

Sautéed *Hijiki* and Chicken Livers

       1/2 oz (15 g) dried *hijiki*
       7 oz (200 g) chicken livers
       2 Tbsp fine julienne cut ginger root
       2 Tbsp sakè
       2 Tbsp soy sauce
       2 Tbsp sugar
       3 Tbsp sesame oil

1.   Thoroughly clean the chicken livers and wash them in water. Place them in a heatproof dish and roast them in the oven just long enough for them to be barely done. Reserve any juices remaining in the baking dish.

2.   In a saucepan combine the pan juice from the liver with sakè, soy sauce, and sugar. Bring to a boil. Add the livers and the julienne cut ginger. Simmer over a low heat.

3.   Soften the *hijiki* in water. Trim till all are approximately the same length. Heat sesame oil in a pan and sauté the *hijiki*. Combine with the liver mixture and simmer till all liquid has evaporated.

Serves four.

Hijiki and Soybeans

       1/3 oz (10 g) dried *hijiki*
       1/2 cup dried soybeans
       2 Tbsp oil

> **2 Tbsp sugar**
> **3 Tbsp soy sauce**

1. Allow the soybeans to soften in water overnight.
2. Soften the *hijiki* in water and cut them all into 1-in (3-cm) lengths.
3. Heat oil in a saucepan. First lightly sauté the soybeans, then add the *hijiki* and sauté further over a medium heat. Add enough water to cover the ingredients and simmer till the beans are tender. Season with sugar and soy sauce and simmer till all the liquid has evaporated.

Serves four.

Hijiki and *Abura-agè*

> **1/3 oz (10 g) dried *hijiki***
> **2 fried bean-curd bags (*abura-agè*)**
> **2 Tbsp oil**
> **2 Tbsp sakè**
> **2 Tbsp sugar**
> **4 Tbsp soy sauce**

1. Soften the *hijiki* in water. Boil for two or three minutes.
2. Julienne cut the *abura-agè* bags.
3. Heat oil over a high heat in a saucepan. Sauté the *hijiki* well. Add the *abura-agè* then the sakè. Next add enough water (or stock) to cover the ingredients and simmer for ten minutes. Season with sugar and soy sauce, and simmer until all liquid has evaporated.

Serves four.

Hijiki-and-shrimp Fritters

> **1/2 cup *hijiki* softened in water**
> **1/4 cup small raw shrimps**
> **1/2 cup stock**
> **1/2 tsp soy sauce**
> **1 tsp *mirin***
> **2 eggs**
> **1 cup flour**
> **1/4 tsp salt**
> **oil for frying**

1. Boil the softened *hijiki* in 1/2 cup stock, soy sauce and *mirin* to flavor it.
2. Shell and devein the shrimps.
3. Lightly beat 2 eggs with 2 Tbsp water. Add 1 cup flour and 1/4 tsp salt and mix briefly to make a batter.

4. Add *hijiki* and shrimps to the batter.
5. Heat oil for frying to 160°C or 320°F. Drop the batter mixture into the hot oil by tablespoonfuls. Fry till golden and heated through. Drain on paper towels.

Serves four.

Vegetarian Sushi with *Hijiki*

> **4 cups rice prepared for sushi (see p. 171)**
> *Kōya* **bean curd topping:**
> > **2 cakes *Kōya* bean curd**
> > **1/2 cup stock**
> > **1-1/2 Tbsp sugar**
> > **1/2 tsp salt**
> > **1/2 tsp soy sauce**
>
> *Hijiki* **topping:**
> > **1/3 oz (10 g) *hijiki***
> > **1/2 cup stock**
> > **1 Tbsp *mirin***
> > **1-1/4 Tbsp sugar**
> > **1/4 tsp salt**
> > **1 tsp soy sauce**
>
> **Carrot and bamboo shoot topping:**
> > **4 oz (120 g) carrot**
> > **5 oz (150 g) bamboo shoot**
> > **1/2 cup stock**
> > **2 Tbsp *mirin***
> > **2-1/2 Tbsp sugar**
> > **1/2 tsp salt**
>
> *Shiitake* **mushroom topping:**
> > **1/3 oz (10 g) dried *shiitake* mushrooms**
> > **1/2 cup stock**
> > **1/2 Tbsp sugar**
> > **1 tsp soy sauce**
> > **1 Tbsp *mirin***
>
> *Fuki* **topping:**
> > **5 oz (150 g) *fuki* (butterbur)**
> > **salt**
>
> **Egg topping:**
> > **2 eggs**
> > **1/2 tsp sugar**
> > **1/5 tsp salt**
>
> **Garnish:**
> > **red pickled ginger**

1. Soften *Kōya* bean curd in hot water. Boil briefly and drain. In a saucepan combine stock, sugar, and salt. Add *Kōya* bean curd and simmer over a low heat. When the liquid has almost all evaporated, add soy sauce and remove from heat.

Allow to stand for a while and then cut in fairly large rectangular slices.

2. Soften the *hijiki* in water. Combine *hijiki*, stock, *mirin*, sugar, salt and soy sauce in a saucepan and simmer over a medium heat till the liquid has evaporated.

3. Cut carrots and bamboo shoots in rectangular slices and parboil. Combine with stock, *mirin*, sugar, and salt in a saucepan and simmer till the liquid has evaporated.

4. Soften the dried *shiitake* mushrooms in water. Slice them. Combine them with 1/2 cup water in which they were soaked, sugar, soy sauce, and *mirin*. Simmer until the liquid has evaporated.

5. Boil the butterbur in lightly salted water. Peel and slice thin on a slanting line. Lightly salt.

6. Mix eggs, sugar, and salt. In a lightly oiled pan, fry half of the egg mixture in a thin omelet. Remove to a chopping board. Fry the other half. Put one omelet on the other and cut in rectangular pieces.

7. Mound sushi rice in individual bowls and sprinkle some of each of these toppings on all servings. Garnish with red pickled ginger.

Serves four.

Hijiki Rice

> 1/2 cup *hijiki* and *abura-agè* prepared according to the recipe on p. 160
> 4 cups cooked rice
> 1/5 tsp salt
> 1 tsp sugar
> 2 eggs
> pickled ginger

1. Chop the *hijiki* and *abura-agè* fine. Mix with the hot rice.

2. Beat the eggs with a small amount of stock or water, salt, and sugar. Heat a frying pan and lightly oil it. Pour the egg mixture in a thin layer over the bottom. Fry till the egg is set. Lift the thin omelet from the pan and cut it into julienne strips. Repeat till all the egg is used.

3. Heap the mixed rice in serving bowls and top with portions of the egg strips and slices of pickled ginger root.

Serves four.

Arame (Eisenia bicyclis)

Since its fibers are tough, *arame* must be softened in water and then boiled before it can be used in food. Though generally preferred cooked with other foods, it may be eaten with a marinade of vinegar, soy sauce, and sugar. It is sometimes used in bean-paste soup and is an especially good addition to the diet since it is rich in iron and calcium.

Arame and Abura-agè

> 1-1/2 oz (15 g) dried *arame*
> 2 fried bean-curd bags (*abura-agè*)
> 3 Tbsp oil
> 1 cup stock or water
> 3 Tbsp soy sauce
> 3 Tbsp sugar
> 3 Tbsp sakè

1. After softening it in water, boil the *arame* for from five to ten minutes or until tender. Cut into 1/2-in (1-cm) pieces.
2. Julienne cut the *abura-agè*.
3. Heat oil in a frying pan over a high heat. Sauté the *arame*. Add the *abura-agè*. Pour in enough stock or water to cover the ingredients and add the soy sauce, sugar, and sakè. Simmer for twenty minutes or until the liquid has evaporated over a medium heat.

Serves four.

Chicken and Vegetable Stew with Arame

> 5-1/2 oz (160 g) chicken meat
> 2 oz (60 g) lotus root
> 2 oz (60 g) burdock root
> 2 oz (60 g) carrot
> 2 oz (60 g) *konnyaku*
> 1/3 oz (10 g) dried *arame*
> 3 Tbsp oil
> 2 cups stock
> 3 Tbsp sugar
> 3 Tbsp soy sauce
> 1-1/2 Tbsp sakè
> 1-1/2 oz (40 g) green peas

1. Cut the chicken meat in bite-size pieces.
2. Peal and chop the lotus root coarse. Scrape and chop the burdock root coarse. Let both stand in water for a while to reduce their astringency. Scrape and chop the carrot coarse.

3. Dip the *konnyaku* in boiling water then either pull it into pieces or dice it.

4. Soften the *arame* in water then boil it for from five to ten minutes, or until tender.

5. Heat oil in a deep pan. First sauté the chicken meat then add the vegetables and sauté them. Add stock and seasonings. Simmer over a low heat till all liquid has evaporated. Just before removing from the heat, add the green peas.

Serves four.

Arame and Pork

> **1/3 oz (10 g) dried *arame***
> **5-1/2 oz (160 g) fat pork**
> **3/4 oz (20 g) ginger**
> **1 Tbsp oil**
> **2 Tbsp sakè**
> **3 Tbsp soy sauce**
> **1 Tbsp sugar**
> **1 cup stock**

1. Prepare the *arame* as in the preceding recipe.
2. Cut the pork into 1-in (3-cm) strips.
3. Peel and julienne cut the ginger.
4. Heat 1 Tbsp oil in a saucepan. Sauté the pork until lightly brown. Remove to a separate dish. Add more oil to the pan and sauté the *arame* thoroughly. Add ginger, seasonings, and stock. Simmer for a while, then add the pork and continue simmering over a medium heat till the liquid has evaporated.

Serves four.

Rice with *Arame*

> **1/3 oz (10 g) dried *arame***
> **1 Tbsp oil**
> **2 cups rice**
> **3-1/2 cups water**
> **1 tsp salt**
> **2 Tbsp sakè**

1. Prepare the *arame* as in the preceding recipes. Sauté in 1 Tbsp oil.
2. Wash rice until wash water runs perfectly clear. Combine with 3-1/2 cups water, *arame*, salt, and sakè. Bring to a boil, lidded, over a high heat. Reduce heat to medium and simmer for fifteen minutes. Allow to stand off the heat and covered for ten minutes.

Serves four.

Asakusa-nori (*Porphyra tenera*)

The fragrance of it when toasted, its crispness, and light flavor make *Asakusa-nori* (*Porphyra tenera*), which is a special product of Japan, a favorite with the Japanese. Difficult now to obtain raw, *Asakusa-nori* is most widely purchased in the form of dried sheets. It is toasted and cut or crumbled for addition to other dishes. Sometimes other kinds of foods are rolled in it. One of its most important uses is as an outer covering for various kinds of rolled sushi. As rich as eggs and meat in proteins, *Asakusa-nori* is richer in practically all vitamins, especially in vitamin A (carotin). Since it is generally stored in airtight containers to preserve its crispness, *Asakusa-nori* maintains its high content of vitamin C for a long time. Its fibers are tenderer than those in other algae; and it is rich in calcium, iron, and iodine. In short, *Asakusa-nori* is practically an ideal food. It is used in soup in winter in some parts of north Europe.

Soups

Broth with Egg Custard

> 1 egg
> salt
> stock or water
> 2-3/4 oz (80 g) *udo* (*Aralia cordata*) (optional)
> 12 stalks (1-1/2 oz or 40 g) trefoil
> 1 sheet *Asakusa-nori*
> Broth:
> > 6 cups stock
> > 2-1/2 tsp salt
> > 1/2 Tbsp soy sauce

1. Lightly beat egg and combine it with a small amount of salt, and twice its volume in stock. Mix well. Pour into a square container and steam till set. Cool and cut in six equal parts.
2. Scrape *udo* and cut it into thin rectangular pieces. Parboil trefoil very briefly and tie into attractive knots.
3. Arrange *udo*, trefoil, and a piece of egg custard in each of six serving bowls.
4. Bring stock to a boil and season with salt and soy sauce. Ladle stock into each of the soup bowls.
5. Beforehand lightly toast the sheet of *Asakusa-nori*. Crush it. Just before serving the soup sprinkle some of the crushed *nori* in each bowl.

The egg custard may be chopped into medium dice, and parsley may be substituted for the trefoil. Consommé may be substituted for the stock.

Serves six.

Consommé à la Colbert

1 quail egg or very small hen egg
1/10 sheet *Asakusa-nori*
1/4 oz (5 g) carrot
1/4 oz (5 g) onion
2 cups stock or water in which one consommé cube is added
salt
pepper

1.   Poach the egg in hot water to which small amounts of salt and vinegar have been added.
2.   Lightly toast the *Asakusa-nori* and either cut it into fine strips with scissors or crush it fine.
3.   Chop carrot and onion into fine dice. Simmer them in stock till tender.
4.   Add poached egg. Season to taste. Pour in a serving bowl, sprinkle on crushed *nori*, and serve at once.

Serves one.

Marinated Dishes

Fresh *Nori* in Lemon Sauce

1 cup fresh raw *nori*
3/4 oz (2 g) ginger root
1 lemon
1 Tbsp soy sauce
2 Tbsp water
1 tsp *mirin* or sugar

1.   Wash the *nori* well in lightly salted water. Drain. Plunge into boiling water. Drain at once.
2.   Julienne cut the ginger root and allow it to stand in water till needed.
3.   Cut four thin slices of lemon and reserve them. Squeeze the juice from the remaining lemon and season it with soy sauce, water, and *mirin* (or sugar) to make the lemon sauce.
4.   Arrange fresh *nori* in four individual serving dishes. Add lemon sauce, and top with ginger and one lemon slice per serving.

Serves four.

Avocado with Grated *Daikon* Radish

1 avocado
11 oz (300 g) *daikon* radish
1 medium cucumber
1 sheet *Asakusa-nori*
1 Tbsp lemon juice
1 tsp salt
1 Tbsp sugar

1. Peel, pit, and dice the avocado.
2. Peel and grate *daikon* radish. Grate unpealed cucumber. Combine the two and lightly press out some of the liquid. Season with lemon juice and salt and sugar to taste.
3. Toast the *Asakusa-nori* on one side over an open flame. Crush it.
4. Arrange diced avocado and grated *daikon* radish and cucumber in individual serving dishes. Top with crushed *Asakusa-nori*.

Serves four.

Avocado and *Nori* Rolls

1/2 avocado
1/4 sheet *Asakusa-nori*
1 tsp grated *wasabi* horseradish
1/2 tsp soy sauce

1. Peel, pit, and slice the avocado lengthwise.
2. Lightly toast the *Asakusa-nori* on one side over an open flame. Cut it into strips 1/2 by 2 in (1 × 5 cm).
3. Wrap each slice of avocado in a strip of *Asakusa-nori*. Serve it with a dab of grated *wasabi* horseradish and soy sauce.

Serves one.

Sashimi

Squid Hakata Roll

1 squid
1 cucumber
1 sheet *Asakusa-nori*
6 green *shiso* leaves
12 *shiso* buds

1/2 tsp salt
5 Tbsp vinegar

1.   Remove the entrails and legs from the squid. Cut and open the flesh. Wash it well in vinegared water. Make vertical incisions in it.

2.   Cut the cucumber in six lengthwise strips. Allow it to stand in salt and vinegar for thirty minutes.

3.   Spread the squid, incised side down, on a clean cloth. Spread *Asakusa-nori* on this. Then add a layer of *shiso* leaves. Line the cucumber strips in the center and roll the squid around it. Cut into six slices. Garnish with *shiso* buds.

Serves six.

Bonito

14 oz (400 g) bonito
1 medium (4 oz or 100 g) cucumber
3 oz (80 g) fresh *ogonori*
1 sheet *Asakusa-nori*
4 green *shiso* leaves
12 *shiso* buds
1/2 tube grated *wasabi* horseradish
1/2 cup soy sauce (dark variety)

1.   Clean and fillet the bonito, leaving the skin intact but removing scales. Trim away the thin flesh in the walls of the abdominal cavity. Cut each fillet in half vertically.

2.   With a wooden mallet, pound each piece till it is fan shaped. Over a high heat, scorch the skin side of the fish. Wrap in a clean, dry towel and refrigerate till needed.

3.   Cut the cucumber into julienne strips 4 in (10 cm) long and allow to stand in ice water.

4.   Wash the *ogonori* in lightly salted water.

5.   Lightly toast the *Asakusa-nori* over an open flame. Crush it.

6.   Trim the pieces of bonito into equal shapes. Cut the trimmings into bite-size chunks and mix with crushed *Asakusa-nori*.

7.   In an individual serving dish, make a mound of sliced cucumbers on the far side. Top with a green *shiso* leaf. On this arrange flat pieces of bonito and a small heap of bonito and *Asakusa-nori*. Serve a small separate dish with dark soy sauce and a dab of *wasabi* horseradish. A more flavorful accompaniment for this dish is *Tosa* sauce made in the following way. Combine 1/2 cup soy sauce, 1 Tbsp *mirin*, and 1/4 oz (5 g) flaked dried bonito in a saucepan. Bring to a boil, strain, and chill. Garnish with *shiso* buds.

Serves six.

Roasted and Fried Dishes

Roast Shrimp with *Nori* and Grated *Daikon* Radish

> 3 shrimp
> soy sauce
> 3-1/2 oz (100 g) *daikon* radish
> 1/2 Tbsp lemon sauce
> 1/4 sheet *Asakusa-nori*

1. Devein the shrimp by cutting through the shells along the back. Leave the shell intact.
2. Broil briefly. Coat with soy sauce. Broil again. Repeat twice taking care not to burn the soy sauce.
3. Peel and grate the *daikon* radish fine. Prepare lemon sauce by combining the ingredients in these proportions: 5 parts lemon juice, 1 part soy sauce, and 3 parts sugar.
4. Lightly toast *Asakusa-nori* and crush it fine.
5. Place the shrimp in a serving dish. Heap the grated *daikon* beside it and top the *daikon* with crushed *nori*.

Serves one.

Kinpura Fried Chicken with *Asakusa-nori* and Eggplants

> 8 boned chicken breasts
> 6 small oriental eggplants
> 1 sheet *Asakusa-nori*
> 1 egg
> 2 egg yolks
> 5 Tbsp flour
> 3 Tbsp water
> 1 Tbsp.sakè
> 1/4 tsp salt
> oil for frying

1. Remove tendons from chicken breasts. Lightly flour them.
2. Cut away the calyxes of the eggplants. Cut each in half lengthwise and allow them to stand in salted water.
3. Cut the *Asakusa-nori* into eighths with scissors.
4. Beat lightly egg and egg yolks. Add water and sakè. Mix then, add flour and mix only briefly to make a somewhat stiff batter.
5. Heat oil for deep frying to 170°C (340°F).
6. Dip the chicken breasts and eggplants in batter and deep fry them. Coat one side only of each piece of *nori* in batter and quickly deep fry them.

7. Serve with salt.

Serves four.

Asakusa-nori and Rice

Oyster Rice

2 cups rice
1 cup shucked oysters
2-2/3 cups stock
1/4 cup soy sauce
1/3 tsp salt
1 cup stock
1/4 cup sakè
1/4 cup light soy sauce
1/2 sheet *Asakusa-nori*
grated *wasabi* **horseradish**
1 Tbsp chopped scallion
1 Tbsp grated *daikon* **radish**

1. One hour before cooking time, wash the rice thoroughly and allow it to drain in a colander.
2. Salt the oysters. Rub them lightly and wash in freshwater. Allow to drain in a colander.
3. Combine rice, 2-2/3 cups stock, oysters, soy sauce, and salt in a heavy lidded pot. Bring to a boil over a high heat. Allow to steam for fifteen minutes over a medium heat. Remove from heat, and allow to stand covered for ten minutes.
4. Combine 1 cup stock, sakè, and light soy sauce in a saucepan. Bring to a boil and remove from heat.
5. Heap oyster rice in individual serving bowls. Top with some of the sauce, toasted and crushed *Asakusa-nori*, grated *wasabi* horseradish, chopped scallion, and grated *daikon* radish.

Serves four.

Salmon Rice Broth

2 oz (60 g) lightly salted salmon
1/6 sheet of *Asakusa-nori*
1 tsp *wasabi* **horseradish**
1/2 tsp toasted white sesame seeds
1 stalk trefoil
1 cup cooked rice
1-1/2 cups freshly prepared green tea

1. Cut the salmon into diagonal slices and quickly toast on both sides.
2. Lightly toast *Asakusa-nori* and cut into julienne strips with scissors.
3. Grate *wasabi* horseradish if fresh. Prepare as directed if canned.
4. Chop sesame seeds.
5. Chop trefoil.
6. Put a small serving of cooked rice in a deep bowl. Sprinkle sesame seeds on it. Add salmon, trefoil, and *nori*. Pour on freshly prepared green tea and add a dab of *wasabi* horseradish.

Serves one.

Sushi

Asakusa-nori goes especially well with the mixture of vinegared rice, fish, and vegetables called sushi. Sometimes it is crushed and sprinkled on top of what is called *chirashi-zushi*. Sometimes it is the outside wrapping of sushi rolls.

Rice for Sushi

> **2 cups rice**
> **1 strip *kombu* 1-1/2 in (4 cm) long or 1/4 oz (8 g) in weight**
> **2-1/4 cups water**
> **1/4 cup vinegar**
> **1 tsp salt**
> **1-1/2 Tbsp sugar**

1. An hour before cooking time, wash the rice well and allow it to drain in a colander.
2. In a deep pan combine water and *kombu*. Bring to a boil, removing the *kombu* just before the boiling point is reached. This stock will be used, hot or cold, to cook the rice.
3. Combine rice and stock in a lidded pot. Bring to a boil over a high heat. Reduce the heat to medium and steam for fifteen minutes. Allow to stand off the heat and lidded for ten minutes.
4. Combine vinegar, salt, and sugar. Put the rice in a large, low-sided container—special wooden tubs are used in Japan—and sprinkle the vinegar mixture on. Mixing constantly with a flat wooden spatula, turn an electric fan on the rice or wave an ordinary fan over it until no more steam rises. It is now ready to be used in any of a variety of sushi dishes.

Serves four.

Thick Sushi Rolls

        8 cups rice prepared for sushi
        4 sheets *nori*
Kōya-style dried bean curd filling:
        1 cake *Kōya*-**style dried bean curd**
        1/2 cup stock
        1-1/2 Tbsp sugar
        1 tsp soy sauce
        pinch of salt
Thick omelet filling:
        2 eggs
        1 Tbsp stock
        3 tsp sugar
        pinch of salt
Mushroom filling:
        10 dried *shiitake* **mushrooms**
        1/3 oz (10 g) dried *kampyō* **gourd**
        1/2 cup water in which mushrooms were softened
        1 Tbsp sugar
        1 Tbsp soy sauce
        20 8-in (20-cm) long stalks trefoil

1.   Soften *Kōya*-style dried bean curd in hot water. Boil for a few minutes and drain in a colander. In a saucepan combine 1/2 cup stock, 1-1/2 Tbsp sugar, and a pinch of salt. Over a medium heat simmer till most of the moisture has evaporated. Add a little soy sauce for color and remove from the heat. Allow the bean curd to stand in the liquid. Later cut it in 1/2-in (1-cm) cubes.

2.   Lightly beat eggs and 1 Tbsp stock, 3 tsp sugar, and a pinch of salt. Over a low heat, warm a Japanese-style omelet pan or an ordinary frying pan. Add enough oil to cover the bottom. Pour in all the egg mixture and fry a thick omelet. Cut in long strips.

3.   Soften *shiitake* mushrooms and *kampyō* gourd in water. Simmer them in 1/2 cup of their soaking water, 1 Tbsp sugar, and 1 Tbsp soy sauce till almost all the liquid has evaporated.

4.   Dip the trefoil briefly in boiling water. Drain and chill.

5.   Toast *nori* over an open flame. This process can be accelerated by holding two sheets together and toasting both sides.

6.   Spread a sheet of toasted *nori* on a bamboo sushi-rolling mat. Top this with a layer of rice (1/4 the total amount) leaving 1/2 in (1-1/2 cm) free at the near side and 3/4 in (2 cm) free at the far side. Make strips of *Kōya*-style bean curd in the center. Add strips of all the other fillings. Lift the near side of the rolling mat and roll the fillings toward the far side. When the roll is complete, before removing the mat, press lightly to adjust the shape.

7.   Cut the roll into eight equal segments. Continue making rolls with the remain-

ing ingredients.

Serves four.

Nori-wrapped Sushi

Cucumber rolls

> 1/2 cup rice prepared for sushi
> 1/2 sheet toasted *nori*
> 1/8 to 1/6 cucumber
> grated *wasabi* horseradish

1. Salt cucumber and roll on a board to soften the peel. Wash it and cut into slender lengthwise strips.
2. With 1/2 sheet lightly toasted *nori*, make rolled sushi with cucumber as the center filling. Cut into four equal pieces.

Serves one.

Pickle rolls

> 1/2 cup rice prepared for sushi
> 1/2 sheet toasted *nori*
> 1 oz (25 g) *takuan* pickled *daikon* radish or 1 slice of canned marinated beet

1. Julienne cut the pickles.
2. Make sushi roll with toasted *nori* and with the pickles as the center filling. Cut into four equal pieces.

Serves one.

Kampyō gourd rolls

> 1/2 cup rice prepared for sushi
> 1/2 sheet toasted *nori*
> 1/8 oz (3 g) boiled and seasoned *kampyō* gourd strips

These are made in exactly the same way as all the others except that *kampyō* is the filling.

Serves one.

Tekka rolls

> 1/2 cup rice prepared for sushi
> 1/2 sheet toasted *nori*
> 1 oz (30 g) fresh tuna fillet
> 1/2 tsp grated *wasabi* horseradish

Cut the tuna in slender strips and use them for the center filling in rolls made according to the preceding method. Dab *wasabi* horseradish on the rice before adding the fish. Cut into four equal pieces.

Serves one.

Sea-urchin-roe rolls

> **1/2 cup rice prepared for sushi**
> **1/2 sheet toasted *nori***
> **1 oz (30 g) sea-urchin roe**
> **green *shiso* leaves (optional)**

Sea-urchin roe is sold in paste form. Use this paste, spread on a bed of *shiso* leaves, as the filling of rolls made according to the method explained above.

Serves one.

Thin-omelet rolls

> **1/2 cup rice prepared for sushi**
> **1/4 sheet toasted *nori***
> **3/4 oz (20 g) carrot**
> **3/4 oz (20 g) *shiitake* mushrooms**
> **3/4 oz (20 g) *kampyō* gourd**
> **serving of thin omelet (see p. 162)**

1. Prepare the carrot, *shiitake* mushrooms, and *kampyō* as for thick sushi rolls (see p. 172).
2. On top of the bamboo rolling mat, spread thin omelet. Top this with the *nori*.
3. Spread rice on top of this and arrange the other ingredients in the center as for other rolled sushi. Roll and cut in the usual manner.

Serves one.

Variations on Rolled Sushi

Wiener rolls

> **4 Wiener sausages**
> **1/2 cup rice prepared for sushi**
> **1/2 sheet toasted *nori***

Sushi rolls with a *nori* outer coating may be made from boiled and cooled Wiener sausages.

Avocado rolls

> **1/2 avocado**
> **2 green *shiso* leaves**

Peel and pit the avocado and cut it into strips with a 1/2-in (1-cm) square section. Lightly salt and wrap in *shiso* leaves. Make sushi rolls with these strips as centers.

Cheese rolls

> **3/4 oz (20 g) cheese**

These are made in the same way as the preceding rolls except the cheese is substituted for the avocado.

Cod-roe rolls

> **10 oz (30 g) lightly salted cod roe**

Remove the thin membrane from the roe. Flake the roe. With the palm of the left hand and the index and middle fingers of the right, squeeze a ball of sushi rice until it is an oblong about 1 in (3 cm) tall. Around the periphery of this, wrap a strip of *nori* so that it projects above the top level of the rice to hold the cod roe in place. Spread a dab of grated *wasabi* horseradish on top of the rice, add some *shiso* buds, and cod roe. Eat at once. Red caviar may be substituted for the cod roe.

Oboro rolls

Thin sushi rolls may be made with *oboro kombu* instead of *Asakusa-nori*. They may be filled with strips of cucumber or the flesh only of salted plums (*umeboshi*).

Buckwheat-noodle Sushi (*Soba-zushi*)

> **4 packages buckwheat noodles (*soba*)**
> **4 sheets *Asakusa-nori***
> **4 dried *shiitake* mushrooms**
> **1/2 carrot**
> **1 Tbsp *mirin***
> **1 Tbsp soy sauce**
> **2 tsp sugar**
> **2 eggs**
> **salt**
> **1/2 tsp sugar**
> **20 16-in (40-cm) long stalks trefoil**
> **1 Tbsp grated *wasabi* horseradish**
> **4 horse mackerel**
> **1-1/2 oz (40 g) edible chrysanthemum leaves**
> **oil for frying**
> **grated *daikon* radish**
> **Batter:**
> > **1-3/4 oz (50 g) flour**
> > **1/2 egg**
> > **1/4 cup ice water**

Dipping sauce:
1 cup stock
1 strip *kombu* **3/4 in (2 cm) long**
dried bonito flakes
4 Tbsp soy sauce
2 tsp sugar
1 Tbsp *mirin*

1. Briefly boil the buckwheat noodles and drain them in a colander.
2. Soften *shiitake* mushrooms in water. Discard the stems. Cut caps in rectangular pieces. Peel carrot and cut in pieces the same size and shape as the *shiitake* mushrooms. Simmer the two together in 1/2 cup of the mushroom-softening water, 1 Tbsp *mirin*, 1 Tbsp soy sauce, 2 tsp sugar till almost all the liquid has evaporated.
3. Lightly beat the eggs with a pinch of salt and 1/2 tsp sugar. Heat oil in a frying pan and make two thin omelets by frying half the egg mixture at a time. Cut the omelets in thin strips.
4. Dip the trefoil briefly in boiling water.
5. Toast a sheet of *nori*. Spread it on a bamboo sushi-rolling mat. Spread the noodles evenly on the *nori*, leaving 1/2 in (1 cm) free on the near side and 1 in (3 cm) free on the far side. In the center make rows of carrot and mushroom, omelet, and trefoil. Roll as for rice sushi (see p. 172). Cut the roll in five or six equal segments.
6. This dish is accompanied by pieces of tempura and a dipping sauce. Fillet the mackerel. Wash the chrysanthemum leaves and cut them in convenient lengths. Prepare a batter by combining flour, 1/2 egg, and water. Mix as little as possible. Heat oil to deep-frying temperature. Dip fish fillets and leaves in batter and fry them till just done. Drain on absorbent paper.
7. The tempura dipping sauce is made by making a stock from water, *kombu*, and dried bonito flakes (see p. 134); straining this; combining it with soy sauce, sugar, and *mirin*; and simmering for five to six minutes. It is served in individual bowls with small mounds of grated *daikon* radish and grated *wasabi* horseradish.

Serves four.

Nori Sandwiches

16 slices sandwich-slice bread
3 oz (80 g) butter
prepared mustard
4 slices processed cheese
4 Tbsp paste of sea-urchin roe
4 sheets *Asakusa-nori*

1. Soften the butter with the mustard and blend well.
2. Spread mustard-butter mixture on one side of each slice of bread.
3. Toast *Asakusa-nori* and, with scissors, cut each sheet in quarters.

4.   Put a slice of cheese, some sea-urchin roe, and a piece of *Asakusa-nori* on the buttered bread, in that order. Top with remaining slices of bread. Press lightly and cut in quarters. (This recipe may be made with half the number of slices of bread, and the sandwiches may be rolled.)

Serves four.

Tosakanori (*Meristotheca papulosa*)

Such red algae as *ogonori (Gracilaria verrucosa)*, *tosakanori (Meristotheca papulosa)*, *funori (Gloiopeltis furcata)*, *tsunomata (Chondrus ocellatus)*, *kirinsai (Eucheuma catrilagineum)*, *komenori (Carpopeltis flabellata)*, and the brown alga *mozuku (Nemacystus decipiens)* are sold in Japan either fresh or salted. The latter variety is soaked in water till desalinated and softened. None of these algae are boiled. Instead they are used as accompaniments for sashimi, in cold dishes served with vinegar or other sauces, and recently in salads with such dressings as mayonnaise. *Ogonori* is the most popular for use with sashimi. *Tosakanori*, though employed in the same way as *ogonori*, more often appears in somewhat expensive foods. It is marketed in white, red, and green varieties. Only the red is natural. The green has been treated with wood ash and then boiled, and the white has been bleached to make it more attractive with fish.

Hors d'oeuvres

Crab Cocktail with *Tosakanori*

> 3-1/2 oz (100 g) green *tosakanori*
> 2 oz (60 g) canned crab meat; shrimp may be substituted
> 1/2 (3/4 oz or 80 g) tomato
> 1/6 (1-1/2 oz or 40 g) onion
> 4 Tbsp cocktail sauce (2 Tbsp ketchup, 1 Tbsp lemon juice, 2 Tbsp
>   Worcestershire sauce, and 1/2 Tbsp prepared mustard)

1. Wash the *tosakanori* in lightly salted water then in freshwater. Drain and refrigerate till well chilled.
2. Pick over the crab to remove all bone or shell.
3. Peel and dice the tomato. Chop the onion fine. Mix these two ingredients with crab meat.
4. Blend cocktail-sauce ingredients.
5. Spread pieces of chilled *tosakanori* in the bottoms of individual cocktail glasses. Add the crab mixture and top with cocktail sauce.

Serves four.

Tosakanori and Pickled Herring

> 1 pickled herring
> 1-1/2 oz (40 g) *tosakanori*
> 1 Tbsp tartar sauce (mayonnaise; chopped hard-boiled egg yolks; and chopped

onion, sweet pickles, and parsley)
1 slice lemon

1. If the herring is large cut it in half sidewise.
2. Wash the *tosakanori* (a mixture of red and green is attractive for this dish) in lightly salted water, wash in freshwater, and chill in the refrigerator.
3. Arrange *tosakanori* in the bottom of an individual serving dish. Add the herring and top with tartar sauce and lemon slice.

Serves one.

Steamed Abalone and *Tosakanori*

1 abalone
2/3 tsp salt
2 Tbsp sakè
2 oz (60 g) green *tosakanori*
4 buds *myōga* (*Zingiber Mioga*; optional)
1/2 cucumber
1 Tbsp stock
2 Tbsp vinegar
3 Tbsp soy sauce
1 tsp grated *wasabi* horseradish

1. Wash the abalone. Salt it and sprinkle it with sakè. In a steamer over a high heat, steam it for from seven to eight minutes. Cool. Remove internal organs, reserving only the muscular foot. Slice this thin.
2. Wash the *tosakanori*. Let it stand in salted water. Then wash it in freshwater.
3. Julienne cut the *myōga* and let it stand in cold water.
4. Make cucumber fans by cutting half a cucumber into 1-1/2-in (4-cm) lengths and then making vertical incisions at close intervals in each length. The incisions must not go all the way to the bottom of the piece of cucumber.
5. Combine stock, vinegar, soy sauce, and grated *wasabi* horseradish.
6. Arrange abalone, *tosakanori*, cucumber fans, and julienne *myōga* in serving dishes and top with the soy-sauce and vinegar mixture.

Serves four.

Squid and Green *Tosakanori*

1/2 squid (*yari-ika*)
2-3/4 oz (80 g) green *tosakanori*
4 quail eggs
1 Tbsp grated *wasabi* horseradish (ground fresh or prepared paste)
4 Tbsp soy sauce

1. Clean and skin the squid. After washing thoroughly, cut into strips the thickness of maccaroni (about 1/2 in or 1 cm). Chill in the refrigerator.
2. Wash the green *tosakanori* well in lightly salted water. Drain.
3. Spread the *tosakanori* in the bottoms of individual serving dishes. Heap the squid on top, making a small well in the top of each heap. Into the well drop one raw quail egg. Season to taste with soy sauce and grated *wasabi* horseradish.

Serves four.

Salads

Tosakanori and Tuna Salad

> **2 oz (60 g) oil packed, canned tuna**
> **3/4 oz (20 g) onion**
> **1 Tbsp mayonnaise**
> **salt**
> **pepper**
> **1-1/2 oz (40 g) green *tosakanori***
> **lemon wedge**

1. Chop onion fine.
2. Flake tuna with a fork and mix with onion and mayonnaise. Season to taste with salt and pepper.
3. Wash *tosakanori* in lightly salted water, then in freshwater. Drain.
4. Spread *tosakanori* in a serving dish. Heap the tuna mixture on top and garnish with a lemon wedge.

Serves one.

Mimosa Salad

> **3-1/2 oz (100 g) green *tosakanori***
> **3-1/2 oz (100 g) red *tosakanori***
> **2 eggs**
> **1 onion**
> **1/2 cup mayonnaise**
> **1 Tbsp sweet pickles chopped fine**
> **12 black olives**

1. Wash *tosakanori* in lightly salted water, then in freshwater. Drain and chill.
2. Hard-boil eggs and chop coarse.
3. Slice onion fine and allow to stand in cold water. Drain.
4. Combine mayonnaise and pickles to make dressing.
5. Arrange red and green *tosakanori* in a salad bowl. Add onion and sprinkle

with chopped egg and black olives. Pour the dressing over the salad.

Serves four.

Avocado and *Tosakanori* Salad

> **7 oz (200 g)** *tosakanori*
> **1 avocado**
> **salt**
> **pepper**
> **8 radishes**
> **4 Tbsp salad dressing**

1. Wash *tosakanori* thoroughly in salted water. Drain. The appearance of the salad is improved if both red and green *tosakanori* are used.
2. Peel and pit the avocado. Slice it 3/4 in (2 cm) thick. Season with salt and pepper.
3. Wash and slice the radishes. Let them stand in cold water.
4. Spread *tosakanori* in a salad bowl. Add radishes and avocado. Chill in the refrigerator. Serve with salad dressing.

Serves four.

Mozuku in Vinegar Sauce

> **4 oz (120 g) fresh** *mozuku*
> **1 cucumber**
> **4 Tbsp vinegar**
> **3 Tbsp soy sauce**
> **1 tsp prepared mustard**
> **4** *shiso* **leaves**

1. Wash *mozuku* well in freshwater. Drain.
2. Julienne cut cucumber. After it has stood a while in cold water, drain.
3. Combine vinegar, soy sauce, and mustard.
4. Place the *shiso* leaves in the bottoms of individual serving dishes. On top of them, arrange *mozuku* and cucumber. Top them with vinegar sauce.

Serves four.

Kanten (Agar)

The jellied product known as *tokoroten*, prepared from a red alga called *tengusa* (*Gelidium amansii*) has been popular with the Japanese—especially when eaten with a combination of vinegar and soy sauce—for centuries. From this *tokoroten* is made *kanten*, a distinctive Japanese product that has industrial as well as culinary applications. *Kanten*, which is eaten alone with soy sauce and vinegar, is used to make jellied dishes with various other ingredients and to perform the role of gelatin in sweets. Foods stiffened with *kanten* are firmer and do not melt readily, as those stiffened with gelatin do. Furthermore, dieters and other people who must watch caloric intake welcome *kanten* since it has no calories at all. As might be expected, *kanten* dishes are popular in summer since they look refreshingly cool. But in winter too, *kanten* can be used to make desserts and aspics. It is easy to use and produces a firm jelly at from 0.8 to 1.5 percent of total volume.

Crab Aspic with *Kanten*

> 1 piece *kanten*
> 2 cups stock
> 1/2 tsp salt
> 1 Tbsp *mirin*
> 1 tsp soy sauce
> 1/2 can canned crab meat
> 3/4 oz (20 g) softened *wakame*
> vinegar
> 1-2/4 oz (50 g) green *tosakanori*
> 1/2 Tbsp grated *wasabi* horseradish
>
> Dipping sauce:
> 1/2 cup stock
> 1/2 Tbsp soy sauce
> 1/2 Tbsp *mirin*

1. Soften *kanten* in water. Wash it thoroughly and dissolve it in 2 cups boiling stock. Season with salt, *mirin*, and soy sauce. Filter through cloth.
2. Pick over the crab meat to remove all bone and shell.
3. Cut the *wakame* into 3/4-in (2-cm) lengths. Dip in boiling water. Drain and sprinkle with vinegar.
4. When the *kanten* liquid is about 50° C (122° F), add the *wakame* and crab. Wet a rectangular mold. Pour the *kanten* mixture in and chill till firm in the refrigerator.
5. Combine stock, soy sauce, and *mirin* to make a sauce. (Mayonnaise may be substituted.)
6. Remove *kanten* aspic from mold and cut in quarters.

7. Place *tosakanori* in individual serving dishes. Add aspic and top with the sauce, and grated *wasabi* horseradish.

Serves four.

Sea-eel Aspic

> **2/3 stick *kanten***
> **5-1/2 oz (160 g) sea eel or white-flesh fish**
> **3/4 oz (20 g) carrot**
> **1/3 oz (10 g) green beans**
> **3 *kikurage***
> **2 cups stock**
> **1/3 tsp salt**
> **1 tsp sakè**
> ***tororo kombu***
> **2 Tbsp soy sauce**
> **grated *wasabi* horseradish**

1. Soften *kanten* in water. Squeeze well. Tear it into small bits and let it stand in stock.
2. Keeping it skin-side down, slice the sea eel thin.
3. Parboil carrots and green beans. Julienne cut both.
4. Soften the *kikurage* in water and julienne cut it.
5. Bring stock and *kanten* to a boil over a medium heat. When the *kanten* has dissolved, add sea eel and simmer for two or three minutes. Remove scum that floats to the surface. Season with salt, sakè, and monosodium glutamate. Remove from heat and add carrots, green beans, *kikurage*, and *tororo kombu*. Wet a rectangular mold. Pour in the aspic mixture and chill till set. Cut in quarters and serve with soy sauce and grated *wasabi* horseradish.

Serves four.

Takigawa Bean Curd

> **1 stick *kanten***
> **1 cake bean curd**
> **1/2 tsp salt**
> **1/2 tsp sugar**
> **2 cups water**
> **3/4 cup stock**
> **1/4 cup soy sauce**
> **1/4 cup *mirin***
> **1 Tbsp grated *wasabi* horseradish**

1. Soften *kanten* in water. Wash well. Allow to stand for thirty minutes in 2 cups water.

2. Dip the bean curd in boiling water. Remove and squeeze between two boards, the top one of which is weighted with a brick. Blend in a blender or kitchen mortar with salt and sugar.

3. Bring the water and *kanten* to a boil. When the *kanten* has dissolved and the mixture has cooled, add bean curd, a little at a time, blending constantly.

4. Wet a rectangular mold. Pour in the bean-curd mixture and chill till firm.

5. Combine stock, soy sauce, and *mirin* to make a sauce.

6. Traditionally this dish is pushed through a special sievelike box that cuts it into uniform square-sectioned strips which come out all together in a bundle suggesting a waterfall in a river (*takigawa*). If this device is unavailable, the bean-curd *kanten* may be cut into attractive, uniform dice. In either case it is served with the sauce (step 5) and a dab of grated *wasabi* horseradish.

Serves four.

Tokoroten

> **1 oz (25 g) dried** *tengusa*
> **9 cups water**
> **1 Tbsp vinegar**
> **1/3 cup vinegar**
> **1/4 Tbsp soy sauce**
> **1 tsp** *aonori*
> **1 tsp prepared mustard**

1. Combine *tengusa* and water and bring to a boil. Simmer for about thirty minutes. Add 1 Tbsp vinegar. Strain through a cloth and pour into a wet, box-shaped mold. Chill till set. Cut into long, thin strips. A traditional press-type cutter is available in Japan for this purpose.

2. Make a sauce by combining 1/3 cup vinegar and 1/4 Tbsp soy sauce. Top the *tokoroten* with the sauce, *aonori* and mustard.

Serves four.

Variations
1) This may be made with 1 strip (3/10 oz or 8 g) of *kanten* to 5 cups of water instead of with *tengusa*.
2) Instead of vinegar and soy sauce, a syrup made by boiling 3 Tbsp brown sugar and 1/2 cup water; roasted and powdered soybeans; a mixture of vinegar, soy sauce, sugar, and salt (p. 147); a mixture of vinegar, soy sauce, and stock (p. 138); a mixture of sugar, vinegar, and bean paste; soy sauce and grated *wasabi* horseradish may be used as a topping.

Liang-pan Xu-qin

> **1/4 oz (6 g) string (*ito*) *kanten***
> **2-1/2 medium (8-1/2 oz or 240 g) cucumbers**
> **1-1/2 oz (40 g) ham**
> **1 egg**
> **pinch of salt**
> **1/6 (1-1/2 oz or 40 g) onion**
> **4 Tbsp vinegar**
> **2 Tbsp soy sauce**
> **1 Tbsp sugar**
> **sesame oil**
> **prepared mustard**
> **parsley**

1. Soften the *kanten* in water and cut into 2-1/2-in (6-cm) lengths.
2. Julienne cut the cucumber and ham in 2-1/2-in (6-cm) lengths.
3. Mix egg and salt. Fry in a thin sheet. When it is cool, julienne cut the thin omelet.
4. Julienne cut the onion and rub it with salt.
5. Combine vinegar, soy sauce, sugar, and sesame oil to make a sauce.
6. Coat the *kanten*, cucumber, ham, and egg well with the sauce and serve garnished with mustard and parsley.

Serves four.

Grapefruit Jelly

> **1 stick square *kanten***
> **3 cups water**
> **1 grapefruit**
> **1 cup sugar**

1. Soak the *kanten* in water. Tear it into small pieces. Wash, squeeze well and allow it to stand in 3 cups freshwater for from thirty minutes to an hour.
2. Halve the grapefruit. Juice the halves to produce about one cup. Scrape the peels clean and reserve.
3. Combine sugar and *kanten* mixture. Bring to a boil and simmer to reduce slightly. Strain grapefruit juice and add it to the *kanten* mixture. Stir well.
4. Pour this mixture into the peel halves and chill till set. Cut each half in half.

Serves four.

Custard Jelly with Fruit Sauce

2 egg yolks
1-1/4 cup milk
1 cup sugar
1/2 strip square *kanten* or 1/5 oz (4 g) agar powder
1-1/4 cup water
lemon flavor

Sauce:

4 canned apricots
1-1/4 cups water
3 Tbsp sugar
4 tsp Curaçao orange liqueur

1. Combine and thoroughly mix egg yolks, milk, and sugar.
2. Purée the apricots. Add water, sugar, and Curaçao to this. Bring to a boil, then chill.
3. Wash the *kanten*. Combine in a saucepan with 1-1/4 cups water. Bring to a boil. When the *kanten* has dissolved, strain through cloth. Return to a saucepan and bring to a boil once again. Remove from heat. Add milk mixture and mix quickly. When the jelly is partly set, add lemon flavor. Allow this to cool. Pour into wet individual jelly molds and chill till firm. Remove from molds and top with apricot sauce before serving.

Serves four.

Mint Jelly

1 strip square *kanten* or 2/5 oz (8 g) agar powder
2 cups water
1-1/3 cups sugar
1/2 bottle lemon soda
1 tsp peppermint extract
2 slices canned yellow peach

1. Wash *kanten*. Boil in water till dissolved. Add sugar and simmer briefly. Add soda and peppermint extract.
2. Cut peach slices into small pieces and place a little in each of six wet individual jelly molds. Pour *kanten* mixture over them and chill till firm.

Serves six.

Strawberry Jelly

1 strip square *kanten* or 2/5 oz (8 g) agar powder
1-1/2 cups water
2 cups sugar

1 cup strawberries
2 egg whites

1.   Wash the *kanten* and soften in water. Boil in 1-1/2 cups water till dissolved. Add sugar and simmer briefly.
2.   Hull and wash the strawberries. Boil them briefly. Cool and purée.
3.   Beat egg whites till they form peaks. Combine egg whites and *kanten* mixture. Add strawberries. Pour into wet jelly molds and chill till firm.

Serves six.

Almond Jelly

1 strip square *kanten* or 2/5 oz (8 g) agar powder
2 cups water
5 Tbsp sugar
1 cup milk
almond extract
  Syrup:
1 cup sugar
4 cups water
almond extract
  Garnish:
6 slices pineapple
6 cherries

1.   Soften *kanten* in water. Boil in 2 cups water till dissolved. Add 5 Tbsp sugar, bring to a boil, and remove from heat.
2.   When this mixture has cooled, add milk and almond extract. Strain through cloth. Pour into a wet mold. Chill till firm.
3.   Prepare a syrup by boiling together 1 cup sugar, 4 cups water, and almond extract.
4.   Cut the almond jelly into medium dice, garnish with pineapple and cherries, and top with syrup.

Serves six.

Mitsumamè

1 strip square *kanten* or 2/5 oz (8 g) agar powder
2-1/2 cups water
1 cup *shiratama* flour
canned fruit or fresh fruit in season
1/2 cup boiled red beans
  Syrup:
1 cup sugar

1/2 cup water
1 Tbsp honey

1.   Soften *kanten* in water. Boil in 2-1/2 cups water till dissolved. Strain through cloth. Pour into a wet square mold and chill till firm.

2.   Mix *shiratama* flour with a little water. Knead well. Divide into thirds. Tint one third pink and one third green with food coloring. Leave the remaining third white. Form into small dumplings, boil briefly, remove from water, and cool.

3.   Combine 1 cup sugar, 1/2 cup water, and 1 Tbsp honey in a saucepan. Simmer till a medium syrup is formed.

4.   Cut firm *kanten* jelly into 1/2-in (1-1/2-cm) dice. In individual serving dishes, combine *kanten* dice, red beans, *shiratama* dumplings, and bite-size pieces of fruit. Top with syrup.

Serves four.

Green Laver (*Enteromorpha*)

Because of its pleasant aroma, green laver is frequently toasted lightly, crushed, and used as a topping for other foods, in soups, and as a coating. It is available in powdered form for similar uses. Richer in proteins than all other algae except *Asakusa-nori*, it has abundant vitamin A, niacin, and vitamin C. It has thirty times more iron than spinach. A small amount of it can correct an iron deficiency. An excellent addition to the diets of weight watchers, it is known as sea lettuce in the West.

Scallop Roast with Sea-urchin

> 12 medium scallops
> salt
> monosodium glutamate
> 1-1/2 Tbsp sea-urchin-roe paste
> 1/2 egg yolk
> *aonori*
> 4 ginger stalks
> 1/2 cup vinegar
> 1 Tbsp sugar
> 1/4 tsp salt

1. Wash and drain the scallops. Season with salt and monosodium glutamate.
2. Combine sea-urchin-roe paste and egg yolk. Mix well.
3. Heat the oven to somewhat more than medium temperature. Place the scallops on a grill in the oven and roast them about five minutes, coating them from time to time with the egg and sea-urchin paste. When they are an attractive gold, sprinkle with *aonori*.
4. Serve garnished with ginger stalks that have been dipped briefly in boiling water and then marinated in a mixture of 1/2 cup vinegar, 1 Tbsp sugar, and 1/4 tsp salt.

Serves six.

Roast Sea Bream

> 4 slices sea bream or other white-flesh fish
> salt
> powdered *aonori*
> 4 ginger stalks
> 1/2 cup vinegar
> 1 Tbsp sugar
> 1/4 tsp salt

1.   One hour before cooking time, lightly salt the fish. Preheat the oven to medium and roast the fish in it for ten minutes. Coat the fish slices in powdered *aonori*.

2.   Dip the ginger stalks in boiling water; then marinate them in a mixture of vinegar, sugar, and salt. Serve as garnish with the fish.

Serves four.

Golden-roast Sea Bass

> **4 slices sea bass or other white-flesh fish**
> **salt**
> **1 egg yolk**
> **1/2 Tbsp** *mirin*
> **1 tsp powdered** *aonori*
> **pickled ginger stalks**

1.   Lightly salt the fish.
2.   Combine egg yolk and *mirin*.
3.   Roast the fish slices, coating them from time to time with the egg mixture. Sprinkle with *aonori*. The roasting should take only a few minutes in a medium oven.
4.   Serve the fish garnished with pickled ginger stalks or with cucumber pickles.

Serves four.

Turnips in Green Laver

> **1 large or two or three small turnips**
> **1/2 cup stock**
> **1 tsp sakè**
> **1/5 tsp salt**
> **1 tsp sugar**
> **1/4 oz (4 g) green laver**

1.   Peel the turnip and trim it into a perfect round. Boil till tender or cook two or three minutes in a electronic range.
2.   Combine stock, sakè, salt, and sugar in a saucepan. Bring to a boil. Add the turnip and simmer briefly to flavor it.
3.   Roll the turnip in chopped green laver or green laver powder.

Serves one.

Index of Scientific Names of Sea Vegetables

Index of Japanese Names of Sea Vegetables

List of Recipes